ECONOMIC INDEPENDENCE FOR WOMEN
The Foundation for Equal Rights

Sage Yearbooks in
WOMEN'S POLICY STUDIES

Series Editors

Jane Roberts Chapman and Margaret Gates
Center for Women Policy Studies
Washington, D.C.

Editorial Board

Volume 1
Sage Yearbooks in WOMEN'S POLICY STUDIES

ECONOMIC INDEPENDENCE FOR WOMEN

The Foundation for Equal Rights

Edited by

JANE ROBERTS CHAPMAN

 SAGE Publications   Beverly Hills / London

For information address:

SAGE PUBLICATIONS, INC.
275 South Beverly Drive
Beverly Hills, California 90212

SAGE PUBLICATIONS LTD
St George's House / 44 Hatton Garden
London EC1N 8ER

Printed in the United States of America

International Standard Book Number 0-8039-0444-4 (cloth)
0-8039-0517-3 (paper)

Library of Congress Catalog Card No. 75-11129

FIRST PRINTING

CONTENTS

Dedicated to
ANN LONDON SCOTT
1930-1975

PREFACE

Economic Independence for Women is the first volume of the Sage Yearbooks in Women's Policy Studies. This series is being edited by the Center for Women Policy Studies and will consist of annual volumes containing research and analysis of major policy issues related to the status of women. Each volume will present the work of contributors who are in the forefront of current efforts directed to the specific policy issue addressed. In the first volume the reader will find a cross-section of recent thinking related to the economic status of women.

The Center for Women Policy Studies was established in 1972 to help meet the need for research directed to the identification of policy needs and actions required to improve the economic and legal status of women. Although this function is a basic aspect of representative government, governmental studies on the status of women have historically been in short supply. This contrasts sharply with the extensive studies and resulting legislation on the problems of other population groups such as racial minorities, the aged, and the poor. Private institutions have also failed to address themselves to women policy issues except such highly specific matters as extension of the right to vote. It is remarkable that even during postwar periods of conversion to peacetime economy when the status of women has received the most extreme and traumatic blows, there have been few calls for special policy, much less opposition, from any source.

The need for policies directed to the welfare and equality of women was articulated in the writings of Abigail Adams and Mary Wollstonecraft in the eighteenth and nineteenth centuries and further nourished by the manifestos of the Seneca Falls Convention in 1848, the first convention on women's rights in the United States. The concept of special policies on the status of women was sorely tested by the postsuffrage indifference which lasted from the 1920s into the 1960s. But the feminists of the late 1960s with their demands for concrete goals such as equal pay and other job rights laid the preconditions for the development of systematic women policy studies.

Research and analysis conducted by the Center for Women Policy Studies is pragmatic in nature and is based on the need to initiate and implement change. This approach recognizes that policy which is not accompanied by resources in the form of programs or other tangible support to insure implementation is nothing more than a statement of intention or position. These Sage Yearbooks will provide a forum for the action-oriented research that is now being produced on the policy issues most central to the emerging independence of women. Volume II of the series, for example, will address the newly identified issues surrounding women and the family; it is tentatively entitled, *Women into Wives: The Legal and Economic Impact of Marriage.*

Women policy issues cannot be successfully superimposed on conventional academic disciplines. Day-care, for example, involves not only the area of child development but also questions of labor force participation rates and trends, access to nontraditional employment, sex roles, health and population trends, and population dispersion and living patterns. Therefore, each Sage Yearbook will be devoted to a single theme, but the theme will receive an interdisciplinary treatment. As in the current volume, contributors will include scholars from relevant disciplines as well as activists, legislators, program directors, and organizers. A mix of this sort approximates reality with respect to policy research, development, and implementation.

The Center gratefully acknowledges the strong support given it by the individuals who are beginning to produce the new body of research which is represented here. We look forward to the future, the maturation of a new discipline, and the opportunity to link the women's rights interests of the activist and the scholar.

—Jane Roberts Chapman
—Margaret Gates
Washington, D.C.

INTRODUCTION

JANE ROBERTS CHAPMAN

> When women can support themselves, have their entry to all the trades and professions, with a house of their own over their heads and a bank account, they will own their bodies and be dictators in the social realm.
>
> —*Elizabeth Cady Stanton, 1890*

The movement to secure equal rights for women has developed historically along four major fronts: political, social, educational, and economic. Perhaps the most critical of these is the economic arena. To the extent that women cannot control their own economic fates or influence the major policy decisions which affect them, they are incapable of changing their status and the conditions of economic dependence under which most of them live. It is impossible for women, or any other group, to achieve adequate political representation without first achieving economic independence and a significant level of economic influence. Political and economic clout are closely intertwined. To an unfortunate degree, it is a fact of American life that politics is linked to property.

This collection of essays is intended to provide a statement of the current economic condition of women, primarily American women. Chapters 2 and 3 provide overviews of the status of women, including a discussion of research and legislation. In chapters 4 and 5, cross-cultural perspectives of the economic standing of women are presented. Other chapters cover more specialized topics—occupational status, trade unions, credit, poverty, blue-collar women, earnings. The volume provides a comprehensive analysis of the disadvantaged status of women in economic terms. But more than that, the evidence presented here strongly suggests as an underlying thesis that the root of the economic problems with which women are chronically afflicted is the general view of women as dependent people.

In minimal terms "economic independence" could be defined as the earning of one's own living. But it may also be argued that no one can be considered economically independent as long as law, custom, and public policy place limits on the freedom to act on his or her own behalf, and that women, as a group, must obtain considerably more freedom before they can be considered to have achieved independence. In 1974, over 38 million adult American women earned no income whatever; of the 30 million women who were employed, their median earnings were $6,335 per year, compared with $11,186 for men. These nonearning or low-earning women cannot be said to have adequate control over their own lives (U.S. Department of Labor, Women's Bureau, forthcoming). They are in one way or another prisoners of economic dependency, a dependency which is intensified by the manner in which it has been institutionalized. The social security system, for example, guarantees a benefit to a dependent wife but penalizes the working wife, and federal and state tax codes impact negatively on families with two working spouses.

The law and other institutions perceive, classify, and treat women as dependents, even when they are not. But this concept of women as economic dependents conflicts sharply with reality and need. Fully 6.8 million women are classified as heads of families; one out of eight American families is headed by a woman. In addition, 43% of all married women are employed (U.S. Department of Labor, Women's Bureau, forthcoming). Public policy and decisions in the marketplace which do not fully take these facts into account must be considered invalid. And, it is fair to say, such failures to perceive the economic role of women further contribute to the economic disadvantages of women.

While women who work outside the home have varying degrees of economic independence, women who are homemakers currently have none, in the terms described above, unless they are among the few enjoying substantial independently owned assets such as stocks or real estate. It must be acknowledged, of course, that a great many married American women who do not engage in paid employment are comfortably situated and that economic dependency is often voluntary. Looking more closely at this group of approximately 45 million persons, the degree of their dependency becomes more apparent. For most of them, their economic circumstances derive from men to whom they are attached in some way. Whether they are fathers, husbands, ex-husbands, or benefactors in other categories, these men are the determinants of a standard of living which usually changes drastically when they or their income is removed from the family. It seems accurate to say, therefore, that few women actually possess middle-class status in their own right—rather, that they enjoy it on loan, through their attachments to middle-class men.

A further question to be examined here is whether or not this kind of dependence is indeed voluntary at all. Aside from factors of conditioning and social pressures, a woman's willingness to accept what is known as a "derived status" (derived from a husband) often reflects less a voluntary choice than the lack of attractive alternatives. The prospect of being identified as Mrs. Prominent-Physician, for example, may have more intrinsic appeal than being known as Ms. Overeducated-Secretary.

That women who are homemakers make an economic contribution to their families is not disputed here. Where measures of this contribution have been attempted over the years (see Kahne, chapter 2), it has been found to be significant in terms of the generation of national wealth. The value of this contribution has been set as high as 25% of GNP in income terms ($350 billion in 1974). But there is a crucial distinction between economic contribution and economic independence. Charlotte Perkins Gilman made the point well in her landmark work, *Women and Economics,* almost 80 years ago:

> For a certain percentage of persons to serve other persons in order that the ones so served may produce more, is a contribution not to be overlooked. The labor of women in the house, certainly, enables men to produce more wealth than they otherwise could; and in this way women are economic factors in society. But so are horses. The labor of horses enables men to produce more wealth than they otherwise could. The horse is an economic factor in society. But the horse is not economically independent, nor is the woman.

It should be recognized that there are different kinds of factors at work, some of them conflicting, which influence the economic status of women. There are the market considerations—the demand for labor, level of education and training, the need for money. But there are also the nonmarket considerations. There is a whole range of social influences which are at work even in early childhood and which have the general effect of reducing the economic independence of women as a group. The collection of papers presented here identifies the full range of factors influencing the status of women in America in the 1970s. Fittingly, not all of the contributors are economists; they are also legislators, political scientists, and sociologists. It is significant that the papers demonstrate the impossibility of separating market from private, social, or psychological considerations concerning the economic status of women.

Barrett (chapter 3), for example, has looked at a number of Western industrialized countries and has found that the ideology of these countries—whether egalitarian or sexist—has not played a large role in determining either the female labor force participation rates or its female wage rates. Rather, it is likely that mechanisms which most effectively keep women in an inferior economic position are those growing out of sex differentiation within the family and, to a lesser degree, the impact of social policy. Barrett investigates these and other explanations for economic disadvantage and what changes would be required to improve the lot of women in the industrialized countries.

Too often the economic condition of women has not been considered in its entirety or with reference to the full range of its manifestations. In the past, attention has been focused primarily on female employment with little attempt made to relate other aspects of the problem. Nor has the fact that these problems may spring from a common cause been given adequate attention. While an independent income (usually in the form of earnings) may be considered the crux of economic independence, other factors adversely affect women's economic position. Among these are social security, taxation, pensions, insurance, and credit. In all of these areas relating to financial opportunities, the perception of women as dependents has been institutionalized in the form of restrictive policies, regulations, practices, and programs which are discriminatory against women as a class. Some of these considerations are discussed by Griffiths in chapter 1 and Kahne in chapter 2.

Thus, it is seen that—fallacious, unrealistic, and grounded solely on traditional expectations though it may be—economic dependence remains in 1975 a basic operational premise of society's legal, social, and economic institutions. Former Congresswoman Martha Griffiths observes, in chapter 1, the "failure of American economic policy to assure equitable reward for work done by women inside or outside the home. Public policy tends to discourage wives from working outside the home and to treat them as second-class workers when they do so. At the same time, public policy ignores the value of homemaking." In the face of this, policy-makers, almost exclusively men, have remained almost entirely indifferent to the situation and, indeed, indifferent to the evidence that a "situation" exists.

The denial of credit to women is a good example of a problem rooted in the notion of dependency, long after the notion has any practical validity. Credit-extending institutions until very recently have behaved as though all women were dependent and financially unaccountable, more often than not denying credit to wage-earning women while awarding it to their husbands, following a head-of-household criterion under which only men could be eligible. Chapter 10 explores this situation and goes on to analyze the economic justification for differentiating by sex and marital status in extending credit.

One measure of the significance of women's economic activity is the difference it makes to those families which have income from a wife's employment. Bell, in chapter 9, analyzes the contribution of wives' earnings to family income and finds that it is greater than commonly assumed by, among other institutions, the Bureau of the Census. This underrating of wives' income is part of society's refusal to treat women as anything but economic dependents. To counter the Bureau of the Census assertion that "most families depend entirely or primarily on" the earnings of the man of the house, Bell presents statistical material showing that there is in fact remarkable diversity in family income patterns.

This sort of underaccounting of "women's work" is evident also when economic development programs incorporating a developed country's values are imposed on a less-developed country. In chapter 4, Tinker cautions that the process of development has tended to restrict the economic independence of women. Traditionally, women in many developing countries have conducted economic activities in addition to their family responsibilities. But development models imported from developed countries tend to threaten the traditional jobs—Western notions of appropriate roles and occupations for women tend to be exported with the aid. It is ironic that modernization may not bring improvement in the lot of women. Barrett and others have pointed this out in our own history, citing the more integrated economic role of women before the industrial revolution.

Nowhere does the disadvantaged economic position of women stand out more dramatically than in the discussion of the poverty population by Ross in chapter 5. Most poor families with children are headed by women. An astounding 70% of nonwhite poor families with children are female-headed. The labor market has offered women so little for so long that their expectations are low, and the alternative of dependency (even the subsistence dependency of welfare) seems preferable to working for many women. But the solution to the increasingly female character of the poverty problem is not welfare, substituting the government for a male provider (substituting The Man for the man). Rather, it is to improve opportunities to become self-supporting, to open up apprenticeships, the skilled trades, all occupations to women.

The concerns of blue-collar women, including the lack of access to many job categories, have received little attention through either research or outreach programs. In the early part of the century, much attention was focused on the poor working and living conditions of women in working-class jobs. Research, coupled with action by the labor movement, resulted in reform legislation and other improvements. But in recent years, Pamela Roby, the author of chapter 6, has found that practically no research has been devoted to women employed in blue-collar industrial or service jobs. The situation is now changing. Dr. Roby's study of the conditions of women in blue-collar jobs and Wertheimer and Nelson's *Trade Union Women* (1975) detail the status and recent organizational efforts of union women. Wertheimer's contribution to the current volume (chapter 7) reviews the position of women in trade unions and finds that, while they hold few national offices in unions, they hold increasing numbers of posts on the local level. The emergence of the National Coalition of Labor Union Women is perhaps one of the most encouraging developments relating to the economic status of women in recent years. It represents an instance of women recognizing the necessity and importance of their labor market activity and organizing in order to take charge of their own fate.

By any of the standard measures—wages, numbers in poverty, level of economic influence—women have been found to be economically disadvantaged. But this has seldom appeared to be a significant factor in the development of public policy. Formulation of public policy, mirroring institutional preference, has taken as a convenient rationale the assumption that women are to be "taken care of" by men, or by transfer payments such as social security or welfare which substitute for the men who are absent. It is no coincidence that welfare mothers as a group are held in low esteem by society since they lack achieving husbands from whom they might derive status. But if the cultural interpretation of the position of women is removed, the precarious economic status of women reveals itself as a problem of exceedingly large proportions. Bell suggests (chapter 9) that

> Most of the ambiguity and ignorance about women's earnings, women's contribution to the economy, and for that matter the economic status of women stem from the automatic identification of a woman as a wife and mother—that is, as the female adult of a family.

Because of the cultural bias with which the status of women is viewed, the needs for research, commitment of resources, legislative action, and other considerations usually given to major social problems have not been fully recognized. The operating assumption in public policy referred to above has generally precluded the recognition of any need to study the status of women as independently derived. Ross states (chapter 5) that "one of the functions of government policy is to correct major imbalances which occur when economic activity rewards some people much more than others." It might also be said that government has an obligation to promulgate policies which are free of bias on the basis of sex or marital status. In addition, because policies are made by institutions outside the government as well, resolution of the economically dependent and disadvantaged status of women must also include review and reform initiated by private institutions—financial, educational, and business. Finally, if the economic status of women is to be improved, there must also be supportive activities such as retraining, affirmative action, and counseling.

The last decade has brought initiatives in all of these areas to some extent. There has been the legislation directed toward employment and education discrimination, and passage by Congress of the Equal Rights Amendment to the Constitution. Certainly, there has been a burgeoning of research on the status of women. Supporting activities have been introduced, ranging from continuing education programs to the establishment of women's banks. But nowhere does the scale of remedial activity approach the scale of the problem. The Equal Employment Opportunity Commission's backlog of almost 6,000 actionable sex discrimination complaints is one evidence of this inadequacy.

It is important to generate interaction among the steps which form the process of social change. Such interaction is particularly important in changing the status of women, since the effects of such change touch the lives of all human beings in society in a profound way. Activists eager to provoke change through specific legislative, litigative, or educational actions may see research as a lengthy process with no concrete results. However, research must precede action programs, if the programs are to address the right problems for the right groups in the right way. Research, on the other hand, should be stimulated and shaped by the issues raised by affected groups in their action projects.

Because of the impossibility of separating many complex influences and considerations, research topics relating to the economic status of women are interdisciplinary. A reform which improves the condition of one segment of the female population might impact negatively on another segment, so issues must be examined from more than one perspective. One way of approaching the complexity of women policy research has been to diversify the kinds of institutions involved, to include not only academic institutions but also private policy-oriented groups, feminist groups with activist links, as well as the traditional women's organizations such as the YWCA and the League of Women Voters.

If women as a group are to be freed of economic dependency, they must first reach the decision that the disadvantages of dependency outweigh its advantages. The pressure which has stimulated the current level of women's rights activity has been brought about by a relatively small proportion of women. However, the attitudes of women in general have changed as well in the recent past, as evidenced by the 48% of respondents in a 1972 poll who asserted support for the objectives of the Women's Movement such as equal rights in employment (Louis Harris and Associates, 1972). Yet in the same year when a Harris Survey asked a national sample of women whether "having a loving husband who is able to take care of me is much more important to me than making it on my own," half of the respondents under 30 years of age said that they frequently felt that the loving husband was more important, and among older women the proportion was even higher (Blake, 1974). Of course, the structure of the question is biased in favor of the response it received. That is, it leaves out the possibility of being independent *and* having a loving husband. In addition it links the idea of a loving husband with the idea of being taken care of (the suggestion of being cared for), while leaving "making it on my own" in an unexplained and more or less pejorative context. A similar survey two years later put the question in more neutral terms (Roper Organization, 1974). A majority of women over 40 still endorsed "a traditional marriage with the husband assuming the responsibility for providing for the family and the wife running the home and taking care of the children." But most women under 40 said they would find a marriage in which husband and wife both worked, and shared homemaking and child-rearing responsibilities, to be the most satisfactory way of life.

Vatter, in chapter 8, predicts that, increasingly, "women will less and less regard themselves as secondary, supplementary, or peripheral workers and more and more be concerned with their labor force status." Other messages consistent with that idea are in the wind. Blue-collar women are organizing themselves, as the Coalition of Labor Union Women (CLUW) has shown, and professional associations are increasingly developing women's caucuses. Related to this has been the increased enrollment of women in professional and technical schools. There is also an apparent increase in the number of women who own their own businesses. While the national policy of the Jaycees is to exclude women from membership, alternatives for women are developing such as the Association of Women Business Owners, organized in Washington, D.C.

The lack of widespread discontent over the derived and dependent status of homemakers jeopardizes the possibility of significantly improving the economic condition of women as a class. And the question of what the future attitudes and behavior of the female homemaker will be remains unanswered. Sociologist Jessie Bernard (1972: 52) has pointed out that many wives, perhaps most,

> have been so completely shaped for their dependency and passivity that the very threat of changes that would force them to greater independence frightens them. They have successfully come to terms with the conditions of their lives. They do not know any other. They do not know that other patterns of living might yield greater satisfactions, or want to know. Their cage can be open. They will stay put.

Numerous social and behavioral scientists have presented evidence for the position stated recently by Judith Blake (1974: 145) in "The Changing Status of Women in Developed Countries" that

There are extremely powerful pressures from all sources to select personality traits and behavior patterns that are believed to be congruent with the status of wife and mother.

One cannot help but feel, however, that if the economic implications of sex-differentiated practices of child-rearing and the resulting dependency of women were better understood, it would not be encouraged by anyone. If parents knew of the disproportionate number of women in poverty; if they knew not only of the high and increasing divorce rate, but also that current statistics show that after four years only 33% of court-awarded child support payments are made, and after 10 years practically none (Nagel and Weitzman, 1971)[1] —if parents were to comprehend these facts, perhaps they would not encourage their daughters' expectations of marriage as a lifetime guarantee of "a loving husband who is able to take care of me" or educate their daughters without regard to occupational goals.

Certainly, it is only by continuing to assert themselves in the marketplace that women can gain the independence which must underlie their achievement of equal rights. The information in the chapters which follow actually describes millions of personal circumstances and ways of arranging personal and family economic affairs. As such, this book tells us that this kind of assertiveness not only exists, but is growing. It also tells us that society has predicated its institutions on the presumption that women are dependents and thereby has created great barriers to overcoming that presumption.

Charlotte Perkins Gilman, a strong outspoken feminist, predicted that the period of women's economic dependence was drawing to a close because its usefulness was wearing out. That was in 1898. The progress of the past 80 years might not strike her as unqualified success. But the Bureau of the Census recently released what might be the most significant information on the status of women in 1975: while the divorce rate has continued to climb, there has been a decline in the number of couples getting married. This should not necessarily be interpreted as an indication of change in conventional notions of male-female relationships, but it might be. It may be that women are beginning to follow their instincts on the subject of independence—choosing, ultimately, to make it on their own.

NOTE

1. Data were gathered by Kenneth Eckhardt from a sample of fathers who were ordered to pay some child support in a metropolitan county of Wisconsin in 1955. Data on the reliability of alimony and child support are scarce, but consistently show that these sources of income are unreliable.

REFERENCES

BERNARD, J. (1972) The Future of Marriage. New York: World.
BLAKE, J. (1974) "The changing status of women in developed countries." Scientific American (December): 137-147.
GILMAN, C. P. (1970) Women and Economics, The Economic Factor Between Men and Women as a Factor in Social Evolution. New York: Harper & Row. (Originally published in 1898 by Small, Maynard & Co., Boston.)
Louis Harris and Associates (1972) The 1972 Virginia Slims American Women's Opinion Poll.
NAGEL, M. and L. WEITZMAN (1971) "Women as litigants." Hastings Law Journal.
ROBY, P. (1975) The Condition of Women in Blue Collar and Service Jobs: A Review of Research, Action and Policy. New York: Russell Sage Foundation.
Roper Organization (1974) The Virginia Slims American Women's Opinion Poll, A Survey on the Attitudes of Women on Marriage, Divorce, the Family and America's Changing Sexual Morality, Vol. III.
U.S. Department of Labor, Women's Bureau (forthcoming) 1975 Handbook on Women Workers. Washington, D.C.: Government Printing Office.
WERTHEIMER, B. and A. H. NELSON (1975) Trade Union Women. New York: Praeger.

1

HOW MUCH IS A WOMAN WORTH?
The American Public Policy

MARTHA W. GRIFFITHS

Contrary to popular belief, women do not control the wealth in this country. In 1973, only 69% of American women, compared with 92% of American men, had money income from any source. Among those with income, the average income for men was $9,289, but for women, only $3,799 (U.S. Census Bureau, 1974b). Female-headed families comprise only 9% of families with incomes above the poverty level, but 45% of those with incomes below (U.S. Census Bureau, 1974a).

Women's inferior economic status results at least in part from the failure of American economic policy to assure equitable reward for work done by women, inside or outside the home. Public policy tends to discourage wives from working outside the home and to treat them as second-class workers when they do so. At the same time, public policy ignores the value of homemaking and often fails to promote the stability of the family, the traditional source of women's economic security.

When viewed separately, sex-based inequities in policies on employment, taxes, social security, private pensions, welfare, child support, and credit may seem unrelated and relatively insignificant. When viewed as a whole, however, these inequities form an overall economic policy overwhelmingly unfavorable to women. The purpose of this chapter is to show the dimensions of that policy and to look at the assumptions and attitudes on which it is based. Part I of the chapter discusses public policy on the economic value of women's employment; Part II examines public policy on the economic value of homemaking.

I. PUBLIC POLICY ON THE ECONOMIC VALUE
OF WOMEN'S EMPLOYMENT

American economic policy toward women who work outside the home reflects the attitude that female earners are secondary earners. True, sex discrimination in employment is illegal. By the Equal Pay Act of 1963 (29 U.S.C. § 206[d] [1970]) and the Civil Rights Act of 1964 (42 U.S.C. § 2000[e] [1970]), Congress prohibited employers from discriminating on the basis of sex. However, efforts to enforce these laws have not been strong. Testifying before the Joint Economic Committee in 1973, Labor Department officials admitted that less than half of the back pay that the Labor Department had found to be owed to women because of violations of the Equal Pay Act had ever been paid (U.S. Congress, Joint Economic Committee, 1973: 103).

Enforcement of the employment provisions of the 1964 Civil Rights Act is no stronger. The Equal Employment Opportunity Commission, which has the task of ending employment discrimination against women, blacks (who together comprise about 44% of the labor force), and other minorities has a budget only one-seventh as large as that of the federal agency charged with forecasting the weather. As a result of understaffing, the Equal Employment Opportunity Commission has a backlog of about 90,000 cases.

The wage gap between men and women reflects the weakness of these enforcement efforts. In 1972, the median earnings of women who worked outside the home full-time and year-round were $5,903 (U.S. Census Bureau, 1973b). This was only 58% as much as the median earnings of men who worked full-time—down from 60% in 1963 and 1964 when the equal employment opportunity laws were passed, and down from 64% in 1955, eight years before their enactment (U.S. Department of Labor, Women's Bureau, 1971).

The average female earner not only receives lower wages than the average male earner, but also feels the brunt of the federal income tax. The internal revenue code's discrimination against two-earner families creates a significant disincentive for married women to work outside the home. Consider the situation of a wife whose husband earns $20,000 a year: if she earned $7,000 in 1974, about 30% of it would go to pay the family's extra federal income tax occasioned by her earnings; if her husband earned $30,000 and she earned $7,000, about 40% of it would go to pay the family's extra federal income tax.[1]

While accompanied by high taxes, women's employment brings low pension benefits. In the first place, female earners are far less likely than male earners to receive a private pension, for women are concentrated in industries and occupations which lack pension coverage. Moreover, women earners who are lucky enough to receive pensions receive considerably lower benefits than men, partly because of their lower wages, on which pension contributions are based. Among social security recipients who retired in 1969-1970 with private pensions, the median annual private pension for men was $2,080, but for women it was only $970 (Kolodrubetz, 1973: 19).

The social security system also devalues the contributions of women earners. Unless a wife's earnings entitle her to a social security benefit larger than half of her husband's (and often they do not)—or, for a widow, a benefit larger than her deceased husband's full benefit—a married woman who pays social security taxes all her life will receive retirement benefits no larger than if she had never paid a dime (see Weinberger, 1973). Even if her earnings do entitle her to a retirement benefit somewhat larger than she would have received as a dependent, for that extra amount she will have paid a disproportionately heavy tax.

Married women earners receive an unfavorable return on their social security taxes in terms of not only retirement benefits, but also dependents' benefits. When a husband dies, retires, or becomes disabled, his wife may draw on his social security regardless of her actual dependence on him; but when a wife dies, retires, or becomes disabled, her husband may draw only if he received at least half of his support from her. Benefits for disabled widowers, but not for disabled widows, are also conditioned on a support test (42 U.S.C. §402[b, c, e, f] [1970]).* (Asterisk refers to Editor's Note, p. 36.)

Like discrimination in employment, taxes, and pensions, discrimination in credit undervalues the work done by women. Dollar for dollar, a woman's paycheck or pension seldom stretches as far as a man's, for credit is less accessible to a woman. In 1972, after holding hearings on sex discrimination in credit, the National Commission on Consumer Finance reported that testimony at the hearings had shown the following: single women have more trouble obtaining credit than single men; creditors generally require a woman upon marriage to reapply for credit (usually in her husband's name), while similar reapplication is not asked of men; creditors are often unwilling to extend credit to a married woman in her own name; creditors are often unwilling to count the wife's income when a married couple applies for credit; and women who are divorced, separated, or widowed have trouble reestablishing credit.[2] Since these hearings, comprehensive legislation has been passed which forbids discrimination in lending on the basis of sex. The new law took effect in October 1975–although it is called the Equal Credit Opportunity Act of 1974.

In considering economic policy toward women workers, one cannot ignore the treatment of women's unemployment. In 1973, women's unemployment rate was 46% above men's, up from 13% above men's in 1961.[3] Federal job training programs reflect legislators' lack of concern about unemployment among women. For example, the Work Incentive (WIN) Program provides job training and employment services for persons who receive welfare under the program of Aid to Families with Dependent Children (AFDC). Although most able-bodied adult AFDC recipients are women, federal law gives fathers first priority for enrollment in WIN; unemployed mothers who volunteer to participate have only second priority (42 U.S.C. § 633[a] [Supp. II, 1972]).

The unemployment insurance system also shows the lack of importance legislators attach to women's unemployment. Women do not receive the same unemployment insurance protection as men. For example, as a result of statutory and administrative definitions of dependency tending to discriminate against women, the 11 states which provided unemployment insurance allowances for dependents in 1972 paid such allowances to over 50% of the male claimants, but to fewer than 10% of the female (Dahm, 1973: 354-355).

In short, American economic policy discourages women from working outside the home and treats them as second-class workers when they do so. Public policy fails to assure equitable reward for women's employment.

Legislative Assumptions and Attitudes Underlying Policy

Traditionally, the law has concerned itself not with the security of women workers, but with the security of men's jobs. Nothing shows this better than the development of so-called "protective" labor legislation. One of the first protective labor laws to be considered by the U.S. Supreme Court was a New York law which provided that no employee could be required or permitted to work in a bakery more than 60 hours per week or 10 hours per day. In *Lochner v. New York* (198 U.S. 45 [1905]), decided in 1905, the Supreme Court ruled that the New York law violated employees' constitutional right to freedom of contract. Noting that the bakery employees affected by the case were men, the Court said that the law had "no such direct relation to and no such substantial effect upon the health of the employee, as to justify us in regarding the section as really a health law" (198 U.S. at 64 [1905]).

Three years later, however, the Supreme Court approved a similar law which applied only to women. In *Muller v. Oregon* (208 U.S. 412 [1908]), the Court upheld an Oregon law which prohibited the employment of women in a "mechanical establishment," factory, or laundry more than 10 hours per day. The Court found no violation of women's freedom of contract. Nor did the Court overrule its previous decision in *Lochner;* to the contrary, the Court explicitly approved it. Explaining why it was applying the Constitution differently to women than to men, the Court commented, "[H]istory discloses the fact that woman has always been dependent upon man. He established his control at the outset by superior physical strength, and this control in various forms, with diminishing intensity, has continued to the present" (208 U.S. at 421 [1908]).

After the *Muller* decision, every state enacted laws affecting women's employment. Many of these laws did not protect women —they protected men's jobs. For example:

- Ohio prohibited women from working as meter readers (U.S. Department of Labor, Women's Bureau, 1969: 278). If Ohio legislators had wanted to protect women who are home while the meter is being read, they would have required female meter readers.

- Six states and Puerto Rico prohibited women from working during certain periods before and after childbirth. Only Puerto Rico provided for women's job security during the required absence (p. 276 in the same source).

- Some states prohibited women from working as bartenders, but not as bar waitresses. North Dakota and Washington prohibited women from working at night, but only as elevator operators. Ohio prohibited women from working at night, but only as taxi drivers (p. 275). Women have always found it possible to work at night as poorly paid scrubwomen.

- Some states limited the amount of weight women could lift or carry on the job. California forbade women to lift more than 50 pounds in some occupations and 25 pounds in others. Massachusetts prohibited women from lifting more than 40 pounds—except in foundries, where they were permitted to lift only 25. The weightlifting laws of New York, Maryland, and Minnesota applied only in foundries and corerooms—certainly not in hospitals, where tiny nurses have always lifted heavy patients (p. 279).

In short, traditionally the law did not counteract discrimination against women workers; the law reinforced it. Until 1963, women had virtually no legal protection against sex discrimination in employment. Directing their attention to the security of men's jobs, legislators have assumed that women's earnings are not necessary to support themselves or their families. Legislators have thought in terms of the traditional male and female stereotypes—that men are breadwinners and women are wives or widows; that men provide necessary income for their families but women do not; in other words, that women are supported by men.

This view of the world never matched reality, but today it is further than ever from the truth. Over 15 million households are not supported by a man.[4] Among families which are supported by a man, husband-wife families where the husband works, almost half of the wives are in the labor force (U.S. Department of Labor, Bureau of Labor Statistics, 1973a: Table 3). Forty-three percent of school-age children and almost 30% of preschool children have mothers who work outside the home (U.S. Department of Labor, Bureau of Labor Statistics, 1973b: Table 2). Sixty percent of all women who work outside the home are single, divorced, widowed, or separated, or have husbands who earn less than $7,000 a year (U.S. Department of Labor, Women's Bureau: 1974).

The development of social security legislation regarding dependents' benefits suggests the history of society's regard for the role of women's earnings in family support. In 1939 Congress amended the Social Security Act to provide benefits to the children, wives, and widows of retired and deceased male earners. However, no social security benefits were provided to the children, husbands, or widowers of female earners until 1950. Not until 1967 were children of female earners permitted to receive benefits on exactly the same basis as children of male earners, and husbands and widowers still may not qualify for benefits on the same basis as wives and widows. In addition, two kinds of benefits available to the dependents of male earners are not yet available to the dependents of female earners. While wives and widows caring for minor children may qualify for "mother's insurance benefits," there are no corresponding "father's insurance benefits" for husbands and widowers. Similarly, there are benefits for divorced wives, but not divorced husbands.[5] Thus, the process of revising the law to reflect the importance of women's earnings in family support has been slow and incomplete.*

Accompanying legislators' traditional idea about the unimportance of women's earnings has been the assumption that employed men have the ability to support their families. Social security protects families against their breadwinners' retirement, death, or disability; unemployment insurance protects against breadwinners' loss of employment; and welfare protects families without full-time breadwinners. However, little federal aid is available to the families of the many men who work full-time, but who do not earn enough to enable their families to enjoy a decent standard of living. In 1972, 4.6 million persons lived in families which had incomes below the poverty line despite year-round full-time work by their breadwinners (U.S. Census Bureau, 1973c: Table 32).

As a result of assumptions about the sufficiency of men's earnings and the insignificance of women's earnings, legislators have not paid adequate attention to the effects of economic policy on the two-earner family. For example, look at the nation's major welfare program, Aid to Families with Dependent Children (AFDC). Twenty-six states do not provide AFDC to families with two able-bodied parents. In order for such a family to qualify, one parent must leave home, and it is usually the father who leaves. In other words, in these states a mother may either live with the father of her children or receive welfare, but not both—since the father is supposed to be the breadwinner, the mother may not have him and welfare too. By "definition," the father does not need welfare.

In the other 24 states, families with two able-bodied parents may receive AFDC, but only if the father is unemployed (see 42 U.S.C. § 607 [1970]). To be considered unemployed, a father must be working less than 100 hours per month (45 C.F.R. § 233.100 [1972]); his family is ineligible for AFDC if he works 100 or more hours per month, no matter how little he earns. While families with an *unemployed father and an employed mother* may qualify for AFDC, families with an *employed father and unemployed mother* may not. In 1961, when Congress first provided federal aid to children who were in need as the result of the unemployment of a parent, such unemployment included that of either a mother or a father. However, in 1968 Congress changed the law to include only the unemployment of the father (42 U.S.C. § 607 [1970]). Such is the strength of the assumption that the father is the breadwinner.

Like the welfare system, the social security system discriminates against two-earner families. For example, when both husband and wife have worked outside the home, a retired couple may receive less in benefits than a single-earner family which had the same total earnings and paid no more in social security taxes. Moreover, such a retired couple may have paid more in social security taxes and yet receive less in benefits than a single-earner family which had lower total earnings. And when both husband and wife have paid the maximum amount in social security taxes each year, paying twice as much in taxes as a single-earner family in which the husband paid the maximum, they will not qualify for twice as much (but only one and one-third times as much) in benefits.

The federal income tax also discriminates against two-earner families. For example, a two-earner family in which each spouse earns $10,000 pays the same tax as a single-earner family where the husband earns $20,000; but the two-earner family has less tax-paying ability because of the extra expenses associated with the wife's employment and because it lacks the value of the nonemployed wife's untaxed labor in the home.

Largely as a result of 1969 changes in the rate structure of the federal income tax, the two-earner family is also at a tax disadvantage in comparison with two single persons who have the same total income. For example, if a woman who earns $2,000 a year marries a man who earns $3,000, together they will pay $184 more in federal income tax for 1974 than if they had remained single. This amount represents almost 60% of their total tax liability. The "marriage penalty" increases as income rises. If a woman who earns $14,000 marries a man with the same income, next January they will owe an extra $984 in federal income tax for the privilege of being husband and wife; if one of them has a child from a previous marriage, their "marriage penalty" will rise to well over $1,000.[6]

By underestimating the role of women's earnings in family support and by overestimating the sufficiency of men's earnings, legislators have thus shaped economic policy in a way which tends to devalue women's employment and discriminate against the two-earner family.

II. PUBLIC POLICY ON THE
ECONOMIC VALUE OF HOMEMAKING

While public policy discourages women from working outside the home, it fails to assure economic rewards for those who work in the home. From childhood on, every American woman is taught to believe that the highest calling in life is to be a wife and mother and that American law will protect her in this calling. However, the law gives little economic protection to the homemaker.

In the first place, the homemaker receives little protection in the form of property rights. In the 42 states with common law property systems, property acquired during marriage belongs to the person who acquires it—this means the person with earnings, not the one who shops. Although the homemaker's unpaid labor makes her husband's employment possible, under the law his earnings belong only to him. During his lifetime, she can gain an ownership interest in his property only if he gives it to her (subject to the gift tax) or sells it to her. In the eight community property states, wives have a theoretical ownership interest in the property of the marital community, but only in recent years have they begun to gain the right to share in the control of that property (Davidson et al., 1974: 165).

During her husband's lifetime, a homemaker is largely dependent on his generosity in providing support. Courts rarely issue a support order when a husband and wife are living together. Theoretically, under the doctrine of necessaries, a wife may enforce her husband's obligation of support by buying what she needs and charging it to him. However, a wife cannot get credit on the strength of her husband's good credit record unless he has one. And even if his credit record is good, merchants hesitate to rely on it for purchases made without his consent; before a court will hold a husband liable for such purchases, the merchant must prove that the goods purchased were "necessaries" not already provided by the husband (Kanowitz, 1969: 69-75; Clark, 1968: 186, 189-192).

If her husband dies, a homemaker's economic situation may be no more secure. In the first place, if her husband leaves to her property of substantial value, the government will take its share in federal estate taxes. Property left to a charity is tax-exempt, but property left to the widow who helped her husband accumulate the property is not.[7]

The widow may or may not receive a pension from her husband's employer. *If* the deceased was covered by a pension plan (many workers are not), *if* the pension plan provides survivors' benefits (many plans do not), *and if* the deceased chose to name his wife as his survivor (he was not required to do so), then—and only then—will the widow receive a pension. And a pension may be barely large enough to pay for postage stamps.

Unless she is disabled or has children under 21, a middle-aged widow will receive no social security. If she has two teen-age children, she can expect a monthly social security check—on the average—of $433 (U.S. Congress, House Ways and Means Committee, 1973: 4). This check may be reduced to $364 a month if she works outside the home. If she has only one child and works outside the home, the check may be reduced to $182. When the children are out of school, even those payments will end. Then what will she do until she qualifies for widows' social security benefits at age 60?

Widowhood is not the only economic crisis that may befall a homemaker. There is also divorce. In 1973, 913,000 divorces occurred in this country, more than double the number of a decade earlier. In 1973 there were two divorces for every five marriages taking place that year.[8] Divorce rates are rising even among those married a long time: federal statistics suggest that almost half of all divorces occur after seven years of marriage and that about one-fourth occur after 14 years (National Center for Health Statistics, 1973: 21-23, Table 19).

A divorced woman's chances of receiving support payments are not good. Courts seldom award alimony and, for women with children, child support is not a sure thing. According to data from the Panel Study on Income Dynamics which is being conducted at the University of Michigan, almost half of all divorced mothers heading families receive no alimony or child support, and the median amount received by those who do is only about $1,350 a year.[9]

If the ex-husband dies, even the divorced woman's meager right to collect support will be gone. And a divorced homemaker may draw on her ex-husband's social security only if she was married to him for at least twenty years.[10] A homemaker who is divorced after five, ten, or even nineteen and one-half years of marriage will not receive social security payments for the years that her ex-husband worked under covered employment while she kept house for him.

Of course, Congress has given homemakers the economic protection of welfare. Under the programs of Food Stamps, Medicaid, and Aid to Families with Dependent Children, a mother and three children who have no other income may receive an average benefit of $4,100 a year, plus free medical care (Storey, 1974: 4). This equals about $5,400 in annual before-tax earnings, which approaches the median earnings of women who work outside the home full-time, year-round.[11] By conditioning benefits on the father's absence, welfare programs provide a substantial financial incentive for families to split up. This is what Congress has done for homemakers.

Legislative Assumptions and Attitudes Underlying Policy

Legislators consistently underestimate the value of work done in the home. Under the Fair Labor Standards Act, for example, American workers in most occupations have had federal minimum wage protection since 1938 (29 U.S.C. § 206 [1970]). Yet paid domestic workers, most of whom are women, did not receive such protection until 1974 (Fair Labor Standards Amendments of 1974, P.L. No. 93-259, § 7 [April 8, 1974]).

Unpaid homemaking is still excluded from employment covered by the social security system. Whether she is married or unmarried, after a lifetime of housework a full-time homemaker may not qualify for social security payments in her own right. When a man retires or becomes disabled, he receives a 50% increase in his social security payment as an allowance for his wife—in other words, he receives an increased payment because he has a dependent, but the homemaker receives no payment in recognition of the work she has performed.

Limitations on the federal income tax deduction for household and child-care services also reflect the lack of value attached to domestic work (26 U.S.C. § 214 [Supp. II, 1972]). In order to deduct the cost of household services, a wife must have a child under 15 (or a dependent or spouse who is incapable of self-care), and many married women in the labor force do not. She must also work full-time—apparently legislators think that a part-time worker, even if she has young children, needs no replacement in the home. In addition, to gain maximum value from the deduction, she must have earnings which, when combined with her husband's, do not exceed $35,000 a year.[12] On the other hand, she must have a high enough income and high enough expenses to make it profitable to itemize deductions; yet of married couples who filed joint tax returns for tax year 1970, 40% of those with adjusted gross incomes less than $15,000 did not itemize deductions.[13] The structure of the present deduction reflects the somewhat limited value that legislators place on work done in the home.

The lack of value which legislators place on homemaking is obvious not only in policies on domestic work, but also in policies on work done outside the home. For example, the social security system's method of determining eligibility for disability payments penalizes women for interrupting their employment to fulfill responsibilities in the home. In order to be eligible for disability benefits, workers not only must be fully insured, but also must have worked five years out of the ten immediately preceding the onset of disability. As a result, only about 40% of women earners, compared to 90% of men earners, are insured for disability under social security (Ball, 1973: 316-317).

The social security system's method of determining benefit amounts also penalizes absences from the paid labor force. Social security benefits are based on average earnings and, in calculating average earnings, years when women have zero earnings because they are rearing their children are included (Ball, 1973: 317).

Like social security, the unemployment insurance system shows the lack of value which legislators place on homemaking. In the first place, by imposing special statutory limitations on the benefit rights of pregnant women, many states penalize women for bearing children. In these states, unemployed women who are able to work, available for work, and otherwise eligible for unemployment insurance, are denied payments simply because they are pregnant.

Similarly, some states have statutory provisions denying unemployment insurance payments to workers who leave their jobs because of domestic or marital obligations. Eligibility provisions applying to all workers prevent payments from being made to persons who are unable to, or unavailable for, work. Under the special provisions, however, workers who leave their jobs to marry; to accompany their spouses to another location; or to fulfill marital, filial, or domestic obligations will be disqualified even when they are again actively seeking work.*

Unemployment insurance requirements of past employment also penalize women for interrupting their employment to fulfill responsibilities in the home. In order to qualify for unemployment insurance payments, an unemployed worker must have worked recently, and for a certain minimum period of time, in covered employment. In effect, requirements of recent past covered employment deny payments to entrants and reentrants into the labor force for nine months to a year after their first day of work, a period of exclusion which may be unnecessarily long. The majority of reentrants into the labor force are female.

Like these statutory disqualifications, the unemployment insurance system's treatment of part-time work reflects the low value which legislators place on homemaking. Under the unemployment insurance system, availability for work has traditionally been interpreted to mean availability for full-time work. Although the wages of part-time workers are subject to unemployment insurance taxes on the same basis as those of full-time workers, an unemployed part-time worker generally may not qualify for unemployment insurance payments while looking for another part-time job. In 1972, 6.4 million women age 20 or over either were voluntarily employed part-time or were unemployed and looking for part-time work; this was about one-fifth of all women workers age 20 or over, and two and two-thirds times the number of men age 20 or over who were in the part-time labor force.[14] Thus, legislators consistently underestimate the value of work done in the home.

In conclusion, current economic policy shows that legislators are still more concerned about men's jobs than the equal treatment of women workers. By underestimating the role of women's earnings in family support, by overestimating the sufficiency of men's earnings, and by ignoring the value of work done in the home, legislators have created a public policy which places lower value on work done by women than on work done by men. Until economic policy equitably recognizes the value of work done by women, women will remain the economic inferiors of men. American economic policy must be reshaped to permit women to become economically equal.

NOTES

1. These examples assume use of the standard deduction. Because a husband's and wife's earnings are taxed as a unit, rather than as two separate incomes, a wife's first dollar of earnings is taxed, in effect, at her husband's highest rate. In addition, her earnings will cause the family to lose all or part of the benefits of income-splitting. See Blumberg (1973).

2. National Commission on Consumer Finance (1972: 152-153). See also U.S. Commission on Civil Rights (1974); Gates and Chapman (1973: 203-210); District of Columbia Commission on the Status of Women (1973a and 1973b).

3. In 1973 women's unemployment rate was 6.0 and men's was 4.1. In 1961 women's unemployment rate was 7.2 and men's was 6.4. See Executive Office of the President (1974: 272, Table A-15).

4. In 1973 there were 6.5 million families headed by a woman and 8.8 million female primary individuals—heads of households with no relatives present. See U.S. Census Bureau (1973a: Table E).

5. For a detailed summary of legislative developments regarding dependents' benefits under social security, see U.S. Congress, Joint Economic Committee, Subcommittee on Fiscal Policy (1972: 35-36).

6. These examples assume use of the standard deduction. The "marriage penalty" results from (1) the higher tax rates for married workers filing separately than for single workers; and (2) the limitation of the maximum standard deduction to $1,000 per married person, as opposed to $2,000 per single person. In addition, upon marriage, a single parent may lose his or her child-care deduction because the upper income limit for deducting child-care expenses applies to the joint income of the two spouses rather than to the individual parent's income.

7. In determining taxable estate, federal law permits a deduction (from the value of the gross estate) equal to the value of property passing to the surviving spouse, but only up to half of the value of the adjusted gross estate (26 U.S.C. §2056 [1970]). No such limitation is imposed upon a deduction for property passing to a charity (26 U.S.C. §2055 [1970]).

8. Information provided by the National Center for Health Statistics, Public Health Service, U.S. Department of Health, Education, and Welfare.

9. Heclo et al. (1973: 13); see also Citizen's Advisory Council on the Status of Women (1972 and 1974).

10. 42 U.S.C. §402(b), 416(d) (1970). If the ex-husband is dead and the ex-wife is caring for a child who is eligible for social security benefits on the basis of the deceased husband's wage record, the 20-year requirement does not apply (42 U.S.C. §§402[g], 416[d] [1970]).

11. The median earnings of women who worked outside the home full-time and year-round in 1973 were $6,335 (U.S. Census Bureau, 1974b: Table 2).

12. For every dollar of joint income over $35,000, the deduction is reduced.

13. Internal Revenue Service (1971: Tables 33 and 46); to claim the deduction, a married couple must file a joint return.

14. U.S. Department of Labor, Bureau of Labor Statistics (1973b: Table A-6). For a full discussion of sex discrimination in unemployment insurance, see Dahm (1973).

EDITOR'S NOTE: Court decisions made after this chapter was written have affected the policies discussed in this paragraph.

REFERENCES

BALL, R. (1973) "Testimony," pp. 316-317 in Economic Problems of Women: Hearings Before the Joint Economic Committee, 93rd Congress, 1st Session. Washington, D.C.: Government Printing Office.

BLUMBERG, G. (1973) "Testimony," pp. 228-235 in Economic Problems of Women: Hearings Before the Joint Economic Committee, 93rd Congress, 1st Session. Washington, D.C.: Government Printing Office.

Citizens Advisory Council on the Status of Women (1974) Recognition of Economic Contribution of Homemakers and Protection of Children in Divorce Law and Practice. Washington, D.C.: Government Printing Office, CACSW Item No. 40-N.

——— (1972) The Equal Rights Amendment and Alimony and Child Support Laws. Washington, D.C.: Government Printing Office, CACSW Item No. 23-N.

CLARK, H. (1968) The Law of Domestic Relations in the United States. St. Paul, Minn.: West.

DAHM, M. (1973) "Testimony," pp. 345-370 in Economic Problems of Women: Hearings Before the Joint Economic Committee, 93rd Congress, 1st Session. Washington, D.C.: Government Printing Office.

DAVIDSON, GINSBURG, and KAY (1974) Text, Cases and Materials on Sex Based Discrimination. St. Paul, Minn: West.

District of Columbia Commission on the Status of Women (1973a) Credit Policies of Department Stores in the Metropolitan Washington Area. Washington, D.C.

--- (1973b) Residential Mortgage Lending Practices of Commercial Banks, Savings and Loan Associations, and Mortgage Bankers. Washington, D.C.

Executive Office of the President (1974) Manpower Report of the President. Washington, D.C.: Government Printing Office.

GATES, M. and J. CHAPMAN (1973) "Testimony," pp. 203-210 in Economic Problems of Women: Hearings Before the Joint Economic Committee, 93rd Congress, 1st Session. Washington, D.C.: Government Printing Office.

HECLO, H., L. RAINWATER, M. REIN, and R. WEISS (1973) "Single-parent families: issues and policies." Working Paper prepared for the Office of Child Development, October.

Internal Revenue Service (1971) Statistics of Income--1970: Individual Income Tax Returns. Washington, D.C.: Government Printing Office.

KANOWITZ, L. (1969) Women and the Law. Albuquerque, N.M.: University of New Mexico Press.

KOLODRUBETZ, W. (1973) "Private retirement benefits and relationship to earnings: survey of new beneficiaries." Social Security Bulletin (May).

National Center for Health Statistics (1973) Divorces: Analysis of Changes. Washington, D.C.: Vital and Health Statistics Series 21, No. 22.

National Commission on Consumer Finance (1972) Consumer Credit in the United States. Washington, D.C.: Government Printing Office.

STOREY, J. (1974) Welfare in the Seventies: A National Study of Benefits Available in 100 Local Areas. Washington, D.C.: Studies in Public Welfare Paper No. 15, Joint Economic Committee, Subcommittee on Fiscal Policy.

U.S. Census Bureau (1974a) "Characteristics of the low-income population: 1973." Current Population Reports, Series P-60, No. 94 (July).

--- (1974b) "Money income in 1973 of families and persons in the United States." Current Population Reports, Series P-60, No. 93 (July).

--- (1973a) "Household and family characteristics: March 1973." Current Population Reports, Series P-20, No. 58.

--- (1973b) "Money income in 1972 of families and persons in the United States." Current Population Reports, Series P-60, No. 90.

--- (1973c) "Characteristics of the low-income population: 1972." Current Population Reports Series P-60, No. 91.

U.S. Commission on Civil Rights (1974) Mortgage Money: Who Gets It? A Case Study in Mortgage Lending Discrimination in Hartford. Washington, D.C.: Civil Rights Commission Clearinghouse Publication No. 48.

U.S. Congress, House Ways and Means Committee (1973) Report to Accompany H.R. 11333, H. R. Report No. 93-627. Washington, D.C.: Government Printing Office.

U.S. Congress, Joint Economic Committee (1973) Economic Problems of Women: Hearings Before the Joint Economic Committee, 93rd Congress, 1st Session. Washington, D.C.: Government Printing Office.

——— Subcommittee on Fiscal Policy (1972) Handbook of Public Income Transfer Programs. Washington, D.C.: Studies in Public Welfare Paper No. 2, Joint Economic Committee, Subcommittee on Fiscal Policy.

U.S. Department of Labor, Bureau of Labor Statistics (1973a) Marital and Family Characteristics of Workers, March 1973. Washington, D.C.: Special Labor Force Report Summary.

——— (1973b) Changes in the Employment Situation in 1972. Washington, D.C.: Special Labor Force Report No. 152.

U.S. Department of Labor, Women's Bureau (1974) Why Women Work. Washington, D.C.: Government Printing Office.

——— (1971) Fact Sheet on the Earnings Gap. Washington, D.C.: Government Printing Office.

——— (1969) "1969 handbook on women workers." Women's Bureau Bulletin 294.

WEINBERGER, C. (1973) "Testimony," pp. 422-444 in Economic Problems of Women: Hearings Before the Joint Economic Committee, 93rd Congress, 1st Session. Washington, D.C.: Government Printing Office.

2

WOMEN'S ROLES IN THE ECONOMY
Economic Investigation and Research Needs

HILDA KAHNE

The purpose of this chapter is to present an overview of the recent economic literature relating to women and to suggest future directions to strengthen its relevance for today's world. The paper identifies the range of topical interests of economists in this field and spells out the content of their findings. It looks primarily at literature that chooses as its central focus issues relating to women's status and roles.[1] The central text seeks neutrality and nontechnical language in reporting, and the views of the author are spelled out primarily in the final section of the paper. It is hoped that this review will provide a base for future interdisciplinary research and exchange.

THE ROLES OF WOMEN IN THE AMERICAN ECONOMY

LABOR FORCE PARTICIPATION

Determinants. Economic research on women's work activities has focused largely on the determinants of labor force participation, with emphasis given primarily to factors influencing supply (Cain, 1966; Mincer, 1962; and Sweet, 1973). Since 1940, there has been a rapid acceleration in women's labor force participation rate despite rising

AUTHOR'S NOTE: Selected portions of a version of this chapter were adapted for an article entitled, "Economic Perspectives on the Roles of Women in the American Economy," which appeared in the December 1975 issue of *Journal of Economic Literature.*

wages and incomes. Demographic changes could not account for this seeming contradiction between women's work activities and rising income. Thus, a number of post-World War II studies (Bancroft, 1958; Durand, 1948) have looked to other explanations.

In his incisive study, Mincer (1962) underscored the family context in which leisure and work decisions are made. He pointed out that

> Other things equal (including family income), an increase in the market wage rate for some family member makes both the consumption of leisure and the production of home services by that individual more costly to the family, and will as a matter of rational family decision encourage greater market labor input by him (her) [p. 66].

In explaining the time allocation of wives among market work, unpaid home work, and leisure, Mincer saw the positive substitution effect between home and market work resulting from women's rising market wages as a much more powerful influence over the course of a lifetime than the long-run negative family income effect. The short-run transitory response of wives to husbands' income has been reflected in cross-sectional studies showing negative relationships between husbands' income and wives' work. Over time this transitory effect disappears and the strong response to their own earnings predominates in paid-work decisions of married women.

Whereas Mincer based his analysis on the experience of white married women as reported in 1950 census data, Cain (1966) analyzed census data relating to both white and nonwhite women for the period 1940 through 1960. His findings for the 1950 data confirmed those of Mincer; but for 1940 and 1960, he found that sometimes income elasticity was stronger than wage elasticity. He agreed that short-run changes in income (transitory income) had a smaller negative effect on wives' employment than did changes in long-run permanent income. But neither measure affected employment decisions as much as the wife's wage variable or "earnings capacity." Cain concluded that the time series increase in work by married women remained only partially explained. He stressed the importance of more specific analysis of these work patterns to understand women's work decisions and as a necessary accompaniment to research relating to economic growth and employment levels; income distribution; taxation; and relationship between female wages, work rates, and birth rates.

Sweet (1973), a demographer and sociologist, contributed to the growing literature on labor force activity of wives by focusing in an analysis of 1960 census data specifically on the relationship between demographic and socioeconomic composition of the family as a unit and the employment characteristics and earnings of married women. He analyzed the relationship between family status (as measured by age of youngest child and number of children) and paid employment of white and nonwhite wives with husband present for different educational and economic classes. His analysis documented the increasing proportion of wives employed with the increasing age of the youngest child to age 12-13, after which time the proportion of working wives remained constant at about 43%. A less strong but independent negative influence on employment of mothers was the number of children in the family under age 18.

While family status variables directly affect wives' employment, they also influence the level of education and the need for additional family income, which likewise affect employment. Sweet found that low levels of educational attainment frequently prevented meeting the economic needs posed by low family income, because jobs were not available or earnings so low as to make the jobs uneconomic to take.

Introducing a different perspective, demographic sociologist Oppenheimer (1970) suggested that the increasing demand for women workers was the major causal influence on women's rising labor force participation rates since 1940. Thus, basic industrial and occupational growth trends led to increased demand for female workers in those occupations and industries that traditionally have been major employers of women. The fact that single and young women constituted a stationary or declining group during the period helped broaden demand to include married and older women, and this facilitated an increase in their supply. Labor force experience, initiated in this way, may well have been an important influence in development of women's interest in having a continuous association with the labor market throughout their lives as well as in providing employers with greater knowledge about women's potential contribution. The existence of the dual labor market provided the structural situation for an increased demand for and employment of women workers.

Additional studies contributed empirical data to the development of a theoretical framework for thinking about women's market activities and provided further statistical documentation about the interrelationships among variables that affect women's labor force participation. Morgan, Sirageldin, and Baerwaldt (1966) identified age of wife, income of husband, and education of wife as the three most important variables affecting positively or negatively the supply of working wives. Bowen and Finegan (1969), using data from the decennial census of 1940-1960 and from monthly surveys of households for the period 1947-1967, analyzed factors determining labor force participation of specific population groups. They looked particularly at the degree of sensitivity of labor force participation rates to the tightness of the labor market. They found that for women higher rates were associated with a strong demand for female labor, demonstrating support for the Oppenheimer thesis. Although for both sexes, of course, individual productivities and market competition influence jobs, Lloyd (1975a) comments that the study confirmed how women, but not men, consider family-related variables in making work decisions. The analysis, grounded in the sex role attitudes of the period, may have less relevance for women today. Aware of this, Lloyd refers to the findings of Smith's dissertation (1972), which showed a greater interdependence between the wage rate of either spouse and labor force participation of the other, though not yet an equal deterrent to work of both marital partners resulting from the presence of children in the home.

Recent research continues to document with updated experience and with specific population groups the general assumptions developed about determinants of women's labor force participation. For example, Kim (1972), using disaggregate data from the National Longitudinal Survey of Labor Market Experience Files,[2] found for a national sample of black and white women aged 30-44 that the impact of a wage rate increase on hours of work offered (substitution effect) was twice as effective as a similar change in the husband's income. Child-care responsibility, measured in terms of numbers and ages of children, was the most powerful deterrent to mothers' market work.

Other studies have looked at a related topic of the impact of unemployment on women's participation rates. Tella (1964), for example, in an examination of employment (including armed forces) and total labor force experience, found that, for women particularly, short-run variations in the labor supply were closely and positively related to variations in employment (i.e., demand). Finegan (1975) discussed the two contradictory influences on wives' employment interests that arise with men's unemployment: unemployment increases the tendency of some wives to work because of increased need, while at the same time it discourages other wives from looking for work because they believe they will be unlikely to find employment. Analyses of both cross-sectional (1960) and time series (1954-1965) data led to Finegan's assertion that only if the period of unemployment were extended (e.g., as in 1958 and 1961 recessions) could one expect the discouragement effect to be dominant, with a consequent dampening influence on women's labor force growth. For short periods of unemployment, such as occurred in 1949 and 1954, the net discouragement effect was likely to be small.

Labor force participation research continues to be important as a reflection of changing attitudes and sex roles. But a number of additional issues, also reflecting the changing times, now vie for attention in labor market-related research.

Labor force participation and fertility. Fertility (the number of children and the timing and spacing of birth), originally an area of interest primarily to demographers and sociologists, is now being studied by economists investigating its relationship to women's work activity. In two successive years, the National Bureau of Economic Research and the Population Council have been joint sponsors of a small invitational conference to develop economic theory and empirical investigation of issues relating to fertility. In contrast to past emphases by economists on effects of aggregate population growth, papers at these conferences focused on fertility decisions of the household—their determinants and implications for family life, work, child-bearing, and child-rearing decisions (see Journal of Political Economy, 1973 and 1974).

Ross' research (1974) looks at the variation among white nonfarm couples in the timing (birth of first child) and spacing (length of interval between childbirths) of children as a reflection of economic forces. She found that both price of time for women and family income affected timing and spacing of births. More highly educated women, for whom the price of time is higher, had their first birth sooner after leaving school and had shorter birth intervals, reflecting Ross' suggestion of cost efficiency in decision-making about child-bearing in a situation where the price of time was high and the earnings profile steeply rising.

In an earlier article, Oppenheimer (1972) established the relationship between fertility and work participation, but was far less certain which was the dependent and which the independent variable. Following review of evidence on both sides, she considered a separate, though related, question of whether the job market in the future was likely to be able to give support to the declining fertility that was being experienced within the society. Her analysis of the limits of traditionally female occupations to fulfill employment needs relate to today's realities. Her message addressed complexities of labor market imbalances which were related not only to fertility, but also to other factors among which were education and attitudinal or sex role changes. It is a message intensified by the economic recession.

Longitudinal work histories. That work history patterns of men and women are different is hardly startling news. The single peaked profile of men's work life rises steadily to about age 30, remains constant until the mid-50s and then falls first gradually and later sharply. The double peak of women's work activities—occurring in the early 20s and again between ages 45-50, related to women leaving the labor market at marriage and birth of first child and their reentry after the last child has entered school—has been a common pattern, at least from the end of World War II through to the present (Kreps, 1970; Suter, 1973). Results of recent research provide additional insight into this work pattern over time. Suter (1973) found that the amount of lifetime work experience was primarily conditioned by motherhood and only secondarily by educational level. Sobel (1973), on the basis of three interviews taking place between 1957 and 1967 with a panel of married white wives of child-bearing age, found the most important influences on labor force participation were expected family size and wife's education. In the late 1960s, at least, marital and maternal factors exerted strong influences on women's labor force behavior.

Polachek (1975), primarily interested in the effect of family characteristics on the size of the male-female wage differentials, has analyzed the relationship of these characteristics to labor force participation. He found that after completion of school, the life cycle of married women differed by age, education, and current work status in the kind and degree of work and home activity. Married women with many children and little education spent the most time out of the labor force to bear and raise children and about four more years devoted to intermittent participation.

Both Polachek and Mallan (1975) foresee a shrinkage of hometime periods for married women with young children. They come to opposite conclusions, however, as to the expected impact on male/female wage differentials. Studies of life cycle work patterns of women have also been related to life cycle earnings of men and to periods of family financial stress. Arising out of an interest in the function of married women's paid employment in families headed by males in different occupational categories, Oppenheimer (1973) has established the existence of two different levels and patterns of peaking of median earnings among men in different occupations. These she compares with the points of financial stress in family needs over the life cycle. The findings underscore the relatively poor synchronization between income and financial need for men with peak median earnings of less than $7,000 in 1959. For married men in this category, which included practically all men in blue-collar and service occupations and about half of men ages 25-64 in white-collar occupations, peak earnings were reached early, were of relatively low level, and were not associated with life cycle family needs. For this group, particularly those in their 40s and 50s with an adolescent child in the home, the potential boost to family well-being that could result from a wife's additional income was clear. Oppenheimer suggests that the identified financial squeeze, a reality for many families, could help to explain the high labor force participation rates of married women over age 35.

Mention should also be made of the ongoing study of the Population Studies Center of the University of Michigan. A 10-year retrospective longitudinal work history survey is in progress analyzing the influence of work experience on women's socioeconomic status and earnings. The findings will be comparable with those collected in the Ohio State National Longitudinal Surveys.

The extent and variability of women's labor market participation has been studied in greater depth than perhaps any other aspect of women's economic role. Analyses with greater specificity for occupational groups and additional studies of socioeconomic and ethnic variability could profitably add to the information on women's work behavior as we move on to trace the effects of changing values and roles and view the new issues which they raise.

THE HOUSEHOLD

Household production. Valuing women's contribution to economic life begins but does not end with a consideration of their market activities. Consumer economists in the 1930s (e.g., Reid, 1934) referred to the household as a producer of goods and services. More recently, Mincer (1962) built nonmarket work activity at home into the model describing women's alternative choices in the allocation of their time. The development of a theory of investment in human capital (Becker, 1964) linked to the scarcity aspects of one basic input—time (Becker, 1965)—firmly established the necessary theoretical framework for considering the household as a producer and for treating work in the home as a nonmarket work activity. By explicitly taking note of the scarcity of time and the need for its competitive allocation among possible uses in household production as well as in choosing among final consumer goods, the household (and its members) are engaged in legitimate, productive activity with utility maximization as a goal (Gronau, 1973a). The household is the economic entity. And the price of time is the key to understanding economic influences on women's decisions in the allocation of work between the market and the home as well as the allocation among family members of work activities in the home. With the wider range of alternative roles now available to both men and women, price of time should also play a major role in determining which family member is to be the major income earner.

Leibowitz (1974c), directing her analysis to time allocation among alternative activities of women, states that while income affects the total amount of work offered by women, its division between home and market depends on wage rates, productivity in the home, and the price and availability of substitutes for the wife's labor time in the home. The more education a woman has, the higher the "cost" of not being in the labor market, since the productivity of her time is raised by education more for labor market work than for home work.

Empirical studies of time spent in household tasks differ among employed and nonemployed women. A 1967-1968 study of wives in Syracuse found that employed wives spent an average of 34 hours per week on household tasks compared with 57 hours for women not employed outside the home (Hedges and Barnett, 1972; Vanek, 1974). In a time budget study of a sample of urban married women, it was found that employed women spent less time each weekday on food preparation, house cleaning, and laundry than did nonemployed women, and about the same amount of time on sleeping (Robinson and Converse, 1966).

Overall, more educated women have smaller time inputs to household production over the life cycle than do other women. Only for the component of child-care is this not so. Within the home (using data collected by Walker and Telling at Cornell University), Leibowitz demonstrates that child-care, unlike other home activities, has greater time inputs with increased education, both overall and per child (1974a). Stafford and Hill (1973) reinforced this finding, showing that home production time caused by the presence of a preschool child is twice as great in high socioeconomic status (SES) families as in low ones. Leibowitz explains this fact, seemingly in contradiction with what would be expected of this time-intensive activity, by reference to the low substitution elasticity with other inputs (babysitters, grandmothers, older children), as contrasted with two other household activities (meal preparation and laundry work), and the high income elasticity for spending more time on this human capital investment in child-care.

Few studies yet report on changing household allocation between husbands and wives. A multinational study of time budgets of persons in 12 countries (Szalai, 1973) indicated that women contributed 32% of all time registered in formal work and accounted for 78% of total time taken up by housework and related obligations. The impact of industrialization hâs not changed in a major way the relative importance of categories on which time is spent: household tasks took about the same amount of time in the industrialized West German towns studied as in the Yugoslavian site that lacked running water.

In the 1960s in the United States, married women spent an average of 40 hours a week keeping house, compared with 4 hours a week for husbands (Morgan, Sirageldin, and Baerwaldt, 1966: 102). A study of dual-career families in the late 1960s found that although husbands and professional wives often shared household tasks, for two-thirds of the couples, household tasks were either performed by the wife with the assistance of hired help or remained the primary responsibility of the wife (Holmstrom, 1972: 67). As our experience with more egalitarian family life styles grows, research can begin to evaluate effects of changing roles as applied to household tasks.

Household tasks comprise the preponderant activity (90%) in nonmarket work, which also includes volunteer activities (5%), education of family head and miscellaneous activities (5%), according to Sirageldin (1969). The collective value of the societal contribution is considerable, but the absence of data on physical inputs, the heterogeneity in the quality of services produced, and the absence of pricing data make it difficult to give precision to the calculations (Gronau, 1973b). To develop value estimates, extensive gathering of time budget data for home production activities (Morgan, Sirageldin, and Baerwaldt, 1966; Hedges and Barnett, 1972) and for volunteer activities (Morgan, Sirageldin, and Baerwaldt, 1966; and U.S. Department of Labor, Manpower Administration, 1969) has taken place. More difficult has been the imputing of prices for services for which there is no market equivalent. Alternative approaches have been suggested for measuring housewives' contributions (Johnson, 1975): valuing homemakers' contributions as equivalent to foregone earnings in the market—opportunity costs (Kreps, 1970; Sirageldin, 1969); summing the results of application of going wage rates to each of the "jobs" performed by housewives (Walker, 1955; Sirageldin, 1969); estimating replacement costs of a substitute mother (Rosen, 1974); or considering the comparative advantage of work in the home and market and hence estimating the value of housewives' time relative to that of wage-earning women (Gronau, 1973a and 1973b). The value of volunteer services has been estimated from an average wage applied to hours expended, obtained through direct inquiry (Morgan, Sirageldin, and Baerwaldt, 1966), and from imputation of an hourly wage applied to estimates of the quantity of volunteers required as provided by recipients of volunteer contributions (Wolozin, 1966).

Morgan, Sirageldin, and Baerwaldt (1966: 5) estimate that inclusion of unpaid work in national accounts in 1964 would have increased the GNP by 38%. Kreps' (1970: 67) report on the NBER in 1918, Kuznets in 1928 and Geller in 1968 each estimated housewives' services at not less than 25% of the value of the GNP. By 1980 it is estimated that volunteer activities, not including home production, may contribute $30 billion a year to the economy (U.S. Department of Labor, Manpower Administration, 1969: 1).

Conversations about how to devise a correct dollar value for these contributions continue, along with discussions of how to incorporate such values into measurements of the GNP and calculations of income for computing social welfare benefits. But the fact of productive contribution is no longer argued, and the research issues surrounding these kinds of work are now being studied (Mueller, 1974).

FAMILY-RELATED ISSUES

It is becoming increasingly clear that market and nonmarket work, marriage, fertility, and education are interrelated questions, decisions about which are both determined by and affect all members of the family unit (Sweet, 1973). To gain insight into the dynamic changes occurring in market and home work and in leisure activities over the life cycle, these activities and their participants must be simultaneously considered. Discussion of some aspects of these topics is arbitrarily placed in this section, although in fact the issues and values to which they are related affect equally market and household functioning. Longitudinal work histories, earlier described, also exemplify this interaction between work and aspects of personal lives.

Marriage. Historically, marriage rates rise with increasing real income, although the reverse has been true in the trend of the past two decades (Santos, 1975). Between 1950 and 1970, there was an increase in the proportion of young single women; the median age at first marriage for females has been creeping up; and the divorce rate has moved markedly upward since 1963, nearly doubling in the past ten years (Hayghe, 1974: 25). Fertility rates are down (U.S. Office of Management and Budget, Statistical Policy Division, 1973: 250). Clearly some major life style changes are taking place.

Economists, no less than other social scientists, are interested in analyzing these trends. For some, analysis has been formulated in terms of economic theory alone; others have been interested in the relationship of the analytic findings to the philosophy of the women's liberation movement. In both cases the primary focus has been on the institution of marriage itself—its structure, function, and future.

Becker (1973) has applied economic maximizing principles and analytic techniques, applicable to the firm, to the initial development of an economic theory of marriage that attempts to explain the existence and variety of marriage choices and patterns. The theories of preferences and utility maximization are used to describe the choice of mate in a "marriage market," which is defined as being in equilibrium in the sense that no person can change mates and be better off. It is further assumed that each person tries to maximize his or her well-being and that there exists a positive correlation between the values of traits (education, physical capital, height, race, and others) of husbands and wives. Gains from marriage over singleness are positively associated with income, relative difference in wage rates, and the level of nonmarket productivity-augmenting variables (e.g., education or beauty). In a subsequent article, Becker (1974) explores a number of questions relating to love and caring, monogamous and polygamous marriages, the relationship between natural selection and assortive mating, and some characteristics of mating in marriages and of marriage dissolutions (divorce).

Johnson (1975), also focusing on the neoclassical economic model, seeks to explain recent changes in marriage and divorce patterns. She describes the expected utility of a marriage as being related to its material and psychic returns. Divorce occurs when expected future returns, relative to cost of being married, are smaller than the expected returns from alternative arrangements. The shift in tastes in favor of labor force activity helps to explain the postponement and decline in marriage, the increase in single-person households, and fewer numbers of children. Divorce is positively and significantly associated with greater job satisfaction, she finds, in an analysis of 1967 data provided by a 5,000-female sample of the National Longitudinal Population Survey. While this cannot be proven to be an effect of the women's movement, she notes a compatibility of this finding with the movement's philosophy with respect to women's roles. Johnson describes additional and reinforcing effects on these trends that can be expected if the feminist recommendations with respect to valuing the contribution of the homemaker are incorporated into our thoughts and our accounts.

Santos (1975) also finds the rise in market work for women to be an important factor in explaining the secular decline in the proportion of married females. This is one of those seemingly innocuous statements that make a startling point—in this instance, suggesting that the increased interest of women to engage in paid work may have far-reaching implications for life styles and intimacy patterns. Even if marriage continues as a societal norm, its prevalence and nature may well be altered.

Throughout this discussion of the economics of marriage, as through consideration of task and time allocation within the household, we are forced to confront major issues facing our society. What is the role of the family in society? What is its future? Does social policy take into account the prevalence of separation and divorce?

Findings of a still ongoing major research project which have a bearing on these questions have recently been published. A panel survey of 5,000 American families, covering the period 1968-1972 (Morgan, 1974) has examined environmental and behavior patterns of individuals and families in an effort to identify variables related to improvement in economic status, particularly for the poor. The findings, dramatic in their implications for family and poverty policy development, suggest that of all the variables influencing changes in well-being, family composition and what takes place within the home are perhaps the most important in their impact on well-being (p. 337). The importance of these findings for poverty policy, and for women, is highlighted when we realize that increasing numbers of poor families are headed by women and that a family's chance of being persistently poor is about twice as great if the head is a woman (p. 336).

Sawhill, Ross, and MacIntosh (1973) approach some of these same questions in a different way. (See also Ross, chapter 5 in this volume.) They review the historical changes in economic functions provided by the family, raise a number of important questions for the future, and speculate that the family may be moving toward a new orientation—that of an income-pooling unit, evolving out of the growing equality of roles of male and female marital partners. Public policy alternatives applicable to the family are explored and evaluated—alternatives such as monitoring legislation to ensure that it contributes to the stabilization of family life, transferring family financial responsibilities to the government, encouraging women's economic independence through programs such as subsidized day-care. Though the policy orientation of each measure is different, they need not be mutually exclusive and could be applied in ways that reinforce one another.

Writing more generally on the relationship between sexism and capitalism, Davies and Reich (1972) find that the role of the family under capitalism appears at the same time to be undermining its traditional structure while benefiting from the maintenance of its sexist character. Finally, in a report prepared for the Office of Child Development, Heclo, Rainwater, Rein, and Weiss (1973) analyze the prevalence, composition, and dynamics of movement into and out of the single-family state and some related emotional and social problems. Both American and European experiences with policy achievement and with unmet needs are evaluated.

While marriage trends are clear, economists' theoretical modeling and supporting empirical studies are incomplete. The models need to take account of the fact that our personal lives are governed by more than profit-maximizing principles. And in empirical studies more questions as well as evaluation of alternative answers need to be considered. Both would increase the reality orientation of the research in an area where the concepts as well as the facts are still undergoing considerable change.

Fertility and child-care. Economists are seeking a framework for interpreting fertility and child-care experience and for assessing their impact both on the work experience of adult family members and on educational attainment and work achievement of the child. They take for granted the human preferences for children, investigate parents' resources for child-bearing and rearing to obtain future satisfaction and productive services, and seek to assess the opportunity costs such choices involve. In sum, they are attempting to provide an analytic approach for explaining lifetime behavior patterns, although research results so far have been restricted to static economic assumptions. The human capital approach (the cost of investment of human time) is the foundation upon which their analytic explanation is developed. And consistent with this approach, time input to the household production function is seen as allocated according to maximization principles among a variety of commodities, of which child-care is only one. The general thrust of argument and review of the literature is contained in *Journal of Economic Literature* review articles on fertility (Leibenstein, 1974) and consumer economics (Ferber, 1973) and in the National Bureau of Economic Research Population Conferences.

One research area to be noted here relates to defining and refining models to explain the quantity and quality of time investment in "child services," an investment that clearly varies at different ages of children and depends on the price of time, family ethos, family income, family member earnings, education, and contraceptive techniques employed (Becker and Lewis, 1973; DeTray, 1973; Willis, 1973; Rosenzweig, 1975). Other research has tested hypotheses relating to the importance of time inputs to children for their later educational attainment, training, and earnings. For example, Hill and Stafford (1974) show that with greater input to child-care, particularly prior to grade school, greater educational attainment and training will be achieved. Leibowitz (1974b) suggests that time spent by educated women with their children affects not only children's early achievement but their ultimate level of schooling as well. She notes that parents' education (proxy for heredity and quality of time) and quantity of time inputs invested in preschool children increased the stock of childhood human capital as measured by children's IQs. Mincer (1962) and Stafford (1974) confirm the importance of education for future education or earnings of children.

Both quantity and quality of time inputs appear to be important to children's development; and for mothers who choose to allocate their time to child-rearing, economists indicate the existence of a positive return. Whether comparable child development can be achieved in alternative ways, for mothers whose choice is for greater time allocation to the market, has not yet been made clear. But alternative market structures for providing child-care, and associated costs, have been studied, and a brief review of this literature is included here.

Day-care in our country dates to 1838 (Boocock, 1973), but not until World War II did programs become widespread, particularly affecting children of women working in the defense industries (U.S. Department of Labor, Women's Bureau, 1971).[3] In the 1960s, associated with increased labor force participation of mothers with young children, interest in child-care was rekindled. Estimates of the use of day-care centers vary (Lave and Angrist, 1973; Keyserling, 1972; Westinghouse Learning Corporation and Westat Research, Inc., 1971; Low and Spindler, 1968), but all agree that the trend in use is upward. The Westinghouse study (1971: VI, VII), for example, estimates that 10.5% of children of working mothers are cared for in day-care centers, 575,000 children receiving full day-care in 17,500 centers and 695,000 additional children in less formal day-care homes. Variation also exists in the estimates of future needs (Ruderman, 1968; Westinghouse . . . , 1971; Zamoff and Lyle, 1971; Angrist and Lave, 1974). The Women's Bureau, for example, projects that by 1980 the number of children under 5 with working mothers will increase from 3.7 million to 5.3 million (Zamoff and Lyle, 1973). The necessity for thinking about alternative approaches to day-care is not trivial.

Costs to users of day-care services depends on goals, services, administrative arrangements, and availability of subsidy. Rowe and Husby (1973) outline the essentials of parents' demands for inexpensive care that is geographically convenient, offered at critical hours, and of the "right" kind. A number of analyses have been made of the costs of services in this labor-intensive industry (Sugarman and Feldman, 1968; Fitzsimmons and Rowe, 1971; Westinghouse . . . , 1971; Weikert, 1972). While cost estimates vary (Rowe and Husby, 1973),[4] there is some agreement that child-care costs are about $2,000 per child-year or $40 a week for full-time care—a much higher figure than parents are willing to pay (Angrist and Lave, 1974: 4). One study indicated, rather, that $22 was the expense families were willing to incur, and this was more consistent with the $24-a-week figure found to be the actual expenditure made.

Studies contribute knowledge to some of the issues that need to be considered for development of future directions. One issue relates to the use of day-care centers as an instrument in fostering child development. Head Start is an example of a child development program, with caretaker functions only incidentally provided. Evaluations have not demonstrated the long-term results hoped for, showing the effects of the program fading by the fourth grade (Angrist and Lave, 1973). While evidence to date justifying programs on the basis of educational externalities (where social benefits exceed private benefits) is still insufficient, other benefits similar to those received from public education—e.g., early detection of children's psychological or physical problems—do exist (Schultze et al., 1972).

A second suggested goal is to provide child-care to permit welfare mothers to engage in paid work. The Work Incentive Program (WIN) has attempted to achieve this result. But from a cost standpoint, at least, there is some evidence that the cost of good day-care exceeds that of the maintenance of welfare payments (Schultze et al., 1972). If this is to be a program objective, nonmonetary gains must provide the rationale.

Alternatively or coincidentally, day-care can be viewed as a service for mothers at all socioeconomic levels who choose to work. Subsidies, voucher programs (Fried et al., 1973), and charging for day-care service on a sliding scale related to income could make this possible. Experience with industrial programs (Curran and Jordan, 1970) and with legislative provisions for tax deductions or credits (Schultze et al., 1972) would then be relevant for deciding about structure and program provisions. Neither approach is problem-free, however.

The conclusion must be reached that evaluative groundwork is incomplete and that research is still needed on such issues as the effect of day-care on child well-being and on the work response of mothers in different socioeconomic groups (Angrist, Lave, and Mickelson, 1975). Experimental research is also needed on innovative day-care approaches and structures (Jusenius and Sandell, 1974). But this must take place within a context of clarity on the purposes day-care is expected to fulfill so that costs can be measured against the private and social benefits desired.

Education. Although the influence of education on aspects of women's roles has been referred to several times in this chapter, it is important to underscore the relevance that education has for family-related issues. The rising numbers and proportions of women with high school and college educations is well known, as is the higher labor force participation rates of women at increasing levels of education. Research informs us, too, that while education presumably raises the productivity and hence the rate of return from market work relative to home production, this rate of return remains lower for women than for men (Leibowitz, 1974c; Madden, 1974). The influence of education on allocation of time among household activities and between market and home production (Leibowitz, 1974) is thus complicated by additional factors.

CHANGING ROLES AND SOCIAL POLICY

This chapter would be incomplete if reference were not made to the importance of economic research on women's roles in legislative and executive policy formulation. The topic is too comprehensive for exhaustive treatment here, but its importance can be documented by reference to three areas where legal and economic issues are closely intertwined.[5] Each is in an area where values and roles are rapidly changing and, perhaps because of the current transitional nature of our value system, divergent for groups in the society. The contribution of economic thinking and research should be valuable in providing guides for policy positions and for legislative change.

INCOME TAX LEGISLATION

Inadequacies in the tax code become more apparent as married women increasingly opt to work in the paid labor market (Groves, 1963; see also Griffiths, chapter 1 in this volume). While married women's labor force attachment has been increasing, income tax provisions are still based on the assumption that the American family has a husband at work in the market and a wife/mother at home. The provisions that reflect this philosophy result in disadvantageous treatment of the two-earner family, and project a strong work disincentive for the wife weighing the benefits and costs of engaging in paid work as an alternative to remaining out of the paid employment market.

The aggregation of income, the filing of joint returns by married couples, and the income-splitting provisions which they permit —while initially introduced to equalize tax burdens between married couples residing within and outside of community property states— have had the additional effect of benefiting most those married couples where the wife limits her activities to the home. With no taxable income for the wife, although with an acknowledge imputed value to her services, such families benefit because the splitting of taxable income between husband and wife lowers the tax bracket into which each income falls. For the wife with a labor market attachment, her first dollar of income is effectively taxes at the primary earner's highest or "marginal" rate, thus reducing her monetary contribution to the family coffers, as well as the effective return for her labors (Blumberg, 1971-1972; Cooper, 1970-1971; Cohen, 1972).

Moreover, unlike the situation found in a number of European countries (Blumberg, 1971-1972), uneven relief is provided to working persons, married or not, in the form of earned income credits or exemptions. While the U.S. internal revenue code does permit a deduction for expenses involved in care of dependents and for household services which are incurred to make it possible for the taxpayer to be gainfully employed, the provisions do have several disadvantageous aspects for women. For married couples, they apply only when both spouses are engaged in substantially full-time employment or when one spouse is incapable of caring for self. They apply only to households containing one or more "qualifying individuals" (dependents under 15 or an incapacitated dependent or spouse), and thus may exclude couples without children or employed single women, both of which groups may also incur expenses in connection with gainful employment. Many divorced spouses also tend to be ineligible for the deductions. Moreover, the cost of household services performed outside the household, though incurred to enable gainful employment to take place, are excluded from coverage (Feld, 1972; Blumberg, 1973).

A variety of corrective suggestions have been offered. To remove the rate inequities resulting from income-splitting and to equalize the tax burden among family units and individuals with the same taxable income, Joseph Pechman (1973: 226) would halve the tax brackets applicable to married couples. At the same time, to meet the two-earner family inequity, he, and others, would enact some form of earned income credit or deduction (Cooper, 1970-1971; Blumberg, 1971-1972; Pechman, 1973) based, for Pechman, on the earned income of the spouse with the lower earnings. Other suggestions include substituting an individual for a spousal taxable unit (Pechman, 1973: 226) or enactment of more rational provisions, either combined or separately constructed, for deduction of costs of child-care or for paid domestic work to replace the wife's work in the home (Bergmann and Adelman, 1973). Proponents of each proposed amendment urge its enactment for one or more reasons—to improve the equity of the tax system, to permit the more accurate reporting of net income after deduction of expenses relating to work (a reflection of capacity to pay), and to help lessen the work disincentive effect of the system as it now operates.

SOCIAL SECURITY LEGISLATION

Some of the proposed revisions of our social security legislation similarly arise from the fact that the basic structure of the system assumes that most married women are economically dependent on their husbands' income. (See also Griffiths, chapter 1 in this volume.) Hence benefits for wives and widows are related in amount to their husbands' benefit. If a wife who has worked in paid employment qualifies for a benefit based on her own earnings that is less than what she would have received as a dependent wife, she automatically receives a supplementary amount equal to this difference. While she is not penalized in the computation of her benefit amount by having qualified for lower benefits on the basis of her own earnings, neither has she gained additional retirement benefits from her tax contributions during her working years.

Suggested solutions—such as basing family retirement income on joint family earnings (Bell, 1973) or lowering the tax rate for married working women (Cooper, 1970-1971: 74)—run into problems of the acceptability of income-splitting arrangements or the equity of special provisions for married as against single working women. The increasing prevalence of divorce also complicates the problem. Without some suitable substitute arrangement, abolition of present provisions that permit linkage of a wife's benefits to her husband's earnings is hardly feasible while a majority of women still are or have been dependent on these earnings. A number of women's groups suggest that credits, presumably at a uniform amount, should be given for service in the home. The appeal of this type of provision, as presented by Carolyn Shaw Bell (1973), for example, is that it would remove the onus of dependency from housewives by giving recognition to their productive contribution. But again, while giving explicit legislative recognition to this contribution is important, devising a system that provides monetary as well as nominal recognition is not easy. For unless credit is accrued in relation to husband's earnings, a housewife's benefits alone, at least for most middle-class women, would be less than that based on a husband's earnings. And for these cases, the present method of benefit computation remains the more favorable alternative. An acceptable benefit formula that incorporates credit for a housewife's activities has yet to be developed.

Much more research and analysis is needed to back up these and other suggestions designed to bring legislation into conformity with current social structures (Merriam, 1972; Reno, 1973). Data on women's lifetime work histories, and their relevance for earning patterns, are still being developed (Mallan, 1974), and it is not at all clear to what extent future patterns of family life or of paid and nonpaid employment will differ from those of today. The relative importance of wives' and husbands' earnings in two-earner families and the extent and character of the economic responsibilities of single women (and men) may also be changing and are worth more analysis by social scientists.

There is a beginning of economic research geared to these current issues. Michael Boskin (1974) provides an overview of some of the important effects of government expenditures and taxes on the supply of male and female labor in the market. He notes the differential effects on men and women of some of the particular tax provisions just discussed, as well as the fact that men and women may offer different amounts of labor in response to a given incentive. He finds that elasticity of wives' market labor supply is positive and much larger than that of husbands', and hence it is negatively affected by taxes. Taxes also reduce the return to (and hence investment in) human capital, and this additionally depresses the female labor supply offered in the market. His work suggests that individual income and payroll taxes in their present form tend to decrease the attractiveness of market work for women and limit human capital accumulation of women relative to men.

Boskin's research addresses both an important tax issue and an important women's issue. But more research on the economic costs and benefits of work for women and how women respond to the work incentives and disincentives in the economy is needed. Such data, combined with knowledge of current living and working patterns, will give the necessary raw materials on which to develop social policy reflective of today's needs.

SOCIAL POLICY AND WOMEN IN POVERTY

For poor women, their economic status and the social legislation to which it gives rise have implications for the roles they play and the way they allocate time between market and home work. The development of constructive social policy with respect to the needs of poor women requires a better understanding of the variables that affect their status and the ways in which legislation influences both their status and their roles. No account of the roles of women can be complete without some references to this group, which is an increasingly important component of our low-income population.

Twenty-three million persons, 11% of the population, were below the poverty level in 1973.[6] Age, sex, and race are closely related to this poverty status. Of the 23 million low-income persons, 18.3 million were in families and 4.7 million were classified as unrelated individuals. Family members included 9.5 million children under age 18, 2.6 million male family heads, 2.2 million female heads, and 4.0 million other family members, many of whom were wives (U.S. Department of Commerce, 1974). Three-fifths of the adult population in poverty were women (U.S. Department of Labor, Bureau of Labor Statistics, 1974). Nineteen percent of low-income women were 65 years of age or over, a considerably higher percentage than their proportion in the population (U.S. Department of Commerce, 1974). Over time the relative importance of male-headed families has decreased, while those with female heads has increased.

Much of the research on poverty has been carried on in an

interdisciplinary environment and has had a policy orientation geared to welfare reform (Barth, Carcagno, and Palmer, 1974). Thurow's basic study (1969) analyzed the causal factors in poverty and considered alternative corrective strategies. Other recent literature has evaluated the experience and effectiveness of ongoing and experimental welfare programs in an effort to identify research needs, policy goals, and programmatic structures that will enable families to move out of poverty to more adequate levels of living (Barth, Carcagno, and Palmer, 1974; U.S. Congress, Joint Economic Committee, 1972-1974). These discussions, directed to the adequacy and improvement of our general welfare policy, relate to all persons in poverty, men and women alike, who comprise the working and nonworking poor.

The sharp rise in the proportion of poor families with female heads has directed some attention to this particular group and has resulted in a number of studies that focus specifically on women's experience and behavior in relation to welfare programs. Jack Meyer (1972), in an analysis of the welfare system of mid-1967 and its influences on work experience for a limited national sample of women aged 30-44, has demonstrated that time spent in paid employment by married women is inversely related to the level of welfare benefits for which they are eligible. Other studies have found a similar increase in the recipient rate for welfare assistance as the benefit size relative to potential earnings increased (Hausman and Kasper, 1971). With rising benefit levels, greater male desertion among poor husband-wife families was also noted in some studies (Honig, 1971; Durbin, 1973).

A number of studies have underscored the complexity of interaction among variables that influence the market labor supply of women—e.g., marital status, earning potential, availability of jobs for men and for women, presence of preschool children, educational levels, and health status (Honig, 1971; Hausman and Kasper, 1971; and Haring, 1973). Shea (1973) has described some of these factors in terms of responses of a group of black and white poor and nonpoor women to a hypothetical job offer. He concluded that while greater job availability, better transportation, and offer of health services might positively affect the work interest level, more efficient child-care arrangements might have little effect.

Some authors have evaluated the potential impact of alternative policy approaches that relate to welfare assistance—e.g., broader coverage of income maintenance programs or increasing benefit levels; to buttressing the position of men as income earners; or to increasing women's ability to achieve economic independence through increasing their work capacities and access to work opportunities (Durbin, 1973; Ross, 1973).

Recent research has continued to identify the problems of existing welfare legislation which inappropriately reinforce certain work and living patterns (Ross, 1973). Several authors have marked out and methodologically developed some of the areas where additional research is needed with respect to income maintenance for women in poverty—studies of marital stability (Lefcowitz, 1971), fertility patterns (Cain, 1971), work incentives (Hausman and Kasper, 1971), among others. The accumulation of data evaluating ongoing programs must continue, while greater clarification is sought with respect to the goals of welfare programs generally and to their impact on female-headed families. A clearer picture of desirable social policy directions with respect to women's roles should help in the development of effective policy and programs that speak to preventative as well as to ameliorative measures.

SOCIETAL CHANGE AND FUTURE DIRECTIONS

The perspective from which one views research by economists on roles of women in the economy must begin with an awareness of the dizzying pace with which societal changes relating to women have been occurring. The advent of the Women's Movement unpegged the stable framework that had permitted investigation into women's labor force participation to proceed comfortably under generally agreed-upon assumptions regarding women's activities.

The mid-1960s witnessed women's rising consciousness of roles, aspirations, and often discriminatory treatment, and at the same time saw the enactment of legislation asserting women's rightful claim to equality of opportunity in the market and equality of treatment in society at large. In the 1970s, despite a diminished bargaining power associated with the economic recession, a two-pronged movement directed to change within the establishment and to alteration of the system itself reinforced the drive for correction of long-persisting inequities. As a result, women are beginning to find broader acceptance within the existing work structures, including placement in jobs and training for jobs that were formerly male occupations. They and their employers are coping with the ramifications of these changes with respect to already employed working persons, many of whom are men. At the same time, both in the workplace and more generally, institutions and structures are beginning to be modified in major ways. The stated desire of the Women's Movement to strengthen the value placed on humane interpersonal relations has been translated into a broader desire to humanize and make more responsive the institutions with which we all must deal.

Bearing in mind the rapidity and thrust of these changes helps to clarify why economic research, suffering from time lags in available analytic data and from delayed publication dates, also fails to focus on the critical issues which these dynamic changes point up. The ongoing changes appear to have a reinforcing rather than a cyclical rhythm; their reflection in personal relationships, living styles, work aspirations, and now institutional and societal structures appears, to this observer at least, to be both dramatic and irreversible. The need for a better understanding of their nature and their impact is imperative.

How should economists deal with all of this? What is the relevance of this commentary for future directions? While research undoubtedly reflects the interests and preferences of research economists, especially those interests that can generate institutional support and those supported researches that can find a publisher, comment can be made about three areas of need—response to which would give the discipline a stronger claim to being at the cutting edge of research related to women's roles and activities.

BOUNDARIES OF THE DISCIPLINE

First, I see a need to consider again, as undoubtedly has been done in the past, just what constitutes legitimate economic research relating to women in terms of assumptions, orientation, and style. In studies of women's roles, as in labor economics (Piore, 1973), the focus of the field on human beings dictates an approach that supports the application of economic tools in ways that enlighten understanding of behavior patterns, rather than abstracting from them in some mechanical way. Human beings embody labor power, but both as acting and reacting agents they are more than an impersonal form of capital. Denial of these facts may make a tidier analytic package, but not a more meaningful one. Since economists are now studying the economics of human beings in their investigations of marriage, divorce, and family relationships, the fence of legitimacy for the discipline should be widened to include consideration of the variables associated with human responses and social relations that influence the human decisions made. Broader consideration of variables will strengthen disciplinary contributions that may begin with application of maximization principles to human decision-making, but seek as an ultimate goal to improve the quality of life for human beings.

Similarly, new values and roles require that research more extensively address itself to challenges of the system itself as well as to studies of modifications or incremental changes within the system. The existing literature on women, for the most part, presumes the values of our mixed economy, and assumptions and findings are developed within this framework. To properly evaluate what is happening, we must give greater visibility in focus and in publication to analyses critical of the existing order and of the way the order impinges on roles and personality traits of workers (Edwards, 1972; Edwards, Reich, and Weisskopf, 1972), and on family behavior (Davies and Reich, 1972), and hence on women.

Not only must the boundaries of legitimate economic research be expanded, but also treatment of many topics still requires an interdisciplinary approach. Labor force participation, work motivation and satisfaction, economics of the family, for example, are all interdisciplinary in nature, and the work of social scientists in disciplines other than economics complement in important ways the thinking of economists (Giele, forthcoming; Gurin, 1974; Laws, forthcoming; Oppenheimer, 1973). Although several education- and government-sponsored conferences have sought to foster interdisciplinary interchange on issues with policy implications, the potential is still greater than the accomplishment. Much could be done to facilitate exchange of ideas and collaborative efforts within institutions rather than to have them take place always among a few leaders in a few interuniversity conferences or within a few major research institutes. Interdisciplinary work could receive important support from presentation of bibliographies in ways that highlight interdisciplinary contributions and integrate the reporting of scholarly research and related programmatic activity.

Moreover, there is a need for an expanded application of research techniques that wed policy implementations and evaluation. These include strategic research techniques that, through the collaborative evaluation and analysis of records, permit time series studies of changes that have taken place as a result of an implemented policy (Reagan and Maynard, 1974; Rivlin, 1974). They include an extension of social experiments to test the feasibility of a suggested policy for achieving a desired goal (Orr, Hollister, and Lefcowitz, 1971). And they include research based on participant observation (Bergmann, 1974). There is need for greater specificity in longitudinal studies of women's work histories in different occupations and in different socioeconomic categories (Kahne, forthcoming; Reagan, Strober, and Moser, 1974). There is need for more case studies to provide a variety of experiential data—e.g., on the performance of men and women in specific occupations (Urban Institute, 1974); on the experience of flexi-time and flexi-work schedules in specific firms (Greenwald, 1974); on the costs and benefits of dual careers carried on in different geographic locations by married couples (Ngai, 1974); and still of critical importance, analysis of occupational and earnings experience of women and men in specific firms and for specific work (Bergmann, 1974). Each of these techniques provides a mechanism for testing and evaluating ongoing changes (or non-changes) in experience and in policy.

RESEARCH ISSUES

There is a need to enlarge the range of issues to be investigated in the light of the rapidly changing social scene. The issues described below are suggestive of the kinds of areas to which researchers might profitably devote attention. They are mentioned as supplements to the already identified research areas which have developed from an awareness of current societal trends and which are now penetrating the literature.

1. There is a continuing need for questioning and redefining vocabulary to ensure that economic terms conform with today's realities. The potentially erroneous interpretations that can follow from imprecise application of value-laden phrases—such as "traditional" and "frictional" unemployment or definitions of the categories of persons who are to be included in enumerations of the labor force—have been commented on in the literature (Bell, 1972 and 1974). But more than this, one must note that concepts are changing

in major ways. For example, there may develop in the future a significant discrepancy between one's job, which is how one earns one's living, and one's work, which is how one spends the rest of one's nonleisure time. Some of the latter is work in the home or volunteer activities; some could relate to other activities such as independent unpaid professional or creative work. Women without institutional affiliation have coped with this problem in the past—becoming volunteer professionals has been one resolution of the dilemma. Economists are beginning to address the economics of volunteer work in a serious way (Mueller, 1975). But the growing numbers of educated persons with interests related to their education, the tight labor market for professional activities, and the disaffection of some persons for career ladders as the appropriate environment for doing their serious work—all combine to reinforce the need to think more thoroughly about the implications of a possible disjunction between jobs and all of the kinds of unpaid work that men and women do. Questions relating to the definition of work; the identification of the workplace and its gradual interface with the home; the measurement of the value of these nonpaid but still professionally productive contributions; their transferability as experience in applying for a market job; and the implications for the individual of work satisfaction, maintenance of occupational networks, and provision of social benefits provide a beginning list of issues to be thought about.

2. The other side of the coin just described relates to jobs—or paid work—and this topic, of course, will continue to be a major aspect of research relating to women's roles. The implications of recession for women's labor market activity, the impact of affirmative action legislation, the potential impact of enactment of the Equal Rights Amendment, the ramifications of male backlash, and the restructuring of time and work are each topics that could benefit from economists' attention. The collection and dissemination of data categorized by sex are of critical importance if we are to understand the statistical patterns of women's employment and earnings.

The possibility of shared jobs is receiving more serious scrutiny now that the beneficial possibilities for academic finances of shared husband-wife appointments become apparent. The issues of flexitime and part-time are no longer being approached as second-best economic solutions for married women who give high priority to home responsibilities, but are seen as a possible positive outcome for both men and women, either because of a lack of full-time job opportunities or because of personal preferences for a more flexible or reduced paid-work commitment. The fact that the proportion of women in part-time jobs is higher than that of men should not obscure the fact that the numbers of men and women who are employed for only part of a year is surprisingly similar. We need studies of the costs and benefits of these kinds of jobs. Further, the study of occupations is beginning to take note of both economic and sociological aspects. Thought is being given to the notion of restructuring traditionally female jobs, such as secretary or nurse, so as to endow them with independence and career potential. The causes and effects of occupational segregation and earnings differentiation must continue to receive concentrated attention.

3. Focus on paid and unpaid work activity must not result in slighting the attention that needs also to be given to issues relating to women in other than labor market relationships. Women in the credit market, as entrepreneurs, home buyers, family providers, and purchasers of insurance may be heard first as activist voices speaking to the need for equal consideration but quickly also fall into place as voices that speak to issues which require research underpinning as an informational and interpretive base (Chapman, 1975).

4. Just begining to be explored are research issues that arise from the realization that—while women share many common concerns and interests relating to their life patterns—work motivation, work pattern and history, career progress, and satisfaction from work may differ among them. The effectively articulated needs of educated women, and the emphasis given the situation of married women and the problems they face in combining marriage and work, have obscured the similarly distinctive problems of single women, for example, and the different individual work patterns over the life cycle that distinguish black from white women and blue-collar from white-collar workers. Economists have not yet engaged in in-depth comparative socioeconomic studies of work patterns of working women. The issues raised move us into more general economic areas, but they also have a specific relevance here for women's roles and suggest logical next steps for research now going on independently on professional women (Johnson and Stafford, 1974; Strober and Quester, forthcoming) and on women in poverty.

In terms of changing patterns of life and work, I am impressed with the full-time continuous commitment and professional competence of educated young professional women. It is possible that they may avoid the problems encountered by their older counterparts, counterparts who have provided researchers with a wealth of data with which to analyze the consequences of following a nonmale work pattern. But I am skeptical that—now that many young women have decided to become professional—all their problems will be solved. More than ever, men and women will have to cope with the frustrations of overlapping roles and the allocative decisions these require. Family income management; economic aspects of alternative life styles; and abortion, fertility, and child-care issues will now provide the basis for research equally important to today's studies analyzing the impact of discontinuities and part-time employment on lifetime earnings experience.

5. Lastly, increasing attention must be given to the experience and policies relating to women in other cultures, not only because of their intrinsic interest, but equally because they are indicators of alternative directions to be considered for American women. Parental leaves of absence from work and pilot studies of the experience of placement of men in women's jobs and vice versa, now being experimented with in Sweden, for example, are immediately relevant for our workplace environment concerns (Barrett, 1973; Giele and Smock, forthcoming).

Economists who are alert to patterns of societal change will find a wealth of issues for investigation, where application of their tools of analysis to the issues raised can contribute understanding and evaluative comment.

POLICY-ORIENTED RESEARCH

Cutting across all of these issues is the question of research orientation. What becomes apparent as one sifts through the literature is the existence of a continuing asymmetry between the developing ways of women's being and their ways of being perceived by existing legislation and in the economy. A large element of discrimination continues to exist in the income rewards of women for the economic contributions they make. Though their economic role within the family is often important and sometimes critical, this is not always acknowledged. Topics in this chapter that serve as intriguing academic exercises for economic researchers represent issues of life-sustaining importance to women seeking equitable consideration for their creative and economically beneficial activities. There is, therefore, a need for continuing and strengthening research concerned with policy issues for women as a disadvantaged group, in order to bring opportunity, treatment, and reward systems more nearly in line with those applicable to men. While such concerns may begin with a quest for simple justice, it is economic reasoning that presses hard for policy priorities. As Sawhill, Ross, and MacIntosh (1973: 3) have recently explained in speaking of the social consequences of discrimination against women:

> First, there is the poverty of female-headed families whose median income is about one-third that of male-headed families and a substantial proportion of whom are now on welfare. Second, there is the fact that segmented labor markets create a dispersion of unemployment rates which shifts the Phillips Curve to the right and makes the achievement of full employment and price stability that much more difficult. Third, if one believes that continued population growth is undesirable for ecological reasons, then women must be provided with opportunities outside the home . . . and I haven't even mentioned . . . an obvious gain in total output from using resources efficiently.

In all the intricacies of generalized model-building, analytic detail, and empirical studies, it is easy to overlook what is the major concern of this field of research, if not indeed the ultimate concern of all of economics. Simple to state, though not simple-minded to comprehend (and, indeed, frequently and patently overlooked), is the fact that what this field is about is the well-being of human beings—individual women and the men and children whose lives are linked to theirs as family, friends, and co-workers. It is no new refrain, but only a new framework for repeating what has been said by economists countless times before: "[While] economics has to do with the aspect of [people] concerned with the satisfaction of . . . material wants . . . it is the whole [person] who acts in economic matters" (Witte, 1957: 14). It is this framework of concern that leads us into interdisciplinary research and into social policy positions. Remembering this will help researchers formulate meaningful as well as challenging questions for study and will help build a body of knowledge that permits both better understanding of the activities of individuals and of the policies that permit human wants to be satisfied in a more satisfying way.

NOTES

1. This review does not cover all of economics that bears on women. It omits a number of areas where a general theoretical or analytic framework also has a relevance for women. Neither consumer economics nor welfare economics—both areas in which women as a group are important in the literature—are covered. In addition, research on male/female differences in earnings and occupational assignment are not reviewed, because this area is touched upon in several other chapters in this book. For a more complete evaluation of economic literature in these areas, see Jusenius and Blau (1975) and Kohen et al. (1975). The latter bibliography is available from the library at the Center for Human Resource Research, Ohio State University, 224 Tenth Avenue, Columbus, Ohio 43201.

2. The National Longitudinal Survey provides a publicly available national data base of demographic characteristics, work and educational experience, and attitudes toward work and school for samples of two groups of women (ages 14-24 and 30-44) and two groups of men (ages 14-24 and 45-59). The sample populations were first surveyed in 1966. A growing number of studies using these data and relating to women's work experience are being initiated. See *NLS Newsletter*, No. 1 (April 1974).

3. This section was developed and written by Dianne S. Hurley, Wellesley, 1970.

4. Rowe and Husby (1973) attribute many differences among the estimates to definitional discrepancies and differences in cost-accounting methods used. Their own estimate—that a full day's care for children under 6 would cost upward of $2,000 per child-year—excluded start-up costs and the administrative costs of federal, state, and local bureaucracies.

5. The author is indebted to Dianne Lund, Harvard Law School, for identifying important recent legal references that analyze changes in women's status under the law. (See Murphy, 1970; Brown et al., 1971; Johnston and Knapp, 1971; Flanders and Anderson, 1973; Getman, 1973.)

6. The poverty level is based on the Social Security Administration's poverty thresholds, adjusted for changes in the Consumer Price Index. For nonfarm households in 1973, the poverty income level for an unrelated individual was set as below $2,247, $2,895 for a couple, and $4,540 for a family of four. The poverty levels for farm households were set at 85% of these amounts.

REFERENCES

American Economic Association, Committee on the Status of Women (1975) Reports on a questionnaire survey of careers of women economists. Papers presented at the annual meeting of the American Economic Association, December 1974, San Francisco, and reported in American Economic Review 65 (May).

AMSDEN, A. H. and C. MOSER (1975) "Job search and affirmative action." American Economic Review 65 (May): 83-91.

ANGRIST, S. S. and J. R. LAVE (1974) "Economic, social and policy aspects of child care: a quantitative analysis of child care arrangements of working mothers." Pittsburgh: Carnegie-Mellon University, School of Urban and Public Affairs, March. (mimeo)

——— (1973) "Issues surrounding day care." Family Coordinator (October): 457-464.

——— and R. MICKELSEN (1975) "How working mothers manage: socioeconomic differences in work, child care, and household tasks." Pittsburgh: Carnegie-Mellon University, School of Urban and Public Affairs. (mimeo)

BANCROFT, G. (1958) The American Labor Force: Its Growth and Changing Composition. New York: John Wiley, 1950 Census Monograph Series.

BARRETT, N. W. (1973) "Have Swedish women achieved equality?" Challenge (November/December): 14-20.

BARTH, M., G. J. CARCAGNO, and J. PALMER (1974) "Towards an effective income support system: problems, prospects and choices." Madison, Wis.: University of Wisconsin, Institute for Research on Poverty.

BECKER, G. S. (1974) "A theory of marriage: part II." Journal of Political Economy 82 (March/April): S11-S26.

——— (1973) "A theory of marriage: part I." Journal of Political Economy 81 (July/August): 813-846.

——— (1965) "A theory of the allocation of time." Economic Journal 75 (September): 495-517.

——— (1964) Human Capital: A Theoretical and Empirical Analysis with Special Reference to Education. New York: National Bureau of Economic Research.

——— and H. G. LEWIS (1973) "On the interaction between the quantity and quality of children." Journal of Political Economy 81 (March/April): S279-S288.

BELL, C. S. (1974) "Women in science: definitions and data for economic analysis," pp. 151-159 in R. Knudsen (ed.) Women and Success: The Anatomy of Achievement. New York: William Morrow.

——— (1973) "Testimony," p. 305 in Economic Problems of Women: Hearings Before the Joint Economic Committee, 93rd Congress, 1st Session, Part 2, July 24-30. Washington, D.C.: Government Printing Office.

——— (1972) "A full employment policy for a pulbic service economy: implications for women." Social Policy (September/October): 12-19.

BERGMANN, B. R. (1974) "Towards more useful modes of research on discrimination in employment and pay." Sloan Management Review 15 (Spring): 43-45.

——— and I. ADELMAN (1973) "The 1973 report of the President's Council of Economic Advisors: the economic role of women." American Economic Review 63 (September): 509-514.

BLUMBERG, G. (1973) "Testimony," pp. 247-252 in Economic Problems of Women: Hearings Before the Joint Economic Committee, 93rd Congress, 1st Session, Part 2, July 24-30. Washington, D.C.: Government Printing Office.

——— (1971-1972) "Sexism in the Code: a comparative study of income taxation of working wives and mothers." Buffalo Law Review 21: 49-98.

BOOCOCK, S. S. (1973) "A cross-cultural analysis of the child care system." New York: Russell Sage Foundation.

BOSKIN, M. J. (1974) "The effects of government expenditures and taxes on female labor." American Economic Review 64 (May): 251-256.

BOWEN, W. G. and T. A. FINEGAN (1969) The Economics of Labor Force Participation. Princeton, N.J.: Princeton University Press.

BROWN, B., T. I. EMERSON, G. FALK, and A. E. FREEDMAN (1971) "The Equal Rights Amendment: a constitutional basis for equal rights for women." Yale Law Journal 80 (April): 871-980.

CAIN, G. (1971) "Experimental income maintenance program to assess the effect of fertility," pp. 89-105 in L. R. Orr, R. G. Hollister, and M. J. Lefcowitz (eds.) Income Maintenance—Interdisciplinary Approaches to Research. Chicago: Markham.

——— (1966) Married Women in the Labor Force. Chicago: University of Chicago Press.

CHAPMAN, J. R. (1975) "Women's access to credit." Challenge (January/February): 40-45.

COHEN, E. S. (1972) "Testimony," before Committee on Ways and Means, House of Representatives, May 1.

COOPER, G. (1970-1971) "Working wives and the tax laws." Rutgers Law Review 25: 67-75.

CURRAN, J. R. and J. W. JORDAN (1970) The KLH Experience: An Evaluative Report of Day Care in Action. Cambridge: KLH Child Development Center.

DAVIES, M. and M. REICH (1972) "On the relationship between sexism and capitalism," pp. 348-356 in R. Edwards et al. (eds.) The Capitalist System. Englewood Cliffs, N.J.: Prentice-Hall.

DAVIS, H. and B. P. RIGAUX (1974) "Role structure in family consumption behavior." Journal of Consumer Research 1 (June).

DeTRAY, D. N. (1973) "Child quality and the demand for children." Journal of Political Economy 81 (March/April): S70-S95.

DURBIN, E. (1973) "Work and welfare: the case of Aid to Families with Dependent Children." Journal of Human Resources 8—supplement (September): 103-125.

Economic Report of the President (1973) Transmitted to Congress January 1973. Washington, D.C.: Government Printing Office.

EDWARDS, R. C. (1972) "Alienation and inequality: capitalist relations of production in bureaucratic enterprises." Ph.D. dissertation, Harvard University, July.

——— M. REICH, and T. E. WEISSKOPF (1972) The Capitalist System. Englewood Cliffs, N.J.: Prentice-Hall.

FELD, A. (1973) "Dissents and concurrences." Tax Law Review 28 (Summer): 535-553.

——— (1972) "Deductibility of expenses for child care and household services: new Section 214." Tax Law Review 27 (Spring): 415-447.

FERBER, R. (1973) "Consumer economics: a survey." Journal of Economic Literature 11 (December): 1303-1342.

——— and L. CHAO (1974) "Husband-wife influence in family purchasing behavior." Journal of Consumer Research 1 (June).

FERBER, R. and F. M. NICOSIA (1972) "Newly married couples and their asset accumulation decisions," in Human Behavior in Economic Affairs: Essays in Honor of George Katona. Amsterdam: North Holland.

FERRIS, A. L. (1970) Indicators of Change in the American Family. New York: Russell Sage Foundation.

FINEGAN, T. A. (1975) "Participation of married women in the labor force," pp. 27-60 in C. Lloyd (ed.) Sex, Discrimination and the Division of Labor. New York: Columbia University Press.

FITZSIMMONS, S. J. and M. P. ROWE (1971) "A study in child care, 1970-71." Prepared for the Office of Economic Opportunity by Abt Associates.

FLANDERS, D. P. and P. E. ANDERSON (1973) "Sex discrimination in employment: theory and practice." Industrial & Labor Relations Review 26 (April): 938-955.

FRIED, E. R. et al. (1973) Setting National Priorities: The 1974 Budget. Washington, D.C.: Brookings.

GALBRAITH, J. K. (1973) "The equitable household and beyond," in Economics and the Public Purpose. Boston: Houghton Mifflin.

GETMAN, J. G. (1973) "The emerging constitutional principle of sexual equality," pp. 157-180 in P. B. Kurland (ed.) The Supreme Court Review. Chicago: University of Chicago Press.

GIELE, J. (forthcoming) American Women and the Future.

——— and A. SMOCK (forthcoming) Women in Society.

GRAMM, W. E. (1975) "Household utility maximization and the working wife." American Economic Review (March): 90-100.

GREENWALD, C. S. (1974) "Part-time work and flexible hours employment." Presented at the Workshop on Research Needed to Improve the Employment and Employability of Women, June 7, 1974. Washington, D.C.: U.S. Department of Labor.

GRONAU, R. (1973a) "The intra-family allocation of time: value of housewives' time." American Economic Review 63 (September): 634-651.

——— (1973b) "The measurement of output of the nonmarket sector: the evaluation of housewives' time," pp. 163-189 in M. Moss (ed.) The Measurement of Economic and Social Performance. New York: Columbia University Press, NBER Studies in Income and Wealth, Vol. 39.

GROVES, H. M. (1963) Federal Tax Treatment of the Family. Washington, D.C.: Brookings.

GURIN, P. (1974) "Psychological issues in the study of employment discrimination." Presented at the M.I.T. Workshop on Equal Employment Opportunity, January 21-22, 1974.

HARING, A. (1973) "Work or welfare? An attitude segmentation of ADC clients." New York: Human Resources Administration, July.

HAUSMAN, L. J. and H. KASPER (1971) "The work effort response of women to income maintenance," pp. 89-105 in L. L. Orr et al. (eds.) Income Maintenance—Interdisciplinary Approaches to Research. Chicago: Markham.

HAYGHE, H. (1973) "Marital and family characteristics of the labor force in March 1973." Montly Labor Review 97 (April): 21-27.

HECLO, H., L. RAINWATER, M. REIN, and R. WEISS (1973) "Single-parent families: issues and policies." Working Paper prepared for the Office of Child Development, October.

HEDGES, J. N. and J. K. BARNETT (1972) "Working women and the division of household tasks." Monthly Labor Review 95 (April): 9-13.

HILL, C. R. and F. P. STAFFORD (1974a) "Family background and lifetime earnings." Paper prepared for Conference on the Distribution of Economic Well-Being, New York, National Bureau of Economic Research, May.

——— (1974b) "Time inputs in children," pp. 319-344 in J. N. Morgan (ed.) Five Thousand American Families—Patterns of Economic Progress, Vol. II. Ann Arbor: University of Michigan, Survey Research Center, Institute for Social Research.

HOLMSTROM, L. L. (1972) The Two Earner Family. Cambridge: Schenkman.

HONIG, M. H. (1971) "The impact of the welfare system on labor supply and family stability: a study of female heads of families." Ph.D. dissertation, Columbia University.

JOHNSON, G. E. and F. P. STAFFORD (1974) "The earnings and promotion of women faculty." American Economic Review (December): 888-903.

JOHNSON, S. B. (1975) "The impact of women's liberation on marriage, divorce, and family life style," pp. 401-426 in C. Lloyd (ed.) Sex, Discrimination and the Division of Labor. New York: Columbia University Press.

JOHNSTON, J. D., Jr. and C. L. KNAPP (1971) "Sex discrimination by law: a study in judicial perspective." New York University Law Review 46: 237-280.

Journal of Political Economy (1974) Volume 82, 2 (March/April).

——— (1973) Volume 81, 2 (March/April).

JUSENIUS, C. L. and F. D. BLAU (1975) "Economists' approaches to sex segregation in the labor market: an assessment." Presented at the Conference on Occupational Segregation, Wellesley College, May 21-23.

JUSENIUS, C. L. and S. SANDELL (1974) "Barriers to entry and re-entry into the labor force." Columbus: Ohio State University, Center for Human Resource Research, June.

KAHNE, H. (forthcoming) "Career patterning of women in selected professional fields." Business and Professional Women's Foundation.

KEYSERLING, M. D. (1972) Windows on Day Care. New York: National Council of Jewish Women.

KIM, S. (1972) "Cross-substitution between husband and wife as one of the factors determining the number of hours of labor supplied by married women." Columbus: Ohio State University, Center for Human Resource Research.

KOHEN, A. I. et al. (1975) "Women and the economy: a bibliography and a review of the literature on sex differentiation in the market." Columbus: Ohio State University, Center for Human Resource Research, March.

KREPS, J. (1970) Sex in the Marketplace: American Women at Work. Baltimore: Johns Hopkins Press.

LAVE, J. R. and S. S. ANGRIST (1973) "Factors affecting child care expenditure of working mothers." Pittsburgh: Carnegie-Mellon University, School of Urban and Public Affairs.

LAWS, J. L. (forthcoming) "Psychological dimensions of women's work force participation," in P. A. Wallace (ed.) Some New Perspectives on Equal Employment Opportunity. Cambridge: M.I.T. Press.

LEFCOWITZ, M. (1971) "Marital stability," pp. 105-110 in L. L. Orr et al. (eds.) Income Maintenance–Interdisciplinary Approaches to Research. Chicago: Markham.

LEIBENSTEIN, H. (1974) "An interpretation of the economic theory of fertility: promising path or blind alley?" Journal of Economic Literature 12 (June): 457-479.

LEIBOWITZ, A. (1974a) "Production within the household." New York: National Bureau of Economic Research Working Paper No. 27, January.

––– (1974b) "Home investments in children." Journal of Political Economy 82 (March/April): S111-S131.

––– (1974c) "Education and home production." American Economic Review 64 (May): 245-250.

LOW, S. and P. G. SPINDLER (1968) Child Care Arrangements of Working Mothers in the United States, 1965. Washington, D.C.: Government Printing Office, U.S. Children's Bureau and U.S. Women's Bureau Publication No. 461.

MADDEN, J. (1974) "Proposal for research evaluating the returns to the education of women." Personal communication from the author.

MALLAN, L. B. (1974a) "Changes in female labor force experience, 1961-1971." Presented at the annual meeting of the American Economic Association, San Francisco, December.

––– (1974b) "Women born in the early 1900's: employment, earnings, and benefit levels." Social Security Bulletin (March): 3-25.

Massachusetts Institute of Technology (1974) Research Workshop on Equal Employment Opportunity, Cambridge, Mass., January 21-22, March 29, and June 5.

MERRIAM, I. C. (1972) "Women and income security." Presented at Conference on Women: Resource for a Changing World. Cambridge: Radcliffe Institute.

MEYER, J. A. (1972) "Labor supply of women potentially eligible for family assistance." Columbus: Ohio State University, Center for Human Resource Research, November.

MINCER, J. (1962) "Labor force participation of married women: a study of labor supply," pp. 63-101 in Bureau of Economic Research (ed.) Aspects of Labor Economics. Princeton, N.J.: Princeton University Press.

MORGAN, J. N. [ed.] (1974) Five Thousand American Families–Patterns of Economic Progress. Volume II: Special Studies on the First Five Years of the Panel Study of Income Dynamics. Ann Arbor: University of Michigan, Survey Research Center, Institute for Social Research.

––– et al. [eds.] (1974) Five Thousand American Families–Patterns of Economic Progress. Volume I: Analysis of the First Five Years of the Panel Study of Income Dynamics. Ann Arbor: University of Michigan, Survey Research Center, Institute for Social Research.

MORGAN, J. N., I. SIRAGELDIN, and N. BAERWALDT (1966) Productive Americans: A Study of How Individuals Contribute to Economic Growth. Ann Arbor: University of Michigan, Institute for Social Research.

MUELLER, M. N. (1974) "Economic determinants of female participation in volunteer work." Presented at the annual meeting of the American Economic Association, San Francisco, December.

MURPHY, T. E. (1970) "Female wage discrimination: a study of the Equal Pay Act, 1963-1970." University of Cincinnati Law Review 39: 615-649.

NGAI, S.Y.A. (1974) "Long-distance commuting as a solution to geographic limitation to career choices of two career families." M.A. thesis, Massachusetts Institute of Technology.

OPPENHEIMER, V. K. (1973) "The life-cycle squeeze: the interaction of men's occupational and family life cycles." September. (mimeo)

――― (1972) "Rising educational attainment, declining fertility and the inadequacies of the female labor market," pp. 309-328 in C. F. Westoff and R. Parke, Jr. (eds.) Commission on Population Growth and the American Future, Final Research Reports. Volume I: Demographic and Social Aspects of Population Growth.

――― (1970) The Female Labor Force in the U.S.: Demographic and Economic Factors Governing Its Growth and Changing Composition. Berkeley: University of California Press, Population Monograph Series No. 5.

ORR, L. L., R. G. HOLLISTER, and M. LEFCOWITZ [eds.] (1971) Income Maintenance– Interdisciplinary Approaches to Research. Chicago: Markham.

PECHMAN, J. (1973) "Testimony," pp. 253-257 in Economic Problems of Women: Hearings Before the Joint Economic Committee, 93rd Congress, 1st Session, Part 2, July 24-30. Washington, D.C.: Government Printing Office.

PIORE, M. (1973) "The importance of human capital theory to labor economics–a dissenting view." Proceedings of the 26th annual meeting of the Industrial Relations Research Association.

POLACHEK, S. W. (1975) "Discontinuous labor force participation and its effect on women's market earnings," pp. 90-122 in C. Lloyd (ed.) Sex, Discrimination and the Division of Labor. New York: Columbia University Press.

REAGAN, B. B. (1975) "Two supply curves for economists? Implications of mobility and career attachment of women." American Economic Review 65 (May): 100-107.

――― and B. J. MAYNARD (1974) "Sex discrimination in universities: an approach through internal labor market analysis." American Association of University Professors Bulletin (Spring): 13-21.

REID, M. (1934) Economics of Household Production. New York: John Wiley.

RENO, V. (1973) "Women newly entitled to retired-worker benefits: survey of new beneficiaries." Washington, D.C.: U.S. Department of Health, Education and Welfare, Social Security Administration, Office of Research and Statistics Report No. 9, April.

RIVLIN, A. M. (1975) "Income distribution–can economists help?" American Economic Review 65 (May): 1-15.

――― (1974) "Social experiments: their uses and limitations." Monthly Labor Review 97 (June): 28-35.

ROBINSON, J. P. and P. CONVERSE (1966) "66 basic tables of time budget data for the United States." Ann Arbor: University of Michigan, Survey Research Center, Institute for Social Research.

ROSEN, H. S. (1974) "The monetary value of a housewife: a replacement cost approach." American Journal of Economics & Sociology 33 (January): 65-75.

ROSENZWEIG, M. R. (1975) "Child investment and women," pp. 269-288 in C. Lloyd (ed.) Sex, Discrimination and the Division of Labor. New York: Columbia University Press.

ROSS, H. L. (1973) "Poverty: women and children last." Washington, D.C.: Urban Institute, Working Paper, December.

ROSS, S. G. (1974) "The timing and spacing of births and women's labor force participation: an economic analysis." New York: National Bureau of Economic Research Working Paper No. 30.

ROWE, M. P. and R. D. HUSBY (1973) "Economics of child care: costs, needs and issues," pp. 98-122 in P. Roby (ed.) Child Care: Who Cares? New York: Basic Books.

RUDERMAN, F. A. (1968) Child Care Arrangements Made for Daytime Care of Children. New York: Child Welfare League of America.

SANTOS, F. B. (1975) "The economics of marital status," pp. 244-268 in C. Lloyd (ed.) Sex, Discrimination and the Division of Labor. New York: Columbia University Press.

SAWHILL, I. V. (1973) Comments on papers presented at the session on Women at Work in the Home and in the Market, at the annual meeting of the American Economic Association, December.

——— H. L. ROSS, and A. MacINTOSH (1973) "The family in transition." Washington, D.C.: Urban Institute Working Paper No. 776-02, September 14.

SCHULTZ, T. W. (1973) "The value of children: an economic perspective." Journal of Political Economy 81 (March/April): S2-S13.

SCHULTZE, C. L. et al. (1972) Setting National Priorities: The 1973 Budget. Washington, D.C.: Brookings.

SHEA, J. R. (1973) "Welfare mothers: barriers to labor force entry." Journal of Human Resources 8–supplement (September): 90-102.

SHORTLIDGE, R. (forthcoming) Study on demands for day care centers and the constraints of children on women's labor force participation. Columbus: Ohio State University, Center for Human Resources Research.

SIRAGELDIN, I. A-H. (1969) "Non-market components of national income." Ann Arbor: University of Michigan, Survey Research Center, Institute for Social Research.

SMITH, J. (1972) "The life cycle allocation of time in a family context." Ph.D. dissertation, University of Chicago.

SOBOL, M. G. (1973) "A dynamic analysis of labor force participation of married women of childbearing age." Journal of Human Resources 8 (Fall): 497-505.

STAFFORD, F. P. and R. C. HILL (1973) "Allocation of time to preschool children and educational opportunity." (mimeo)

STROBER, M. H. (1975a) "Formal extrafamily child care—some economic observations," pp. 346-375 in C. Lloyd (ed.) Sex, Discrimination and the Division of Labor. New York: Columbia University Press.

——— (1975b) "Women economists: career aspirations, education, and training." American Economic Review 65 (May): 92-99.

——— and A. QUESTER (forthcoming) "Comments on Johnson and Stafford's 'The earnings and promotion of women faculty'."

SUGARMAN, J. and L. FELDMAN (1968) "Standards and costs for child care." Washington, D.C.: U.S. Department of Health, Education and Welfare, Children's Bureau.

SUTER, L. E. (1973) "Occupation, employment and the lifetime work experience of women." Washington, D.C.: U.S. Department of Commerce.

SWEET, J. A. (1973) Women in the Labor Force. New York: Seminar.

SZALAI, A. [ed.] (1973) The Use of Time: Daily Activities of Urban and Suburban Populations in Twelve Countries. The Hague: Mouton.

TELLA, A. (1964) "The relation of labor force to employment." Industrial & Labor Relations Review 17 (April): 454-469.

THUROW, L. C. (1969) Poverty and Discrimination. Washington, D.C.: Brookings.

Urban Institute (1974) Study of policewomen prepared for the Police Foundation. Washington, D.C.: Police Foundation.

U.S. Congress, Joint Economic Committee, Subcommittee on Fiscal Policy (1972-1974) Studies in Public Welfare. Washington, D.C.: Government Printing Office.

U.S. Department of Commerce (1974) "Consumer income." Current Population Reports, Series P-60.

U.S. Department of Labor, Bureau of Labor Statistics (1974) Press release of June 10.

U.S. Department of Labor, Manpower Administration (1969) "Americans Volunteer."
Washington, D.C.: Government Printing Office, Manpower/Automation Research
Monograph No. 10, April.

U.S. Department of Labor, Women's Bureau (1974) Workshop on Research Needed to
Improve the Employment and Employability of Women, Washington, D.C., June 7.

――― (1971) "Day care services: industry's involvement." Bulletin 296. Washington, D.C.:
Government Printing Office.

U.S. Office of Management and Budget, Statistical Policy Division (1973) Social Indicators.
Washington, D.C.: Government Printing Office.

Valparaiso University Law Review (1971) "Women and the Law." Symposium Issue No. 5.

VANEK, J. (1974) "Time spent in housework." Scientific American 231 (November):
116-120.

WALDMAN, E. and R. WHITMORE (1974) "Children of working mothers, March 1973."
Monthly Labor Review 97 (May): 50-58.

WALKER, K. E. (1955) "Homemaking work units for New York State households." Ph.D.
dissertation, Cornell University.

WEIKART, D. P. (1972) "A decision for a national day care cost-effectiveness experiment."
Prepared for the Division of Research and Evaluation, Office of Economic Opportunity.
Ypsilanti, Mich.: High/Scope Educational Research Foundation.

Westinghouse Learning Corporation and Westat Research, Inc. (1971) Day Care Survey–
1970: Summary Report and Basic Analysis. Prepared for Evaluation Division, Office of
Economic Opportunity. Washington, D.C.

WILLIS, R. J. (1973) "A new approach to the economic theory of fertility behavior."
Journal of Political Economy 81 (March/April): S14-S64.

WITTE, E. E. (1957) "Economics and public policy." American Economic Review 47
(March): 1-21.

WOLOZIN, H. (1966) "The value of volunteer services in the U.S. economy." Delivered at
the annual meeting of the Southern Economic Association, Atlanta, November.

ZAMOFF, R. B. and J. R. LYLE (1973) "Who needs what kind of day care center?" Child
Welfare 52 (June): 351-358.

ZAMOFF, R. B. (1971) "Assessment of day care services and needs at the community
level." Washington, D.C.: Urban Institute Paper 714-1-1, November.

3

WOMEN IN INDUSTRIAL SOCIETY
An International Perspective

NANCY SMITH BARRETT

During the 1960s, women's rights movements gained increasing momentum in most of the industrial countries. Although the form these movements took and the social reaction to them varied from country to country, they all relfected a growing malaise among women—particularly middle-class and upper-class women—that most observers attribute primarily to changes in economic conditions.

While radical feminist activity accompanied demands for social reform in most countries, it is a mistake to attribute changes in attitudes of women in industrialized countries toward work, family, and society in general to a radical fringe. Although the severity of the problem may vary from country to country and the solutions may be different, there is no question that industrial development has rendered nonfunctional certain types of sex role differentiation and that this has produced the potential for social conflict between the sexes.

Opinions vary as to how widespread are the feelings of discontent. One purpose of this paper will be to shed some light on the nature and magnitude of the problem. However, whether or not traditional attitudes about appropriate activities for women are deeply in-grained, there is no question that equality for women will become more, rather than less, of a social issue in the industrial countries. This is because economic and social changes have rendered the woman's role within the family less time-consuming and less fulfilling without at the same time offering her alternative channels to achieve status and self-esteem.

HOW WE GOT WHERE WE ARE

Most theories of sex role differentiation in modern society point, ultimately, to changes in the requirements of the economic system as the motive force for shifts in sex roles and changes in the status of women (Holter, 1971: 2-12). The social conflict associated with women's rights movements that has become increasingly apparent in most industrial societies can be viewed as an attempt to restore the artificial gap between the activities of the sexes created by the industrial revolution.

Preindustrial society was characterized by family-based agriculture and cottage industry, and most economic activity took place in the home. The family unit was also the basic unit of production, and income was realized either in kind or from the sale of goods and services produced jointly by the family members. Not only did women have an important economic function, but there was no question of separating the incomes of husband and wife. So the problem of whose activities had greater worth or who was economically dependent upon whom did not arise in the manner in which it does today.

Social status was more related to family connections than income or occupation, and such connections could come through a person of either sex. Who one was, rather than what one did, was most important. And while a woman could potentially improve her status through marriage, the same was also possible for a man. Although high income was certainly a source of social status, income was generally obtained through inheritance and landownership, rather than labor force activity. In fact, of course, the concept of a labor force did not appear until the process of industrialization began (Polyani, 1957). Thus, while there was sex differentiation in preindustrial society—with women specializing in child-bearing and child-rearing activities—it produced little alienation between the sexes in the economic sphere.

Many aspects of the industrial revolution served to develop sources of conflict between the sexes. The shift of the most lucrative economic activities out of the home into the factory had a number of effects. Because of the child-rearing responsibilities of the woman, the man was usually first to leave the home, and factory products soon displaced home-produced goods in the market economy. The growth of the money economy meant that the man became the principal source of money income within the family. And as traditional society began to crumble, money income became an important source of social status. Thus, not only did the economic activities of the sexes become physically separated, but the social value of the man's activities, measured in money, became separated from his wife's. Because household economic activity was not given a market value, a woman had no way to achieve economic status independent of her husband.

Other aspects of the industrial revolution were the urbanization process and the increase in geographical mobility which produced more socially isolated families. Thus, at the same time that family-based economic activity declined in importance, extended family ties were ruptured and an important source of social status and self-esteem for women was lost. Although more egalitarian relationships between spouses are likely to develop in the nuclear family than the extended family (Holter, 1971: 3), the potential conflict based on inequality of economic status increases.

The factory system of the nineteenth century was physically and mentally debilitating, and the liberation of women from the factories to the home was one focus of women's rights movements during that period. The idea of women as the "weaker sex," to be protected by men, was most fully developed in this period, particularly the Victorian era of the late nineteenth century. The nonworking wife was indeed a symbol of economic success; and the more servants she had and the more she spent on frivolous but conspicuous consumption, the more prestige was afforded the husband and family. Remnants of these attitudes can still be seen in working-class families today. Labor force participation rates are lowest for women in the income and educational groups that reflect low-middle-class status, suggesting that the pressures for these women to stay at home despite the potential rewards from labor force activity are greatest for this group.[1]

Such were the developments during the industrial revolution that simultaneously moved men into labor force activity, attached social status to that activity, and encouraged women to remain at home (Pinchbeck, 1930). A woman's social status became determined by her husband, and the socially acceptable mechanism for gaining self-esteem became the fulfillment of family responsibilities. This being the norm, unmarried women were viewed as a social anomaly and, except in rare circumstances, afforded little opportunity to

TABLE 1: Labor Force Participation Rates in Sweden and the United States, 1950-1972[1]

	Sweden				United States			
	Men	Women			Men	Women		
		Single[2]	Married	With Children Under 7		Single	Married[3]	With Children Under 6[4]
1950	88.7	60.0	16.0		86.8	47.0	23.8	11.9
1960	86.2	60.0	26.0		84.0	42.1	30.5	18.6
1965	84.0	57.4	44.0	36.9	81.5	39.6	34.7	23.3
1966	83.2	56.8	45.9	38.2	81.4	40.2	35.4	24.2
1967	82.4	54.5	46.2	40.3	81.5	41.8	36.8	26.5
1968	82.1	55.2	47.8	42.1	81.2	45.7	38.3	27.6
1969	81.3	55.2	49.5	45.8	80.9	45.7	39.6	28.5
1970	80.6	55.1	51.5	49.7	80.6	46.8	40.8	30.3
1971	80.3	55.4	53.2	52.1	80.0	45.8	40.8	29.6
1972	79.7	55.2	54.5	53.7	79.7	47.2	41.5	30.1

1. For Sweden, labor force participation rates are expressed as a percentage of the population between ages 16 and 74. For the United States, they are percentage of the population over 13 years of age until 1966, and over 15 years thereafter.
2. Includes widowed and divorced.
3. Only with spouse present in the household; all other women are included in the "single" category.
4. Only for married women with spouse present. For Sweden all women with children under 7 are included.

Sources: Sweden—Statistiska Centralbyrån, *Arbetskraftsundersokningen*; United States—Bureau of Labor Statistics, *Current Population Survey*.

achieve status on their own initiative. The wife of a doctor who performs no economic function still has considerably more social status than an unmarried nurse.

In more recent years, certain social changes have produced a growing dissatisfaction among women who stay at home. The life expectancy of women has increased dramatically since the turn of the century, and this longevity has coincided with a reduction in family size. In many countries the marriage age has also declined, and this means that the age at which the average woman bears her last child has fallen to 30 or below in many countries. Consequently, a woman may easily look forward to 20 or 25 years of life after her last child has left home.

While the demands of child-bearing now take up a smaller proportion of a woman's life, modern technology has also eased the burden of housework in general. No advanced technology can reduce the problems of child-care in the early years (although child-care centers could help significantly), so many women view homemaking as less than a full-time job once the children are in school. Thus, in most all of the industrial countries after World War II, there has been a rapid growth in the participation of women in the labor force. This phenomenon has been widespread and constitutes perhaps the most important structural change in the labor markets of the advanced countries in the past 25 years.

Table 1 shows changes since 1950 in female labor force participation rates in Sweden and the United States, where the changes were most dramatic, but the trend is clear in all the industrialized countries. Not only has the proportion of women in the labor force been increasing rapidly, but the age and class composition of the female labor force has also changed. Because of the expectation of a longer child-free lifespan, many women interrupt their labor force activity only for a year or two (if at all) for child-bearing. As shown in Table 1, labor force participation in the 1960s grew the most dramatically for married women and particularly for women with small children. This has meant that associated with increasing labor force activity in recent years has been a growing need for the provision of child-care facilities—a concern not voiced so strongly in the 1950s, when the female labor force was composed principally of very young women, single women, and older married women.

In recent years there has also been a recognition that a woman's career prospects are endangered by her dropping out of the labor force and, consequently, women seem to have developed more permanent labor force attachments. This development also increases representation of women in the 25-35 age group, who now drop out less frequently or for shorter periods to have children. Rising incomes and increased educational opportunities for women have shifted the occupational composition of the female labor force from industrial and domestic employment to white-collar work. These developments have also contributed to the difficulties associated with the provision of child-care, since less domestic help is available relative to the demand and more communal child-care arrangements are necessitated.

Although the trends toward increasing labor force participation and labor force attachment of women, particularly young women, have been fairly long-term ones, there has been no fundamental reorganization in industrial societies that would make these developments beneficial to all concerned. The reluctance of most governments to recognize that child-care is a social concern, not an individual problem, is only one example. Therefore, industrial development increased women's motives and opportunities to work, but the economic system based on sex role differentiation has failed to respond to these changes. The resulting need for some fundamental reorganization of the division of economic activity between the sexes has become apparent.

Feminist movements have arisen to demand equal employment opportunities and legal rights and responsibilities for women. At the same time, housewives have become increasingly discontented; and the need for positive reinforcement of cultural values supportive of the homeworking wife has become critical to the maintenance of the social fabric. The mass media—television, women's magazines—have been strident in their efforts to bolster the self-esteem of the housewife. The constant reassertion that the homeworking wife is the mainstay of modern society is sometimes almost pathetic in its insistence. Myrdal and Klein (1956: 10) point to the political implications of this need to reinforce anachronistic cultural values, arguing that "because they have been given the vote they [housewives] are constantly courted, appealed to and glorified by governments and politicians." But the results of this campaign are to set women against each other and to force the individual woman to deal with the seemingly unreconcilable personal conflict between the lack of challenge of the housewife role versus the feeling of obligation to her family and the society that glorifies it. As Myrdal and Klein (1956: 136-137) observe:

> many women feel that as women, they have to cope with an almost insoluble conflict of aims. Yet their position at the crossroads is by no means as eternal as it appears to its unfortunate victims. It is not the result of a "Law of Nature," but of contradictory trends and ideals within our society.

In countries, such as Sweden, which have adopted the official view that women should participate in the labor force even when they have small children, there is a growing awareness of a need for psychological counseling for older women who have never had any labor force experiences. Other countries, such as the United States, with a less receptive social attitude toward working women have done very little to help mothers combine the two roles.

Although the industrial countries vary with respect to their ideological commitment to equality for women, it is widely recognized that role differentiation on the basis of sex is deeply ingrained in the social fabric—the family system, personality development of boys and girls, expectations about labor force prospects for women—so that the exclusion of women from the male-oriented status structure that grew out of the industrial revolution is strongly self-reinforcing. Furthermore, the fact that men and women live together in the closest of all human relationships renders any attempt to change attitudes about traditional sex roles the subject of extreme emotional reaction. Holter (1971: 5) and other sociologists have observed that "sex differentiation contains less of a dynamic potential for conflict and change than, for example, social classes or technological change. Therefore, the very stability of sex discrimination should be exposed."

Thus, while economic growth has brought increasing labor force participation among women and while the direction of social change is toward emancipation, the residue of competitive disadvantage for women associated with child-bearing still shapes certain attitudes that may serve as a barrier to occupational achievement for women for many decades, irrespective of ideology. The idea that men are the protectors and providers of these child-bearers is still responsible for discriminatory attitudes toward women, particularly during periods of economic stagnation. Women are viewed as a reserve army of labor whose interests should be given the lowest priority in hard times. As Sullerot (1971: 44) observes:

the trade unions are certainly not anti-feministic but are they not sometimes afraid to "provoke discontent among categories accustomed to a measure of priority as regards wages?" Women trade unionists have few weapons with which to fight this traditional reaction except appeals to democratic conscience and continuous, resolute pressure.

Psychologists observe that when sex differentiation becomes nonfunctional from an economic perspective, society must rely on differences in personality formation of boys and girls to maintain such differentiation. Thus, the argument that girls are not suited for high-status positions requiring masculine behavior traits is circular. But when equality for women becomes a question of interfering in the self-perpetuating system of personality formation on the basis of sex, the matter of the appropriate limits of social policy becomes extremely controversial.

Clearly, however, industrial societies are facing a serious problem in the growing dissatisfaction of women with their lot. An international perspective can shed some light on the way sex differences in labor force status are perpetuated. In addition, we can evaluate the impact of differences in attitudes and the success of social policy in reconciling some sources of conflict.

INTERNATIONAL TRENDS AND NATIONAL IDIOSYNCRACIES

There are a number of reasons for making an international comparison of the status of women in industrial society. First, we have put forward the view that the position of women in postindustrial society can be viewed as the result of economic forces that occurred during the industrial revolution that not only separated the economic function of men and women, but also excluded women from the predominant sources of social status. As demographic and technological developments reduced the length of the child-bearing period in relation to the life cycle and alleviated the burden of housework, women began to seek fulfillment outside the home.

Ideology supportive not only of equal rights for women, but of full integration of women into the social status system tied to labor force activities, has proceeded at a different pace in different countries. Socialist political systems generally have more egalitarian attitudes toward women, at least in official rhetoric. But we have also suggested that the traditional view that a woman's place is in the home is deeply ingrained. This view allows women to enter only a small number of occupations that are seen as "suitable" for women, in the sense that either they are extensions of housewife role—nurse, teacher of small children, secretary (man's helper), interior decorator—or permit flexible schedules that do not interfere with household responsibilities. Because women are excluded from other kinds of work, they crowd into these occupations and, as more women enter the labor force, their wages are depressed relative to male wages. Thus, unless ideology can overcome traditional attitudes about the sex-specific nature of certain activities—attitudes that are closely tied to sex roles within the family—it will not go very far in achieving equality between the sexes in the labor force.

As shown in Table 2, there does not seem to be any clear relationship between ideology and the extent of female labor force participation. A country like Norway, with a strong egalitarian ideology, has one of the lowest rates in all of Western Europe. On the other hand, the countries with strong egalitarian ideologies seem to have had the greatest rates of change of female labor force participation since the mid-1950s, particularly of married women, although again this development is by no means uniform. Austria, for instance, with extremely traditional views about women's role, particularly in the middle class, experienced greater changes in female labor force participation than any of the Scandinavian countries.

The positive relationship observed between income level and female labor force participation is undoubtedly related largely to the fact that participation in the industrial labor force is higher in the more industrialized countries for both sexes. Data for 1953 suggest much less variation in the percentages of the labor force female, by income category. But these figures are misleading since they do not take into account the radical changes in the occupational and class composition of the female labor force that occur in the postindustrialization stage.

Some studies have attempted to establish a relationship between economic development and female labor force participation, but the studies all suffer from definitional problems associated with agricultural activities and work in the service sector. In fact, estimates of female labor force participation rates vary so widely in many countries that it is difficult to know which is the best estimate. When domestic employment is included, the relative participation of

TABLE 2: International Comparison of Female Labor Force Participation by Income Class and Ideology (1953 and 1963 or most recent year)

Ideology	Income Class* (1963)	% of Women in Labor Force (1953)	(1963)	% of Married Women in Labor Force (1953)	(1963)
Strong Egalitarian					
Sweden	1	28	32.6	16.0	32.0
Norway	1	–	17.8		9.4
Denmark	1	–	31.9		22.0
Israel	2	24	30.6		26.0
USSR	2	24	57.3		––
Poland	2	18			59.8
Yugoslavia	4	8			
India	4	8			
Less Egalitarian					
United States	1	28	34.5	23.8	34.7
Canada	1	23	29.7	––	22.0
Australia	1	25	28.9	––	16.7
New Zealand	1	23	28.9	––	15.8
France	1	32	35.0	23.1	26.7
W. Germany	1	24	30.4	––	––
United Kingdom	1	38	42.2	22.0	51.0
Netherlands	2	–	22.6		6.7
Austria	2	24	44.5		39.9
Puerto Rico	3	–	20.0		19.0
Ireland	3	25	28.6		5.2
Panama	4		24.7		16.1
Hong Kong	4		36.8		28.4
Peru	4		21.8		11.7
Morocco	4		8.8		5.5

*Income Class is determined by GNP per capita in 1963: Class 1 = over $1,500; 2 = $1,000-1,500; 3 = $500-1,000; and 4 = under $500.

Sources: Wilensky (1968) and Safilios-Rothschild (1971).

women increases for the less advanced countries. But while the link between economic development and female participation is unclear, it is evident that the influx of women into the industrial sector is a phenomenon that has occurred in the advanced countries irrespective of ideology.

Not only does ideology play a rather minor role in the determination of female labor force participation rates in the advanced countries, but there seems to be no relation between ideology and female standing with respect to earnings. Although comparable earnings data are extremely difficult to obtain, most studies show women at the lowest end of the earnings spectrum in all the countries of Europe, the United States, and Canada. Table 3 presents some measures of sex differences in earnings in Sweden. These can be compared with the earnings data by occupation for the United States (Table 4). Although most countries present data by income class, rather than as averages for the population as a whole, most estimates place the earnings of full-time year-round female

TABLE 3: Measures of Earnings by Sex Difference in Sweden

A. Average Hourly Earnings of Workers in Mining and Manufacturing (1960 = 100)

Year	Men	Women	Women/Men
1950	043	042	70.3
1960	100	100	68.8
1965	149	162	74.9
1966	162	181	76.5
1967	175	198	77.6
1968	187	213	78.2
1969	203	234	79.1
1970	226	263	80.0
1971	248	296	82.0

Source: Statistiska Centralbyrån, Am 1972: 65.

B. Distribution of Full-Time Year-Round Workers by Earnings (in Swedish crowns)

Decile*	Men	Women	Women/Men
0.5	12,320	5,310	.43
1	15,680	8,180	.52
2	18,820	11,570	.61
3	20,750	13,240	.64
4	22,330	14,630	.66
5	24,150	15,900	.66
6	26,330	17,040	.65
7	29,190	18,610	.64
8	33,660	20,880	.62
9	41,620	24,400	.59
9.5	51,960	29,230	.56

*This means, for instance, that 10% of the men working full-time year-round earned less than 15,680 Swedish crowns.
Source: Arbetsgruppen för Låginkomstfrågor, Kompendium om Låginkomstutredningen [Low Income Report], 1971.

C. Salaries of Government Employees by Salary Grade (October 1969)

Salary Grade	Men	% Distribution	Women	% Distribution	% Women
1- 9	11,808	7.8	35,917	51.3	76
10-19	112,571	74.3	31,878	45.5	22
20-30	27,146	17.9	2,273	3.2	8
1-30	151,525	100.0	70,068	100.0	32

Source: Statens Avtalsverk, 1969.

workers between 40 and 65% of the male rate in the industrialized noncommunist countries, irrespective of ideology. Although female workers in manufacturing enterprises seem to be gaining more rapidly relative to men in the socialist countries than in the less egalitarian societies, it is important to bear in mind that in all of the industrialized countries about 80% of the women in the labor force are employed in the service sector—crowded into female-dominated occupations that have experienced a deterioration in wages relative to men, even for full-time year-round workers. In the Scandinavian countries, wages in the industrial sector reported in the official statistics are those negotiated by trade unions. Wage drift, or deviations of actual wages from those officially negotiated, are not reported; but most studies show that men are much more likely to benefit from wage drift than women.

If ideology does not have much effect on female labor force participation and earnings, an international comparison may shed some light on the role of ideology and other national institutional features in determining the mechanisms through which women are kept in an inferior economic position. We have suggested that sex-linked personality development and attitudes toward women growing out of sex differentiation within the family might produce rather uniform mechanisms for excluding women from the status

TABLE 4: Ratio of Total Money Earnings of Full-Time Year-Round
Women/Men Workers in the United States, 1939-1971

Occupational Group	1939	1949	1956	1960	1965	1969	1971
TOTAL			63.3	60.7	59.9	58.9	59.5
Professional and technical	60.8	60.6	62.4	61.3	65.2	62.2	66.4
Teachers—primary and secondary schools				75.6	79.9	72.4	82.0
Managers, officials, and proprietors	54.0	57.3	59.1	52.9	53.2	53.1	53.0
Clerical workers	78.5	70.2	71.7	67.6	67.2	65.0	62.4
Sales workers	51.3	49.3	41.8	40.9	40.5	40.2	42.1
Craftsmen and foremen	63.7	67.2			56.7	56.7	56.4
Operatives	58.5	64.9	62.1	59.4	56.6	58.7	60.5
Service workers, excluding private household	59.6	58.2	55.4	57.2	55.4	57.4	58.5

Sources: *Economic Report of the President* (various years) and U.S. Department of Commerce publications.

structure in Western countries, irrespective of egalitarian attitudes. A related issue is the impact of social policy on women's status. Some of the European countries, most notably the Scandinavians, have developed rather elaborate policy schemes to promote equality for women. Others, such as the United States, have reluctantly allowed women to benefit from the civil rights activities of minority groups, but have explicitly refrained from introducing policy changes that might disrupt traditional family ties. Consequently, an international comparison might also focus on the success or failure of these policy objectives.

INDICATORS OF WOMEN'S STATUS

The intent of this paper is not to present detailed information on the status of women in each of the industrial countries, but instead to provide the reader with some perspectives with which to evaluate such information. The current section examines more specifically some indicators of economic status in some of the industrial countries. This will aid in the development of some models of women's roles found in industrial societies today.

Indicators of women's status are subject to a number of different interpretations. For instance, in most of the Western European countries, the United States, and Canada, instances of unequal pay for exactly the same work are rare (although they do occur). The major reason women earn less than men is that they are in different jobs and do not work as many hours. To dispute whether or not this condition can justifiably be called "discrimination" is to beg the issue. More important are the issues of why women are economically disadvantaged, why they have not made more inroads into the power structure, and what changes would be required to improve their lot.

LABOR FORCE PARTICIPATION AND HOUSEWORK

Perhaps the most striking change in the position of women in the industrialized countries since the 1930s has been the change in attitude of married women toward work. During the Great Depression and World War II, many women entered the labor force out of economic necessity and feelings of patriotism and, for the first time, experienced the financial and psychological independence that an income and activity outside the home could afford. During the 1950s, increasing affluence brought with it modern conveniences that shortened the time required for household responsibilities, and there was a steady rise in labor force activity of married women over 35. For reasons described earlier, the change was greatest for middle-class women who could afford the option of staying at home, and the consequent disruption to family life was greatest in the middle class. Not only was there the charge that the woman was "deserting her family for a career" (a question that does not arise when the mother works out of necessity), but also the nature of the work was more likely to represent a distraction from household responsibilities.

Rising living standards also meant that more families could afford to send their female children to high school and college. These women, better educated than their mothers, were attracted into the labor force by the possibility of higher pay. Thus, during the 1960s, there was a dramatic increase in the number of women with small children who also had jobs. This development produced a new set of problems. Although more advanced household technology had facilitated the entry of older women into the labor force, there was no easy solution for the problems of child-care faced by the younger women. Again, the problems of middle-class women were more severe since the suburban nuclear family is much more characteristic of middle-class life than the extended family patterns of the poor.

The response of governments to this problem has varied considerably. In the Scandinavian countries, much of the attention of the women's rights movement has been centered on state-supported child-care for working mothers. In other countries, such as the United States, Canada, and France, there has not only been no attempt to facilitate labor force participation of mothers through the provision of child-care facilities, but deeply ingrained cultural values dictate that mothers should provide 24-hour child-care for their children, at least until they enter school. Thus, there seems to be a fear in some quarters that the provision of collective child-care facilities will produce psychological damage to children with undesirable results for the future social order. Sullerot (1971: 49) observes, however, that even in those countries that have attempted to provide child-care facilities, these are viewed as "an expensive social venture rather than a social obligation." Furthermore, the idea that child-care facilities are the key to increased economic activity of women explicitly suggests that the responsibility for child-care lies with the mother, rather than with both parents.

The Scandinavian countries have promoted women's rights with the proposition that "the subdivision of functions as between the sexes must be changed in such a way that both the man and the woman in the family are afforded the same practical opportunities of participating in both active parenthood and gainful employment" (Swedish Institute, 1968: 4). However, although labor force participation rates of young women in Scandinavia are rising, there is no evidence that their husbands have assumed a much greater share of household responsibilities. The concern of women's rights advocates over the provision of child-care is evidence of this. Furthermore, studies of the division of labor within the Swedish home indicate that very few husbands participate at all, and the few who do undertake at most a fourth of the workload (Joint Female Labor Council, 1971: 68).

In a 1965 survey of 2,610 households in Denmark with both spouses present, 50% of the women were in the labor force (Noordhoek and Smith, 1971). The division of labor in the household between husband and wife was measured by adding the responses based on seven questions relating to whether the husband helped with preparing breakfast, cooking dinner, daily housecleaning, making beds, doing dishes, washing shirts and socks, and shopping. On the average, the husband helped (but was not completely responsible for) less than one activity. The husband's participation in the household increased slightly when the wife was employed full-time, but remained at a very low level. The average participation increased from 0.5 for nonemployed wives to 1.8 for wives employed full-time (0.8 for part-time working wives) on an index with a maximum of 7. Perhaps the most astonishing aspect of this study was that 74% of the women said they were satisfied with their husband's participation in the housework. Despite the fact that Denmark has adopted an explicit governmental position supportive of equality for women and the encouragement of shared household responsibilities that would free women for labor force activity, most of the women in the 1965 survey apparently accepted traditional sex roles.

Most studies show that, even in those countries with the most advanced ideologies, working women do most of the housework. Thus, labor force participation produces a double burden. An OECD study of household activity of women shows that the average woman

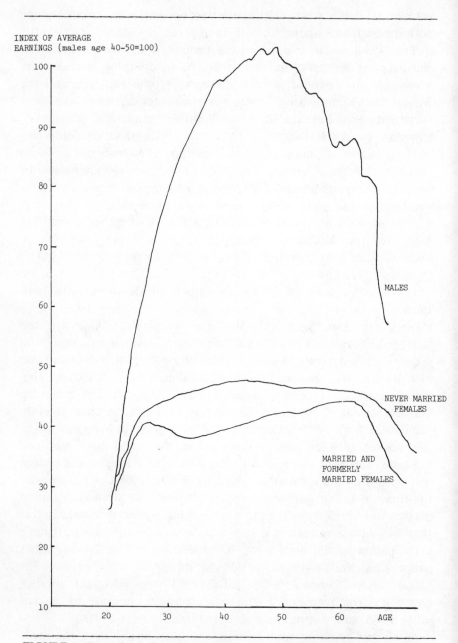

INDEX OF AVERAGE
EARNINGS (males age 40-50=100)

FIGURE 1: Typical Age-Earnings Profile by Sex and Marital Status

working full-time outside the home devotes approximately 30 hours per week to housework (Klein, 1965b: 75-77). If one takes into account the time spent going to and from work as well as time spent on the job, this suggests that the average working woman has practically no leisure. Not only is she overworked, but the unequal distribution of household responsibilities between the spouses is likely to produce resentment and marital tension that ultimately generate unfavorable attitudes toward the wife's career within the family as a whole.[2]

In none of the countries of Western Europe, the United States, or Canada has there been a radical shift in the assignment of household responsibilities by sex, even though it has been widely recognized (although officially stated only in the more progressive societies) that this must precede any serious change in the labor force status of women. This has meant that women are more often forced to interrupt their labor force activity during the peak years of child-care, take part-time work, or search for work with flexible hours.

It is important to make the distinction between labor force participation and labor force attachment. Low-income families, for instance, have a high rate of female labor force participation, on the average, but the women interrupt their labor force activity frequently for child-bearing or other household responsibilities. In the Danish study previously cited, 20% of the women who had worked outside the home in 1964 had left the labor force by spring of 1965 (Noordhoek and Smith, 1971).

Labor force attachment is important because it affects the ability of a woman to improve her earnings in later years. As shown in Figure 1, men's earnings generally rise dramatically throughout their thirties and early forties, declining thereafter. For women, on the other hand, the age-earnings profile is relatively flat. Some people attribute the flat female age-earnings profile to their weak labor force attachment. Yet studies of never married women (who presumably have a stronger labor force attachment than married women) also show flat age-earnings profiles. This suggests that because employers anticipate a weak labor force attachment, they do not train women for career-oriented positions in which they might improve their earnings.

Barbara Bergmann points out (and cites convincing empirical evidence) that it is not fewer years of experience which determines the lower pay of women, but the inferior quality of their work experiences. She points out that this qualitative deficiency in women's work experience is also closely linked to occupational segregation of the sexes:

> Compare, for example, the learning opportunities of the 22-year-old male management trainee and his 22-year-old female secretary, both of them possibly graduates of the same college. It's no wonder that, when they get into their forties, he will be earning five times what she is. And the ratio of his earnings to hers will really depend very little on the number of babies she has dropped out to have, or even whether she has dropped out at all [Bergmann, 1973: 153-154].

One important image for women to overcome, if they are to gain entry to high-paying positions, is to change the social perception that their labor force attachment is weak. Women's rights advocates are themselves divided on whether women should be granted lengthy periods of paid maternity leave with a guarantee of reemployment. Certainly the cost of such leave should not be borne by the employer (since it is a social, not a private cost), but rather by the state. Yet in most countries where maternity leave is guaranteed by law, the employer is forced to bear the burden. Thus, the employer considers the potential cost of maternity leave whenever a woman is hired, even if she expects never to bear children.

The philosophy of the Scandinavian countries, reflected in the statements of Alva Myrdal and others, is actively supportive of state-subsidized maternity leaves for mothers. They view the role of both men and women as combining family and labor force responsibilities with neither predominant. Although lip-service is paid to providing child-care leaves for fathers, the effect is to institutionalize sporadic movements in and out of the labor force by young women (since fathers rarely participate equally—or, for that matter, much at all—in the care of very young children). But some feminist ideologists reject the Myrdal proposals as a mechanism which will perpetuate the view of the woman as an unreliable worker, particularly in jobs where continuous employment is the key to success.

It should be emphasized that there is a sort of vicious circle at work here. Women drop out in part because they see no benefit from staying in: the kinds of jobs open to them are unchallenging and offer no opportunities for advancement. Then the propensity of these bored women to drop out and devote themselves to housewifery for a while is precisely the excuse used by employers to exclude them from management jobs and training programs that pay off only when the employee remains on the job for a reasonably long time.

PART-TIME EMPLOYMENT

The demands of housework and child-rearing often cause women to seek part-time employment as a compromise solution to the conflicting demands of industrial society. Part-time employment seems to be even more prevalent in those countries with explicitly stated views that women should work. Women in these countries seem to have been made to feel less satisfied with staying at home full-time or, alternatively, they have not been led to believe that they can gain complete personal fulfillment through taking care of their families. Table 5 shows the percentage of men and women in voluntary part-time employment in seven countries. In all of the countries, part-time work is predominantly done by women, again despite lip-service paid to the view (particularly in Scandinavia) that both men and women should begin to combine household activities with labor force work.

There are two types of part-time work. Some jobs by their nature are carried out during a limited number of hours—such as school crossing guards and cafeteria workers, relief work during peak hours in restaurants and shops, and the like. A second kind of part-time work artificially imposes split schedules in jobs requiring a full-time shift.

TABLE 5: Percentage of Employed Persons with Voluntary Part-Time Schedules (1965 or nearest year)

Country	Men	Women		Total
		Married	Unmarried	
Belgium	–	– –	– –	17.0
Canada	2.6	– –	– –	14.0
Denmark	1.6	47.9	4.7	– –
Germany	–	– –	– –	11.3
Sweden	7.2	54.9	19.4	40.5
United Kingdom	–	45.0	– –	– –
United States	3.0	24.7	23.5	24.3

Source: Hallaire (1968).

The first type of work is available almost everywhere. It involves little opportunity for advancement, is crowded by women, and is consequently low-paying. Whether or not employers should be forced or encouraged to provide part-time work of the second type to facilitate labor force activity of married women is (like the question of paid maternity leave) the subject of some controversy among women's rights advocates. Although part-time work has the potential of freeing men to assume household tasks, the evidence is that this has not been a very widespread phenomenon. Consequently, part-time work is essentially viewed as a means to reconcile women's household responsibilities with her desire to pursue some labor force activity. This reinforces the view that a woman's labor force attachment is tenuous at best and is secondary to her commitment to the family (otherwise, she would have taken a full-time job).

Yet many women do desire to combine their household responsibilities with labor force activities and, in recognition of this, some governments and trade unions have made an active effort to encourage firms to provide part-time shift work. The emphasis on provision of part-time work is greatest in the Scandinavian countries, particularly in Sweden, where the influence of the Myrdal concept of combining home and work roles is strong. However, the evidence suggests that, while the majority of married women in Sweden have accepted that view, most men work full-time and accept minimal responsibilities for housework.

Part-time work generally carries with it fewer opportunities for advancement than full-time positions, since employers view part-time workers as having a weak attachment to the labor force. The view is reinforced when the large majority of part-time workers are women. Because the crowding theory applies here—keeping wages in part-time jobs relatively low—the age-earnings profiles of part-time workers are likely to be even flatter than those for full-time female workers. Thus, the provision of part-time work is an additional mechanism for segregation of women into low-paying job categories, a mechanism that permits firms to circumvent official equal pay provisions.

Many women complain that they are unable to find full-time work, particularly in slack periods of economic activity. It is far more common for women than for men to be placed on involuntary part-time schedules. Some women's rights advocates argue that, as long as many women voluntarily accept part-time work, employers feel justified in placing any woman in a part-time position even though she would prefer to be in a job more conducive to advancement and career development. There does not seem to be a clear answer to the dilemma of whether the provision of part-time employment benefits or hurts the economic status of women. To the extent that it increases a woman's options, it is clearly beneficial. But when it reinforces traditional attitudes about women's roles, it impedes the cause of equality.

EARNINGS

During the process of industrial development in most countries, women typically received lower rates of pay than men for the same work. This practice is becoming increasingly rare. Most governments and trade unions have accepted the principle of equal pay for equal work. Indeed, the European Economic Community wrote an equal pay article into its Charter. However, in all countries, earnings of full-time year-round female workers are substantially below those of male workers.

Throughout a given national economy, female earnings range between 40% and 65% of male earnings, although differentials are smaller in the industrial sector (as opposed to the service sector) in most countries. The major reason for these differentials is segregation of women into a few occupations where "crowding" has caused deterioration of their earnings relative to male earnings. Associated with this occupational segregation is the failure of older women to achieve significantly higher wages as a result of seniority. Although this may be related to their sporadic dropping out of the labor force, the evidence indicates that women are generally not given jobs with career-building potential to begin with, whether or not they eventually interrupt their employment. Even in female-dominated occupations, such as elementary school teaching, supervisory positions are usually held by men. Conversely, when women manage to penetrate male professions, they receive lower salaries and the less important jobs.

Progress in the unionized industrial sector is slow, but encouraging. We have seen the rapid relative gain of women in the Swedish manufacturing industry from 1960 to 1970. In France, women's hourly rates are nearly 80% of the male rates. But in the Netherlands and Luxemburg, a 1968 study showed female hourly rates in industry were less than 60% of the male rates.

Sullerot (1971: 43), in a study of the EEC countries, found that over the 1960s disparities in hourly wage rates became smaller in countries where they were large initially, but are persisting in those where the average female hourly rates are about 80% of the male level. How does this square with the equal pay provisions of union contracts and the EEC Charter? Sullerot (1971: 44) claims that

legal or contractual subterfuges are used nearly everywhere in order to classify women in lower wage categories. The introduction of "light work" categories as in Germany, the female monopoly of some tasks as in Italy and the Netherlands, the exploitation of classifications as in Belgium and in France, all circumvent the decision on equal pay and thus contribute to making it meaningless.

But data on industrial wages are relatively insignificant when applied to women, since most of them work outside the industrial sector. The service sector is largely nonunionized, and women are heavily concentrated in a few occupations. In Sweden, one of the most advanced countries with respect to attempts to eliminate sex stereotyping, about 85% of Swedish women are concentrated in a few female-dominated occupations. Furthermore, recent surveys of high school seniors in Sweden (who were presumably most influenced by the anti-sexist ideology of the 1960s that permeated the Swedish educational system) show that most of the young women are still planning to enter traditional female occupations (Chapman, 1973: 7).

In all countries, women's earnings within occupations are systematically lower than men's, as we saw in the U.S. data (Table 4). Where women succeed in penetrating male occupations, it is usually in the lowest-paying jobs. While it is not unusual to find a female bus driver in Sweden, for instance, the representation of women in the management of the bus company would be minimal at best.

From this evidence, it seems that equal pay provisions are not the key to improving the earnings position of women in any substantial way. Two phenomena seem to play the key role. First, women need to penetrate male occupations and job categories. Second, they need to achieve access to positions where seniority plays a role in earnings, requiring investment in on-the-job training. Formal education plays a part, but is not a key factor, since in some countries such as the United States women have achieved a higher level of formal education than men, but still are barred from administrative positions. Because advancement requires on-the-job training, women will gain access to managerial posts only if employers are convinced that their labor force attachment is as permanent as men's.

We have noted that sex stereotyping of occupations and the failure of women to achieve responsible positions because of the view that their labor force attachment is weak are both self-reinforcing phenomena. Indeed, this is why the situation is so persistent and so difficult to change with simple legislation such as equal pay rules. In most of the industrial countries, the overwhelming majority of persons in the lowest income and earnings categories are women. Rising divorce rates have increased the representation of female-headed families in the poverty ranks, and governments are increasingly recognizing this as a major social problem.[3] Yet the factors that keep women's earnings so low are deeply ingrained in the social fabric and reinforced by sex-typed personality development. Thus, measures that would substantially affect women's earnings invariably carry with them social consequences that would of necessity disrupt traditional relationships and institutions.

UNEMPLOYMENT

Given the attitude that women's work is a source of "pin money," a secondary income, it is not surprising to find female unemployment rates rising more than male rates during periods of slack economic activity. Conversely, equality for women seems to make the most progress where there is a high level of economic activity and an excess demand for labor. It surely is not coincidental that the women's rights movement in both Scandinavia and the United States had its strongest support (or in the U.S. case, the weakest resistance) during periods of buoyant economic activity. In the early 1970s in Sweden, however, as the rising unemployment rate became an embarrassing political problem for the Social Democratic government, some people began to say that perhaps women had been drawn into the labor force too fast, and there was some retrenchment from the original view that equality should be achieved as quickly as possible.

However, the unemployment concept itself is extremely ambiguous when applied to women whose labor force attachment is tenuous at best. To be counted as unemployed one must (depending on the country) either register with a labor exchange or else respond in a labor market survey that one has actively sought work during the previous week. Many women do neither, but undoubtedly would take a job if they thought a satisfactory one could be found or if they could solve their child-care problem. A Swedish survey in 1968 showed that, of persons not actively in the labor force, 10% of the women and only 1% of the men said that they would have looked for work if they had thought they could find it (Joint Female Labor Council, 1971: 47). Of women with children, 40% of the married women and 50% of the unmarried women expressed the desire to work if their child-supervision problem could be solved (Joint Female Labor Council, 1971: 49). A survey by the French National Institute of Statistics and Economic Studies (Hallaire, 1968: 25) showed that of 4.4 million women under 55 with no gainful employment, more than 1 million would have been willing to work at least part-time if they thought the opportunity were available. And in a survey of British housewives (Klein, 1965a: 47), 52% said they were not presently employed because they could find no satisfactory child-care arrangements.

Unemployment can be viewed as a disequilibrium between supply and demand in the labor market. Given the fact of the occupational segregation of women, coupled with the dramatic increase in female labor force participation rates in most countries, it is not surprising that female unemployment is a problem, and that many women believe there are no jobs available and drop out of the labor force. Indeed, without the relative expansion of the tertiary sector in industrialized countries, which has occurred concurrently with the growth of female labor force participation, the situation would undoubtedly be much worse. And crowding has caused a relative deterioration of women's wages in most of the economy as well as unemployment.

One could take the position that occupational segregation is not the only reason why women experience high unemployment rates. Indeed, to the extent that female occupations are cyclically less sensitive to fluctuations in economic activity, women should experience less unemployment in the downswing than men.[4] Another view is that women are a reserve army of labor. Women are conveniently socialized to seek fulfillment outside the labor force, but can also be mobilized either by offers of high pay or attractive working conditions or through feelings of patriotism in periods of excess demand for labor. It is tempting to analyze the extent to which official policies supportive of women's rights are related to the state of the economy.

TABLE 6: Female Representation in the Professions in Norway, 1960

Profession	Total	Women
Professors	291	5
Chief physicians	339	3
Physicians	3,500	392
Architects	1,506	167
Chief engineers	1,172	4
Engineers	7,805	47
Consultants, secretaries in the central government	7,040	289
School principals	1,071	58

Source: Holter (1966: 393).

WOMEN IN THE POWER STRUCTURE

In none of the industrial countries have women made significant inroads into the power structure. It is astonishing that such a categorical statement can be made, but it is nonetheless accurate. The data in Table 6, on female representation in the professions in Norway, are typical of most countries. But these figures do not tell the whole story because, within those professions, women rarely achieve senior posts. Table 7 shows the number of men and women who hold senior posts in banking in Norway, by educational level. Although over half of the men achieved these posts without higher education, higher education was almost a prerequisite for those few women who achieved such status. In Yugoslavia, enterprises are managed by democratically elected workers' councils, and women make up over 30% of the labor force. In 1970, of the 199 newly nominated directors of enterprises, not one was a woman. Of the 985 reelected directors, only 19 were female (Statistical Yearbook . . . , 1972: 70).

TABLE 7: Percentages of Men and Women Who Hold Senior Banking Posts by Age and Education in Norway

Age	With Grammar School or Commercial College Education		Without Grammar School or Higher Education	
	Men	Women	Men	Women
Under 30	4	0	1	0
30-39	26	4	15	3
40-49	48	12	31	2
50-59	63	13	43	4

Source: Vangsnes (1971: 388).

It has been observed that, when women make significant inroads into a previously male-dominated profession, the occupation loses status. This is certainly the case of the medical profession in the USSR and of dentistry in Scandinavia. Harriet Holter (1971: 7) has put forth the ingenious suggestion that female influence increases in those institutions that are losing social influence. This was true of the institution of the family in the nineteenth century. More recently, she argues, since World War II, in countries where parliaments have become less powerful, women have increased participation. The same argument could be made for universities and the church in countries where these are losing influence. But in no country do women have any more than token representation (and then usually through inheritance) on the boards of banks, insurance companies and industrial concerns.

SOCIETAL ATTITUDES TOWARD WOMEN'S ROLES

Although each country has its own particular view of the "appropriate" role of women, a few basic attitudinal models stand out. Associated with each of these is a set of social policy measures. One could rank these models from the least to the most egalitarian, although some might disagree with the ranking.

Model I: Some societies are characterized by a strong sex role delineation and a decided preference for the married woman to stay at home. In many of these countries, there is a high female labor force participation rate, but the maternal role and labor force activity are perceived to be incompatible. The United States, Canada, France, the United Kingdom, and West Germany all fall into this category. Cultural values dictate that a woman should provide 24-hour maternal child-care, and the scarcity of domestic help has meant that women must break up a career to have children. Safilios-Rothschild (1971: 102) observes that "because of these cultural values, no significant societal effort has been made to help mothers to combine the two roles and the extreme emphasis placed upon the occupational success of the husband has up to now precluded any marital role redefinition that would require time and effort on his part."

Women in these countries are also the most highly educated in the world. Studies in the United States show that more highly educated women spend significantly more time on child-care, and that the achievement ethic that permeates the society and is encouraged in the higher education system induces these women to find the source of their self-esteem through their children (Leibowitz, 1974). Thus, children are placed under considerable pressure from their mothers to perform. This not only renders questionable the concept of 24-hour maternal care under these conditions, but also is a considerable source of conflict between women who stay home and those who do not.

Model II: Another model characterizes some countries at a lower level of development, but in which increasing attention is being paid to the role of women. In countries like Japan, Argentina, Greece, and Austria, the abundance of cheap domestic help and extended families free middle-class women of household responsibilities almost entirely. But female labor force participation is smaller both because of lower levels of education (or segregation of the sexes in the educational system in a manner that leaves women unprepared for labor force activity) and traditional attitudes. In some countries, such as Pakistan, India, and Colombia, traditional taboos against women working outside the home make labor force activity almost prohibitive for middle- and upper-class women. Nevertheless, the lack of emphasis on housework and child-care *per se* renders these countries ripe for a true revolution in sex roles (similar to that experienced in the USSR and the Eastern European countries discussed below), if traditional attitudes can be changed. Since these attitudes are less tied to the role of women in the family and the stability of the social order (as they are in the United States and Western European countries), the inferior position of women seems to contain more dynamic potentialities for change than elsewhere.

Model III: The Eastern European countries, Finland, and the USSR typify another model of women's roles. With a high level of female labor force participation, women in these countries have penetrated male occupations to a much greater extent than in other countries. Yet women still seem to perform fairly specialized roles within these professions, and men generally dominate the supervisory and administrative positions. When substantial female representation occurs (such as in the medical profession in the USSR), the occupation loses some of its status. And there is no evidence that women have made significant encroachments into the power structure in these countries.

Although (with the exception of Finland) cultural values do not demand full-time maternal care of children, and extended families and state-supported communal child-care facilities greatly alleviate the burden of child-care for working women, traditional sex roles within the family do not seem to be much affected by egalitarian attitudes toward women in the labor force. However, housework is less time-consuming in most of these countries, since houses are smaller. Consequently, family responsibilities that fall primarily on women are not a major source of conflict and so are not as prohibitive to full-time female labor force participation and attachment as in the Western European countries, the United States, and Canada.

Model IV: An equalitarian pattern associated with Alva Myrdal and Viola Klein (1956) has developed in the Scandinavian countries: family responsibilities and labor force activities should be shared equally by men and women, and both should seek fulfillment from both types of activities. Both men and women should be expected to interrupt their labor force activity or to take part-time work at some stage to devote attention to children, but expectations with respect to labor force commitment should be the same for both men and women. The actual practice in Scandinavia gives very little evidence of change in male attitudes toward their own work, although men are much more receptive to their wives' working than in Model I.[5] Cultural values are supportive of communal child-care and strong efforts are being made by governments to provide adequate facilities for working mothers.

Although labor force participation rates of married women have risen rapidly—particularly in Sweden, where they rose from 16% in 1950 to 26% in 1960 to 54.5% in 1972—women still bear the bulk of the household responsibilities. Consequently, they drop out of the labor force during child-bearing years and show a strong preference for part-time employment. Women's rights advocates campaign vigorously for paid maternity leave and the provision of part-time work, reinforcing the view that women desire to divide their time between labor force activity and homework. Penetration into male occupations is at a very low level, lower in fact than in the United States or other countries typifying Model I. As seen in Table 8, about 85% of Swedish women are concentrated in a few female-dominated occupations, despite efforts to eliminate sex-typing of jobs.

Thus, although there is much lip-service paid to redefining sex

TABLE 8: Occupations Employing More than 10,000 Women in Sweden

Occupation	Number of Women	% Women in the Occupation
Shop assistant	127,898	80
Secretary, typist	74,592	96
Farmer	62,351	54
Cleaner	57,346	91
Nurse's aid	56,381	98
Maid, child's nurse	52,221	100
Special office employee	50,713	68
Clerical assistant	36,422	82
Seamstress	35,909	98
Bookkeeper, cashier	35,638	70
Waitress	28,884	89
Teacher (grades 1-6)	27,980	75
Nurse	25,658	100
Kitchen assistant	24,904	95
Telephone operator	21,497	99
Shopkeeper	18,905	29
Hairdresser	17,728	74
Home helper	17,578	100
Textile worker	14,352	55
Cook	13,960	82
Rancher	13,206	73
Packer	12,603	66
Lab technician	11,517	57
Cashier	11,337	98
Home economist	10,583	77
Total	860,163	
Women in other fields	105,364	

Source: Population census.

roles within the family and humanizing modern society by turning emphasis away from the work ethic toward "sharing in the life and activities of the community" (Myrdal and Klein, 1956: 190), this ideological position has not been successfully put into practice. Consequently, although most women expect to spend most of their lives in the labor force, they are not gaining access to high-paying jobs and positions in the power structure at a rate consistent with their society's stated ideology.

Model V: Finally, many women's rights advocates see the ultimate liberation of women as being possible only within the context of a fifth model.[6] Advocates of this view argue that, although men are not likely to assume a substantial share of household responsibilities, women will never achieve equal status with men unless they demonstrate an equally strong labor force attachment. This means a continuous career pattern with minimal interruption for maternity, no part-time work, and no special maternity leaves for women. This is not to suggest that child-rearing and other family responsibilities should be ignored. Work schedules could be made more flexible and, ideally, the work week shortened; but shorter work weeks and flexible hours would be made compulsory for all workers. House-work should be viewed as a social responsibility, and flexible work schedules and the provision of child-care should not be viewed as special favors to married women that, in turn, are viewed as a cost of employing them.

Within this model, women must train for careers and be socialized into accepting traditionally male responsibilities. The educational system and vocational counseling should be purged of sexist references. Girls should take technical classes equally with boys, and boys participate in homemaking courses equally with girls. Care should be taken to avoid sex-based personality development in the home and schools. Textbooks and vocational material should be checked for any tendency to present men and women predominantly in traditional sex-typed roles.

Although it must be recognized that women will be economically disadvantaged in the short run for historical reasons, this must again be viewed as a social problem, not the responsibility of their husbands: "The common assumption of Western society that a wife has a right to be supported by her husband must be combatted, for it discourages her from making a serious commitment to a career which is needed for her own and her family's welfare" (Fogarty et al., 1971: 108). So social policy must remove any differences in family-related financial obligations based on sex. Taxation should be based on an individual's income, not his or her family status. Men and women have an equal obligation to provide financial support for themselves and their dependent children.

The official policy of the Swedish government, outlined in a report to the United Nations in 1968, comes the closest of any Western country to that model:

> a policy which attempts to give women an equal place with men in economic life while at the same time confirming woman's traditional responsibility for care of the home and children has no prospect of fullfilling . . . these aims. . . . The subdivision of functions as between the sexes must be changed in such a way that both the man and the woman in a family are afforded the same practical opportunities of participating in both active parenthood and gainful employment [Swedish Institute, 1968: 4].

This bold statement is certainly closer to the Model V view than to the Myrdal and Klein model described earlier. On the other hand, in Sweden there is strong emphasis on the provision of part-time work, paid maternity leave, and the like—an emphasis which is not consistent with the philosophy that women must demonstrate an equally strong labor force commitment if they expect to achieve equality with men, particularly in high-status positions and in the power structure. So the Swedish case can be viewed as intermediate between the Myrdal and Klein model and the more extreme feminist position.

WHERE ARE WE NOW AND WHERE DO WE GO FROM HERE?

Despite the wide range of ideological views of appropriate roles for women in the industrial countries, the practical achievements are not very much different, at least in the noncommunist world. In Sweden as in the United States, the two noncommunist countries with perhaps the most divergent ideological views of the desirability of equality between the sexes, women still interrupt their careers for child-care and are segregated into a few female-dominated occupations characterized either by activities that are qualitatively similar to housework or by activities that require little on-the-job training, no career continuity, and provide little, if any, opportunities for advancement. The rising rates of female labor force participation in both countries have resulted in a crowding of women into these occupations and a relative deterioration in female/male earnings ratios.

There are two major problems impeding action that could result from changing social attitudes toward women. The first is the powerful self-reinforcing nature of sex role differentiation in industrial society. The family system and sex-typed personality development have been uniformly successful through the Western world. Traditional attitudes are not the only problem. Expectations also play a role. Women are caught in a vicious circle: they lack career commitment because they are placed in jobs with no future. The concept of the role model, associated with affirmative action in the United States, is an attempt to modify female expectations about their chances for success in male occupations and to help them achieve high-status positions throughout the economy. But affirmative action is a difficult process in a country with such a weak commitment to women's rights in general. Women in high positions in the United States often feel resented and unwanted when they have been placed in their jobs over the objections of fellow workers and employers. Such attitudes are not conducive to high levels of motivation and achievement for these women, and only the toughest manage to persevere.

A second set of problems is associated with the transition process. What about the generations of women who were taught to seek fulfillment through their families? Now they are told the rules of the game have changed. Most countries have recognized the need to make special provisions to facilitate reentry of older married women into the labor force, and their adaption to changing social perspectives (Seear, 1971). But retraining and refresher courses are not the whole answer. In Scandinavia, where the social environment has become less and less supportive of the homeworking wife and mother, there is the recognition that many psychological adjustments are required by a woman and her family if she is to return to work and remain happily there. In 1966, a national scheme for publicizing job opportunities for older women and providing special vocational guidance courses was launched by the National Labor Market Board in Sweden in cooperation with an employers' association. A special radio series, "Hemmafru byter yrke [The Housewife Changes Her Occupation]," was broadcast. In conjunction with these programs, special conferences were arranged by local labor market boards in which women's organizations, educational associations, employer and employee organizations, and governmental representatives participated. Special counseling and training are also available for persons applying to the local labor exchange for a job, and by far the largest users of these services are older married women (Seear, 1971).

In countries with less egalitarian social attitudes, the role of the housewife is still glorified in the mass media, allowing older women who may well be dissatisfied with their lot to rationalize the existing state of affairs. The response to the growing feminist tide in these countries has been an equally strong defensiveness about traditional sex roles—with housewives viewing working women not only as a threat to their husbands' jobs and status, but also as a threat to their own life style in which they have invested "the best years of their lives." In the United States, for instance, much of the opposition to the Equal Rights Amendment to the Constitution (which, at this writing, is still unratified) has come from women. So women's rights groups in the United States have chosen to work through the legal channels of involuntary force—the path used by blacks to achieve equality. Whether such a policy can be successful in the absence of any significant change in social attitudes is difficult to predict. Certainly the personal abuse and aggravation for women in American society are greater than in countries with more receptive attitudes. And the adverse impact on relations between men and women is also painfully apparent.

In conclusion, two points are clear. First, ideological changes are not in themselves sufficient to achieve equality between the sexes. But differences in attitudes among the industrial countries suggest different mechanisms through which equality can ultimately be achieved. If feminism in countries like the United States, France, and the United Kingdom is unsuccessful in changing attitudes toward women's role, then feminist tactics must of necessity be different from those in the Scandinavian countries where ideology is far more advanced than its practical application. Women in Eastern Europe and the USSR have achieved gains in labor force status that are not matched by achievements within the family, the power structure, and other areas; and these women may face an entirely different set of social problems in the future.

From an international perspective, women in industrial societies face many common problems as a result of similar economic, social, and demographic factors associated with industrial development. But while they have much to learn from each other, their struggles for equality must be made within the ideology and institutions that form their own particular society. Women, unlike some ethnic minorities, cannot find their own separate solutions independent of the other, nonfemale, half of the societies in which they live. This represents the most difficult, but also the most provocative, challenge.

NOTES

1. An argument could be made, however, that the low labor force participation rates of this group reflect a lack of attractive job opportunities relative to more highly educated women, rather than a stronger pressure to stay at home. Undoubtedly, both influences are operative. A more affluent family does not feel the need to demonstrate its financial security by having the women stay at home.

2. In the USSR and Eastern Europe, the housing shortage has meant that families have smaller houses to tend and cultural values requiring full-time maternal care are less

prevalent. Extended family arrangements as well as communal facilities make the child-care problem less severe. So women in these countries have been able to manage their labor force activity with neither significant changes in sex roles within the family nor marital conflict.

3. Female-headed families in the United States and their associated economic and social problems are the subject of a large-scale research project, headed by Heather Ross, Isabel Sawhill, and Anita MacIntosh, at the Urban Institute.

4. In the United States, female unemployment rates do fall relative to the male rate in recessions; but this is not the case in the Western European countries.

5. It is interesting that many men who encourage their wives to work maintain hostile attitudes toward working with a woman peer or supervisor. The reverse is also true in many cases. Clearly, the psychology of the two attitudes is different and should not be confused in delineating equalitarian perspectives.

6. The distinction between this model and the Myrdal and Klein model is explicated in Fogarty et al. (1971: 104-109).

REFERENCES

Acta Sociologica (1971) Special issue on "Sex Roles." Vol. 14, No. 1-2.

BARRETT, N. (1973) "Have Swedish women achieved equality?" Challenge (November/ December): 14-20.

BERGMANN, B. (1973) "Sex discrimination in wages: comment," pp. 153-154 in Ashenfelter and Rees (eds.) Discrimination in Labor Markets. Princeton, N.J.: Princeton University Press.

CHAPMAN, J. R. (1973) "Employment-related programs with impact on women in selected Western countries." Presented at the annual meeting of the American Political Science Association, New Orleans.

COLLVER, A. and E. LANGLOIS (1962) "The female labor force in metropolitan areas: an international comparison." Economic Development & Cultural Change 10 (July): 367-385.

Council of Economic Advisors (1973) "The economic role of women," p. 91 in Economic Report of the President. Washington, D.C.: Government Printing Office.

FOGARTY, M. P. et al. (1971) Sex, Career, and Family. London: George Allen & Unwin.

HILLAIRE, J. (1968) Part-time Employment: Its Extent and Problems. Paris: OECD.

HOLTER, H. (1971) "Sex roles and social change." Acta Sociologica 14, 1-2: 2-12.

――― (1966) "Women's occupational situation in Scandinavia." International Labor Review 93 (April): 383-400.

JEPHCOTT, P. et al. (1962) Married Women Working. London: George Allen & Unwin.

Joint Female Labor Council (1971) Women in Sweden in the Light of Statistics. Stockholm: Joint Female Labor Council.

KLEIN, V. (1965a) Britain's Married Women Workers. London: Routledge & Kegan Paul.

――― (1965b) Women Workers: Working Hours and Services. Paris: OECD.

LEIBOWITZ, A. (1974) "Education and home production." American Economic Review 64 (May): 243-250.

LEIJON, A. (1968) Swedish Women—Swedish Men. Stockholm: Swedish Institute.

MICHEL, A. (1966) "Needs and aspirations of married women workers in France." International Labor Review 94 (July): 39-53.

MINCER, J. (1962) "Labor force participation of married women," in National Bureau of Economic Research (ed.) Aspects of Labor Economics. Princeton, N.J.: Princeton University Press.

MYRDAL, A. (1971) Towards Equality. Stockholm: Prisma.

––– and V. KLEIN (1956) Women's Two Roles: Home and Work. London: Routledge & Kegan Paul.

NOORDHOEK, J. and Y. SMITH (1971) "Family and work." Acta Sociologica 14, 1-2: 43-51.

OPPENHEIMER, V. (1968) "The sex labeling of jobs." Industrial Relations 7 (May): 219-234.

PINCHBECK, I. (1930) Women Workers and the Industrial Revolution. London: G. Routledge.

POLYANI, K. (1957) The Great Transformation. Boston: Beacon.

SAFILIOS-ROTHSCHILD, C. (1971) "A cross-cultural examination of women's marital, educational, and occupational options." Acta Sociologica 14, 1-2: 96-113.

SEEAR, B. N. (1971) Re-entry of Women to the Labour Market After an Interruption in Employment. Paris: OECD.

SILVER, C. B. (1973) "Salon, foyer, bureau: women and the professions in France." American Journal of Sociology 78 (January): 836-851.

Statistical Yearbook of the Socialist Federal Republic of Yugoslavia (1972) Belgrade.

SULLEROT, E. (1971) The Employment of Women and the Problems It Raises in the Member States of the European Community. Abridged version. Geneva: Commission of the European Community.

Swedish Institute (1968) The Status of Women in Sweden, Official Report to the United Nations. Stockholm: Swedish Institute.

United Nations (1973) Equal Rights for Women–A Call for Action. New York: United Nations.

––– (1970) Participation of Women in the Economic and Social Development of Their Countries. New York: United Nations.

VANGSNES, K. (1971) "Equal pay in Norway." International Labor Review 103 (April): 379-392.

WILENSKY, H. L. (1968) "Women's work: economic growth, ideology, structure." Industrial Relations 7 (May): 235-248.

Annals of the American Academy of Political and Social Science (1968) "Women around the world." No. 375 (January).

4

WOMEN IN DEVELOPING SOCIETIES
Economic Independence Is Not Enough

IRENE TINKER

Women in many developing countries are celebrated for their role in economic activities; customary law recognized and protected these roles. Tradition also specified appropriate occupations for each sex, but since many jobs were done by men and women working together, there has been considerable leeway in many cultures for the individual woman. The gradual penetration of modern concepts concerning law, occupations, economic development, or education is necessarily affecting traditional patterns both in towns and in the rural areas. Since the developing world was directly or indirectly influenced by colonialism, the laws and ideas introduced have come largely from Western Europe and the United States. Most developmental aid similarly comes from the "West." Such aid carries with it occupational stereotypes current in the West which reinforce attitudes of modernization held by Western-educated indigenous planners. This vision of future society places women in the home and so encourages planners to ignore women's present contributions to the economy. For this reason, women around the world are too often adversely affected by development because their economic independence is eroded.

To talk of economic roles is not to argue that women are equal to men. Contrary to the premise of this book embodied in its title, *Economic Independence for Women: The Foundation for Equal Rights,* traditional economic activity of women in most of the world has taken place in addition to family responsibilities which circumscribed their economic role. Thus, a woman might make money in the markets, but still be subject to her husband's sexual demands or her father's plans for her marriage; children of a divorced woman or those born outside marriage frequently belong to the husband's tribe or family. The variation in traditional roles and their patterns, which may add up to amazing independence or to near-serfdom, are discussed in some detail below. What is important at the outset is to recognize the linkages between economic activity, family roles, and both personal and political power which make up that elusive concept of status. What is also important is to understand that development will continue, and should, for women lead exhausting lives in most of the world. But development should enhance their lives, not further degrade their status.

INTRODUCTION

It is imperative, in a book directed to an English-speaking audience, to reiterate the dangers of making culture-bound assumptions in comparing women's status across cultures. We must especially beware of seeing women as mirrors of ourselves (Simmons, 1974: 1). For example, Americans tend to view the nuclear family as confining and search out new forms of marriage. Yet several observers of Asian women argue that the nuclear family is the primary liberating force from the patriarchal dominance of the extended family (Mehta, 1970: 203; Ward, 1963). Latin American observers, on the other hand, suggest that the kin network which typifies their traditional extended families actually allow for more female equality because of the shared obligations and duties within the family (Pescatello, 1973: xiv).

Similarly, the practice of seclusion, or purdah, is regarded by us as an extreme form of backwardness. Yet such seclusion is spreading today in parts of Africa and Asia: it is perceived as an improvement of status, an emulation of the upper classes. Among the Hausa of northern Nigeria, farming is done by animist rural women, but the urban Muslim Hausa women are reported to have refused to farm and preferred seclusion. Slave women to the Hausa also worked in the fields; with the abolition of slavery, these women also sought to improve their status by refusing to farm (Smith, 1954: 22-23). This may account for the continued willingness of Hausa women to maintain purdah. A recent study found that "most women inter-viewed claimed they preferred to be kept in seclusion on the grounds that it reduced their workload and raised their prestige" (Barkow, 1972: 323). The process of Sanskritization among Hindus—emulating the caste above your own—has led families who can afford it to stop their women from working in the fields so they may stay at home. In a searching study of purdah, Hanna Papanek (1971: 519) has also observed an increase in the number of women following the custom in Bangladesh.

Family pattern and seclusion may be linked both to religion, culture, and to economics. Ester Boserup (1970: 35), who has thoroughly explored women's role in economic development in her book of that title, describes sex roles in farming as follows:

> in very sparsely populated regions where shifting cultivation is used, men do little farm work, the women doing most. In somewhat more densely populated regions, where the agricultural system is that of extensive plough cultivation, women do little farm work and men do much more. Finally, in regions of intensive cultivation of irrigated land, both men and women must put hard work into agriculture in order to earn enough to support a family on a small piece of land.

In those areas where women farm and land belongs to the tribe, women are entitled to sell the surplus crops after feeding the family and keep any profit. When men with draft animals do most of the farming, women are generally confined within the home. With intensive farming, increasingly true today due to the population pressure, women must come out of the home to help with harvesting and weeding, and more recently, with the fertilizing.

What does her farming role have to do with a woman's status? In subsistence agricultural economies, a woman's work is recognized: a man buys her labor in the form of a bride price. Indeed, women who could afford to buy the work of other women could have wives (Uchendu, 1965: 7)! Wives became an investment, and polygyny was common. However, when customs changed, as among the Hausa women who refused to farm, men could not as easily afford second wives who had become an economic liability, not an asset. Thus, with seclusion, a father often had to provide his daughter's economic contribution to her prospective husband by giving her a dowry. Under some circumstances, the dowry then became the property of the man; but under Islam, with its easy divorce procedure, the dowry belonged to the woman and was returned to her should she be sent home. There are changes as a result of modernization. With the more intensive cultivation brought about by the "green revolution," women in the Punjab are returning to the fields and the marriage age has increased. Elsewhere in India, it has been reported that bride price has replaced the dowry as women begin to earn their keep. Lower castes have always paid a bride price, in any case.

In Southeast Asia, where women have long participated in the rice cultivation, neither extreme of buying or selling the woman is typical. In nominal Muslim areas such as Java, a bride's family may give a token payment to the groom's family; lower-class parents may sell their virgin daughter to a wealthy man who subsequently divorces her. But in Thailand, Vietnam, and the Philippines, women play fairly equal roles in marriage, as in the economy.

To talk about patterns of economic development is not to assume that all societies will pass through equivalent stages, nor is it to assume that a subsequent stage is an improvement on the first. To do so is to ignore the realities of history. Women's status has clearly fluctuated over the centuries, as civilizations have risen and fallen. Sullerot (1971: 19) asserts:

> As a rule it is in the early periods of each civilization that the least difference exists between the position of men and that of women. As a civilization asserts and refines itself, the gap between the relative status of men and women widens.

She argues that this gap is due to the imposition of concepts of private property and the patriarchal family system on simpler societies where women had more options. Ebihara (1974) notes similar reductions of women's status in Southeast Asia: a Chinese visitor to the Khmer empire in Angkor Wat in the thirteenth century recorded that women held many positions in the court; yet within a century, due to the influx of Chinese influence after the fall of the empire, women were reduced to being legal minors of their husbands.

These older civilizations spawned many cities with highly stratified societies, although the majority of the population continued to live in rural areas. Women in urban areas in these countries may be more traditional than their rural sisters; cities will often be a conglomeration of old and new, traditional and Western. Further, the stratification of the society means that the middle- and upper-class women live very different lives than do women of the lower classes. Therefore, after discussing women in the relatively egalitarian subsistence economies, we must treat the women of the older stratified societies separately.

A major question is whether our civilization, with its impetus toward urbanization and westernization, will similarly cause or exacerbate stratification of societies in the face of an ideology which speaks of equality. In both the subsistence and stratified societies, an educated elite is being created which imbibes Western values and supports Western laws. Like converts, they are often stronger in their faith than those of us born in the West. Indeed, it is this attachment to Western values exhibited by the indigenous national leadership which reinforces stereotypes of what is proper for women to do. They observe the traditional occupations of women in their cultures and measure them against the Western scale of values. Traditional women, on the other hand, adapt to Western influences, but remain primarily within an indigenous environment. Thus, there is a widening gap which grows with each succeeding generation. For this reason, the attitudes and status of this elite will be discussed separately in each section.

For a time after World War II, there was great optimism about the ability of the world to proceed apace with economic development. Today there is a growing realization that development is a more elusive concept than had been previously thought. Even where countries are able to boast a rising GNP in the face of population growth, it is recognized that Western-style development has tended to make the rich richer and the poor poorer, both within a country and among countries. It is not only women, then, but the poor generally who have been left out. (For an excellent review of the adverse impact of development on women, see Snyder and Tesba, 1973.)

Not surprisingly, many economists are looking for alternative paths to development and are expressing increasing interest in the experiences of such non-Western countries as the Soviet Union, Japan, and China. A review of women's place in these countries raises a different set of questions about women's status; but again it is clear that whatever the impact of the women on their own societies, these models cannot and should not be exported without major adaptation, or they, too, will undermine women's traditional roles in many countries.

If women's economic independence is not enough, and if this independence is likely to fall before modern development of any type, then the political role of women becomes crucial. Here again the impact of Western middle-class values seems to limit, rather than expand, opportunities for political participation. In most countries it would seem that women's place is going to get worse before it gets better, unless women in the developing world can force recognition of their traditional status upon the developers, both indigenous and foreign.

SUBSISTENCE AGRICULTURAL ECONOMIES

In subsistence economies, every family member has traditionally been assigned roles which are essential for the survival of the unit, whether it be a small nuclear household or an extended family. This has been true in nomadic cultures and in hunting and gathering societies, as well as in the early farming communities. Men and women, girls and boys, young and old—all play important roles, and there is much evidence today to indicate that family units limited the number of members to the availability of resources. Thus, many societies practiced abstinence, abortion, or infanticide, while other societies pushed out members who were no longer useful—old people in the case of the Eskimos, or landless people in the case of some of the Pacific Islanders.

In such societies assigned jobs were sex-specific, but they were not always the same jobs from culture to culture. In some areas women might do all the farming, while in others men did most or all of such work. Men generally hunted while women gathered, but both men and women variously attended flocks. In present-day Cambodia, Ebihara (1974: 27) comments that: "The wife is a necessary co-worker in the rice fields; for while the men do the heavy work such as preparing dikes and plowing and harrowing, women do the sowing, transplanting, much of the harvesting, and winnowing of rice."

Women who were farmers had rights to land. Under tribal custom these were user rights; but as private property became common, women became owners. European colonials felt uncomfortable with customary land tenure rights and often converted land to private ownership without any understanding of the local traditions. Again, they and the Chinese in Southeast Asia failed to recognize women's right to land (Boserup, 1970: 57ff.). As a result, a woman was left with the right to work on land belonging to her lineage or to that of her husband's, even where inheritance was through the female line.

Inheritance of land and the obligations of succoring children in many places go together. Where the woman's clan inherits land and the wife works both on her brother's and husband's plots, she is likely to work harder on her brother's crops because it is her brother who is responsible for her children. Indeed, among the Ashanti in Ghana, wives live more often with their matrilineal kin group than with their husbands (Fortas, 1954: 270). Elsewhere in West Africa, the man's tribe automatically keeps his children when he divorces his wife or when he has children out of wedlock. While this seems counter to our assumptions, such rights give the child some guarantee to a share of the land, which is often the only source of livelihood. Today Wipper (1972: 348) notes that in East Africa there is a breakdown of corporate responsibility by the clan. An act requiring men to contribute to the support of their illegitimate children was repealed by an all-male National Assembly of Kenya, leaving women to support their children alone.

Besides farming, women in subsistence economies have traditionally spun fibers and woven cloth, drawn water, and processed and preserved food. While women in Southeast Asia boiled palm sugar, West African women brewed beer, and women in parts of Mexico made pottery from coils of clay. Women from all of these cultures might sell their surplus food or goods in local markets. Profits belonged to the women themselves. Thus, women in many parts of the world became known for their astuteness in the market. Javanese women are still viewed as being thrifty and foresighted with money, while Javanese men consider themselves incapable of handling it wisely (Geertz, 1961: 123). In Nicaragua the women continue to dominate the indigenous stalls catering to the lower classes in the same vicinity with supermarkets where the middle class goes to be waited on by men (Hagen, 1972: 27). Women in West Africa have gone beyond local markets into transport, importing goods, and manufacturing. Ester Ocloo (1974: 2), a Ghanaian manufacturer, writes about this development:

> By the end of 1940 the scene in our marketplaces, especially in the big towns, began to change. Many of the locally produced goods began to disappear, giving place to foreign ones. Improved marketplaces were built in the big towns with well-protected display stalls for textiles and other foreign goods. It was during this period that we had the market women dividing themselves into two main groups: the first group comprise women who sell farm produce, fish and locally manufactured products such as

clay pots, wooden spoons, beads, etc.; and the second group, who form the rich or well-to-do ones, sell textiles, shoes, cosmetics, tobacco and all sorts of imported items (some also make clothes in the market).

In contrast, Hindu and Arab women are never seen in the markets as sellers and seldom as buyers. Thus, in markets of West Africa the Muslim men sell the leather goods from the north next to coastal women selling local produce. In Southeast Asia the men prefer jobs in the bureaucracy, while women and foreign men dominate the trading sector.

Technology has had considerable impact on these customary activities. Transport has opened new markets for goods which can compete with cheaply made artifacts. In Mexico the greater demand for ceramic animal figures has brought increased income (Stolmaker, 1971: 23), but traditional coil pots are still made in preference to pots thrown on a kick wheel. Women everywhere sew clothing instead of making cloth. Piped water, grinding mills, as well as bus trips into town for amusement, have eased the drudgery of rural life (Ward, 1970: 96).

On the other hand, many traditional occupations have become redundant. The circle of local markets may be bypassed by traders direct from towns, undercutting women traders in the outlying villages. The importation of Coca Cola ruined the local soft drink manufacturers on Java, as the importation of Australian ice cream did to the local sweets industry. Both enterprises had been dominated by women. Sago processing by women in Sarawak was replaced by machine processing run by overseas Chinese (Ward, 1970: 100). Men's enterprises have also suffered from competition from national or international firms. A study of governmental policies in Zaria (Remy and Weeks, 1973: 9) showed that the small informal sectors of the economy, run by men, suffered from the lack of services, particularly water, light, and credit; this prevented their expansion. On the other hand, the large tobacco factory and the textile factory were fostered by governmental policy.

While men as well as women suffer under the dislocation of change, men typically have better access to alternate jobs. Emigration in both Africa and Asia was, at first, predominantly male. Since Asian women did not earn at home, they tended to follow their husbands more quickly than did African women, who stayed at home and farmed. As a result woman-headed households are appearing with increasing frequency throughout rural Africa; in

Kenya the 1969 census recorded that one-third of rural households were headed by a woman. Elsewhere in Africa, women maintain their families alone much of the year, with the men returning only for planting or harvesting (Reining, 1973: 150). Mines and plantations are sources for male employment, although the expansion of plantation lands has been restricted in Africa by the land tenure system (Okediji, 1974: 8). Further, from the earliest days of colonialism in Africa, men were assessed a head tax in order to force them to work for wages. At the same time, women were discouraged from planting cash crops (Dobert, 1974: 3). When agricultural experts from Taiwan came into Liberia in 1973 to instruct in rice planting, it was the men who were taught. The men came because they were paid to attend, but it is the women who typically farm.

Similarly, education has been biased in favor of men around the world. In Africa today, nine out of ten women are illiterate (Sullerot, 1971: 169). The fact that there are only 20% more literate men than women in Africa is a commentary on the elite character of the missionary education system. In Asia the figures go from 87% illiteracy of women in India to 52% in Hong Kong. Yet in that colonial city women are five times more likely to be illiterate than men. The higher the level of education, the fewer the women. In Africa some 20-30% of primary students are girls; in secondary school this falls to 10-20% (Little, 1973: 30). In South Asia where only 2½% of the adult population continue in school after 14 years, about one-fifth are women. In Latin America nearly half the students in higher education are women, although only 2-10% of adults have had any postsecondary education (Boserup, 1970: 119-120).

In traditional pursuits, the lack of education was no problem. Parents often kept girls from attending schools, feeling that education merely delayed marriage. Girls were removed from school at the first sign of puberty in some societies. But as the modern sector invades the traditional sphere, uneducated women in the markets, for example, are at a disadvantage. Thus, the Economic Commission of Africa has launched an African Women's Development Task Force to upgrade the position of the rural women by teaching them such skills as bookkeeping, setting up credit and food cooperatives, teaching the use of labor-saving devices, and devising adult education courses which include farming as well as nutrition. Even more impressive is the attempt to train the educated elite to work with the rural women for this purpose (Pan-African Women's

Centre . . . , 1974; see also Economic Commission for Africa . . . , 1974).

The lack of education limits a woman's options even more when she migrates to the city. If she moves with her husband, she may be able to continue household crafts or petty trading. But trading on a small scale takes place within an established circle of customers; too-frequent moving can destroy a business (Remy, 1975). Seamstresses had to compete with male tailors, for example, who had easier access to credit and therefore could carry a wider supply of fabrics. Remy (1975), who studied the economic activity of women in Zaria, comments: "Without exception, the women in my sample who had been able to earn a substantial independent income had attended primary school. . . . All of the women had learned to read, write, and speak some English."

While the married woman finds her economic independence severely limited in towns, she at least has a husband. But in Africa and parts of Asia where divorce is easy, she may not stay married long. Where divorce is more difficult, many women are not married, since everywhere men tend to marry much younger women and population growth has produced increasingly larger younger generations. Thus, single women and divorcees migrate to the cities. In Dahomey surveys indicated that from 25 to 30% of women living in towns were on their own (Dobert, 1974: 7), while in Ethiopia women outnumber men in the towns due to a high divorce rate (Economic Commission for Africa . . . , 1974). In Latin America, young women seek domestic service in towns and also migrate in larger numbers than men.

Single untrained women have few options in urban settings: domestic service and prostitution are often mentioned as primary forms of employment. Domestic service is the dominant occupation in Latin America (Smith, 1973), where a large number of shop assistants are also women. In Africa, in addition to trading, selling, or working in homes, many women become "walk-about women" (Little, 1973: ch. 6), or prostitutes, femmes libres—something between a geisha and a call girl, or a mistress. The heroine of Ekwensi's novel, *Jagua Nana*, wavers between the latter two types (see also Little, 1973: ch. 7).

Polygyny is still more or less acceptable in Africa. Thus, mistresses often become second wives. Such an arrangement may be secret; but it also may be honored by a declaration ceremony which has social, if not legal, meaning. Since laws requiring monogamy have been passed in most countries, the second wife's position is more precarious now than under customary law. Because bearing children can give the second wife a stronger claim on her husband, such liaisons lead to high fertility (Okediji, 1974: 21). More men have multiple wives in areas where women work than in those where women are kept in seclusion (Pool, 1972: 250). The cost of polygyny has tended to limit its continuance in cities to the middle and upper classes. Lower-class men, both in Africa and in Indonesia, tend to have only one wife at a time, but ease of divorce allows for frequent changes of partner. Economic independence of women and the phenomenon of multiple liaisons seem to go hand in hand.

Interestingly, many market women in Africa argue in favor of polygyny—85%, according to a survey conducted in the Ivory Coast in the 1960s! According to Dobert (1974), the women believe that "in a monogamous marriage power accrues to the man as head of the household whereas formerly both men and women had to defer to the head of the lineage." Further, co-wives share the burden of household work and cooking; one woman can go off trading while another stays home.

Such sharing is an anathema to the educated woman who strongly supports monogamy. Thus, the urban pattern of "illegal" polygyny includes dual households, and women-headed households therefore abound in much of Africa (and in East London as well; Gugler, 1972: 298). Throughout Latin America and the Caribbean, a pattern of serial liaisons is typical (Tracer, 1973: 214). Indeed, one study suggests that women purposely select different fathers for their children so that the potential support network for themselves and their children is enlarged (Stack, 1974). Nonetheless, it is the woman who must support herself: she does have economic independence.

In contrast to the average woman in subsistence societies, the educated elite woman has adopted Western values along with her Western education and language. Nursing and teaching are considered suitable occupations for respectable women; but beyond those occupations, the modern sector in Africa is largely closed to them (Little, 1973: 33). Thus, many educated women lose their economic independence and are forced to depend more on their husbands whose authoritarianism is reinforced (Gugler, 1972: 298). As a result, many educated African women become militantly feminist (Dobert, 1974: 8). Yet one highly placed female government servant argued that such activity was only for the housewife—she was too busy working to worry about feminism (interview with the author in Accra, Ghana, August 6, 1974).

In Southeast Asia the men dominate the bureaucracies and military, but commerce is open to women. In Jakarta wives of the upper civil servants run shops and make jewelry. In Thailand several large hotels are owned and run by women. Philippine women are adept in real estate, as stockbrokers, and running businesses; today in the Philippines more women than men attended private schools—a clear indicator of the value placed on women's ability to learn and to earn (Green, 1973: 17). Yet these women of Southeast Asia appear to us gentle and highly feminine.

Hoskins (n.d.), in her study of Vietnamese women, explains this seeming contradiction. Women in Vietnam have traditionally been seen as pivotal to the family. Any activity which ensures the continuity or aids in the comfort of her family is acceptable. In the rural area she farmed or traded; in the urban setting she responded to opportunity. During the long years of war, the bureaucracy was opened to women. Such equality is a reassertion of traditional values, only partially overlaid by both the Chinese and French influences. Since economic activity is expected and accepted, Vietnamese women do not need to appear as men. Indeed, because the traditional roles of men were more narrowly defined, they have had more difficulty in adapting themselves to the urban scene (Hoskins, n.d.: 6). Also, because women are assumed to be working to benefit their families, there is no assumption on the part of male co-workers that the women are "available"—an assumption greatly annoying to many African working women (Remy, forthcoming).

Throughout Africa, Latin America, and Southeast Asia the highly educated woman can generally find employment. With only a small percentage of the population so trained, these countries need all willing minds. But trends elsewhere suggest that as a higher percentage of the population receives higher education, pressures on the job market will mean that fewer and fewer women are employed. In the United States, for instance, the percentage of women in technical and professional jobs peaked in the decade 1910-1920. Middle-class attitudes of both the individual woman and the society limited women's job opportunities and ambitions (see Tinker, 1973). Similar ideas of woman's place have long been part of the value structure of the "old-urban" societies discussed below.

To summarize: the position of women in subsistence agricultural economies was relatively equal, particularly in economic matters. In her classic, *Women of Tropical Africa,* Denise Paulme (1971: 8) wrote:

> Since the arrival of the Europeans, the new modes of life introduced by them have altered the distribution of tasks in a way that has too often been disadvantageous for women. . . . and while the introduction of cash crops may have provided the men with a substitute for their former warlike activities, women have found that this has only imposed new burdens on them.

In Southeast Asia the response to Westernization has been spread over a longer time; thus, the dislocations are less severe, and the position of women fairly equal within an appropriate family structure. In Latin America and Africa women's equality seems largely to be outside "acceptable" marriage patterns, with the official wife losing independence unless she is a highly trained professional.

"OLD-URBAN" SOCIETIES

While historically all societies were subsistence-level, the development of great civilizations began in 4,000 B.C. in what is now Egypt, Iran, Pakistan, and China. Yet today these countries are included in the list of "developing" nations. While it is indeed true that the rural areas of these countries greatly resemble those in subsistence economies, the residue of a more complex civilization (in the form of stratification and religion) has long since restricted the status of women in all but the lowest and the highest levels of society. To some extent, parts of Latin America could similarly be classed, due to the transplanting of traditional religion and the development of a rigid class structure.

Two major institutions have tended to restrict and protect the woman in these old-urban societies: the family and the religion. As societies become more stratified due to occupational differentiation, the families of the ruling class feel an increasing need to protect their women. While upper-class men could exploit lower-class women, there seems to be universal fear of the reverse. Thus, increasingly "civilized" countries have tended to segregate their women and restrict their contacts, especially with other men. The romantic myths and chivalric codes of the Middle Ages were such an attempt to elevate the position of women in Europe. The extreme isolation of women in harems and purdah characterized the high civilizations of the Hindu and Moslem empires. In China, bound feet were a symbol of restricted movement of women. Extending the concept of protection, families arranged the marriages of their daughters, preferably before or just after puberty, so that the recipient family could be guaranteed a chaste bride.

The major religions of the old-urban societies—Hinduism, Islam, and Buddhism—all allow men to have multiple wives while restricting the wives' rights. Only in Christianity, perhaps because every person is deemed to have a soul of equal value, are men formally not allowed two wives. Nonetheless, the concept of the extramarital mistress has pervaded the upper classes of most European societies.

As occupational differentiation separated the society into classes, it also separated the domain of the men from the women. In most of these countries the woman's role within the domestic sphere was very strong, but she was expected to have no role whatsoever in the public sphere of men (Rosaldo, 1974). Where women did develop outside interests, they were restricted entirely to meeting with other women. In traditional societies this was often an important role, especially in the areas of South and Southeast Asia, where much of the worship was left to the women.

Even in the countryside, the patterns of social segregation and seclusion tended to be imitated. Typically, the lower class tried to imitate middle-class restrictions in order to achieve upward mobility. Among Hindus this process has been termed "Sanskritization" —lower castes adopted food restrictions, methods of worship, and seclusion of women. At the other end of the class spectrum were the upper-class women who had sufficient free time to train in arts, music, painting, and sometimes to get an education, because they were brought up in homes with many servants. Throughout history there are cases of the unusual woman nurtured in such a secluded environment who excels. Because it is essentially the family which enforces the mores, women in the upper classes have often been relatively free of restrictions simply because their families have been so confident of their own worth. Thus, today we have female prime ministers of India and Sri Lanka, just as we have had occasional empresses and queens. Despite such exceptions, most women in stratified societies lost privileges as they moved upward. Inheritance tended to be passed through the family rather than through the woman herself. Even in Islam, which does provide some inheritance protection directly for the woman, the property is often turned over to her male protectors (Youssef, 1974).

Women of the middle class in these old-urban societies tended to live in built-up cities—packed towns with many-storied houses, often having purdah quarters open only to tiny gardens or to the roof. These were frequently centered around the court and developed in response to the demand for large numbers of artisans and traders. Because these cities are so crowded, women in these old-urban centers generally do not raise vegetables or animals in the town. In contrast, in parts of Africa and Southeast Asia today, many modern cities are a conglomerate of Western urban development and village-type compounds where people live as they would in the rural areas.

The impact of development on such societies has, if anything, only increased the role differentiation between men and women. The gap between men and women increases with the introduction of advanced technology and science, which are everywhere typically men's subjects. In contrast, the lower classes continue to live in these societies in patterns more like the subsistence economies discussed above. Omvedt (1973), in her study of lower-class women in India, for example, establishes the fact that there is divorce and remarriage among the Maha, whom she studied. She further points to statistics demonstrating that, even in supposedly secluded India, some 45% of all agricultural labor is done by women, while 33% of all cultivators are women—a clear indication of economic need increasing female participation in agriculture. It is well known that most construction work in North India is done by Rajput women.

Youssef (1974) has analyzed the work opportunities and economic independence of women in the Middle East and in Latin America. She argues that the coincidence of religious authority and family authority under Islam so restricts the options available to any woman that she can only with great difficulty choose to leave the protection of the family. Even the fact that Middle East women are typically divorced several times does not alter their dependence on the family: the divorcee returns to her own family with the expectation of remarriage. Thus, children are assigned to the grandparents, first on her side and then on his, so that she will not be encumbered in a new marriage with children from a former one. Marriage perhaps provides more freedom than living at home, but in neither case is it thought proper for a woman to work outside the house in the Middle East.

It is interesting to compare this restrictive concept of women's role in Islam with the somewhat more open concepts typical in northern Africa. In northern Nigeria urban women continue to observe purdah, but they work within the confines of their homes and sell their products through the good offices of children or male relatives. Further, on Java, where Islam mixes lightly with more indigenous beliefs, only the divorce laws seem to have served to undercut the highly independent role of women in the traditional society.

Unlike Islam, which has no organized church, Catholicism has provided women in Latin America with an alternative source of authority to the family. Youssef further argues that the Hispanic tradition has never thoroughly penetrated the society, so that there are still appeals to indigenous beliefs. Thus, instead of only one pattern of proper behavior, there are several—a factor which allows women some choice for their personal behavior. This flexibility has led to a greater differentiation among classes in Latin America than in the Middle East. Lower-class women work; their economic role gives them some measure of independence to the point where they may not bother to marry. Upper-class women with servants have a measure of freedom and often become active in voluntary associations or choose a profession. Still, professions related to motherhood are predominant. It is the middle-class woman who typically leads the most circumscribed life (Tracer, 1973). As lower-class women struggle to rise on the social scale, they lose many prerogatives, a process clearly evident in the novels of Latin America (Jaquette, 1973).

In Hindu society, as in Islam, the women were secluded; but while in Islam this seclusion was from outsiders with much less restriction within the family compound, among the Hindus the restrictions were from any males (Papanek, 1973). The conflict between this extreme seclusion and the European concept of husband and wife entertaining socially together was clearly a strain on the westernized Indians who entered the British civil service. Mehta (1970) has shown how the first generation of these women pulled away from their caste community and sent their daughters to missionary schools to learn English. The clarity of the impact of the educational system is shown on the second generation of young women, who married before independence. Traditional Hinduism preaches duty and austerity. Duty was especially directed toward the joint family and the acceptance of family members within the household on request. The second generation of women increasingly resented what they began to see as intrusions by their families into their own nuclear households. More recent studies on working women in India by Promilla Kapur (1972) have indicated that a woman's ability to work is increasingly seen as an economic asset when arranging a marriage. That the woman works for her family and that she is a professional only during the day allow a complete separation of work and home. Thus, sex is never an issue in offices in India, which most observers feel relieves Indian women of this strain common in Western society.

Until the communist revolution, class stratification was predominant in China—with the same exploitation of women and men of the poorer classes, great restriction on the mobility of middle-class women, and relative freedom and education for elite women. Following the communist concept of development, every adult becomes an economic producer and every adult becomes equal. There have been massive attempts to undermine the family system and Confucian thought and to attack educational elitism by requiring college students to do physical work on farms or public work projects. Government publications suggest that the ideal of equality has been achieved, but typically the military and bureaucratic leaders are almost entirely men (Kallgren, 1973). Even the most influential Chinese woman today, Chiang Ching, wife of Mao Tse-tung, operates on the periphery (Witke, 1974). Recent visitors to China have been impressed by the efforts to achieve female equality. Nonetheless, even the Chinese delegates to the UN Commission on the Status of Women admitted the men in the outlying areas of the country do not yet understand that women are equal.

In the old-urban societies, then, class stratification tended to leave lower-class women with economic opportunities within their own class level. With upward mobility, economic independence was extremely constricted, as were women's movements outside the home. The elite women in traditional societies enjoyed somewhat greater mobility, if not freedom; and once foreign-style education was grafted onto the traditional structure, some very unusual women leaders emerged. In addition, some middle-class women are beginning to work outside the home, an effort seen as part of their traditional role in relation to the family. Generally, however, their jobs are within spheres related to the nurturing role and are particularly strong where there is still segregation of clients, as in schools and clinics.

POLITICAL POWER

In traditional societies there have always been unusual women who have themselves, or in concert with men, played an important political role. For example, among some groups in West Africa, women were frequently elected to be chiefs. British colonials refused to recognize such chiefdoms and tried to circumvent this aberration (Hoffer, 1972). Igbo women had their own political institutions and participated in village meetings along with men. Particularly effective was the use of nonviolent hazing of men who had interfered in the market or mistreated their wives. This technique, known as "sitting on a man," achieved justice by shaming the guilty person. Use of this technique was escalated against the British: clashes led first to burning, then to shooting. History records such an eruption in 1929 as the "Women's War" (Van Allen, 1972). The tradition of politically active women in Nigeria continued after independence; women played leadership roles and had a separate party during the several election campaigns. Indeed, it was the strong role of women in West Africa which prompted General de Gaulle in 1944 to offer equal suffrage to many women in the African colonies. Only belatedly did he recognize that it would then be necessary to extend the right to vote to French women as well (Dobert, 1974). In Ghana the women strongly supported Nkrumah, while women in Guinea wield power by influencing Sekou Touré (Dobert, 1974). Again, it would seem that their economic independence is necessarily related to their political role.

In Asia elite women took a strong role in the struggle for independence. Such women were drawn from the educated elite and frequently began their political careers when their husbands were detained or imprisoned. These daughters were generally as well educated as their brothers; after all, a nationalist insisting that he was equal to the colonial man could not turn around and discriminate between men and women. Unfortunately, this surge of women in political activity during nationalist periods tended to wane once independence was secured. There are several explanations for this demise. With increasing economic pressures, families frequently cannot educate both sons and daughters. Statistics frequently indicate a higher percentage of men in college. Secondly, the increasing number of educated individuals suggests that fewer and fewer women are likely to get jobs when there are men who are unemployed. While the availability of leisure time might encourage some women to become politically active, economic dependence and cultural pressures recommend a more subservient role.

An alternate explanation for the decreasing number of women participating in the parties of developing countries is the demise of the role of the independent professional. As we have noted, most of the women active in the revolutionary period were drawn from an educated elite. One of the reasons these professionals, men and women, joined the revolutionary movement was that under colonial rule they did not get the recognition they felt they should have had—simply because they were not members of the colonial ethnic group. With independence, their relative position changed. Increasingly, their sons and daughters were educated abroad for many years and lost touch with home. Furthermore, they became more highly specialized in their professions—losing the "class" solidarity associated with being in the literate minority. As a result, professionals themselves began to lose power to the organized bureaucracies of the military and administrative services (Dieter-Evers, n.d.). Neither of these services has been at all receptive to women. Not surprisingly, in those countries that have been taken over by military regimes or by military personnel in collusion with the civil service, fewer women are visible in the governments.

Obviously, a woman's inability to play a role in government impacts upon her economic position. Furthermore, both the military and civil bureaucracies in the developing countries are modern services whose members have imbibed all of the middle-class values of the developed world. Thus, they feel that woman's place is in the home. Even traditional women's occupations are difficult to follow if husbands move from place to place, as they must do in both the military and administrative services.

The erosion of women's political and economic roles in many developing countries, then, is a result of changing opportunities for the professional elite. On the other hand, women in Latin America have never played a very strong political role. Educated elite women, influenced by the persistence of Iberian traditions, work in nurturing occupations, if they work at all. Further, the style of politics typical in Latin America has not been conducive to the development of political parties. The military, as we have seen, has nowhere really admitted women to its ranks. However, in several Latin American countries, there have been serious women candidates for elective political offices. It is noteworthy that restrictions on expatriate employment in the bureaucracies are credited with opening up positions for women in their own countries. In some cases, a developing industrial sector has drawn off men from the bureaucracy, leaving more positions open to women. Again, there would seem to be a connection between economic independence and political activity.

CONCLUSION

The process of development in subsistence economies has tended to restrict the economic independence of women as their traditional jobs are challenged by new methods and technologies. Because Western stereotypes of appropriate roles and occupations for women tend to be exported with aid, modernization continually increases the gap between women's and men's ability to cope with the modern world. Elites in these countries are imbued with Western values and tend to accept the Western notion of women's subordinate place. Thus, women in many developing societies are compelled to trade economic independence for economic dependency, while not yet benefitting from the legal equalities brought in along with Western values.[1]

In the old-urban societies where social stratification had already taken place, modernization and development have tended only to increase the inequities of the system and the gaps between men and women of the lower and middle classes. On the other hand, elite women in these societies have benefitted from Western education and ideals of greater freedom. Only in the Islamic countries has there been restricted response because of the tight control which male relatives hold over their women. This control is also reflected in the extraordinarily high fertility rate everywhere among Moslem women (Youssef, 1974).

An alternative model is practiced in the USSR and Eastern Europe, where women are treated solely as economic units, but still are given economically less important roles. Because women's role as mothers has been largely ignored by these societies, there has been a great drop in fertility rates. Men are still not taking on their share of household duties, and the women are in fact even more oppressed by two jobs—wage work and housework—than they are in many other developed countries (see Tinker, 1974).

The dislocation which development causes in the traditional economic roles of women in subsistence societies encourages the search for alternate models for development. What is needed is not an imported model, but rather an adaptation of development goals to each society. Only then can women now active in the economy be assured that their position will improve, and that development is not a boon for men only.

NOTE

1. For further readings in the area of women in development, see the forthcoming two-volume proceedings of the seminar held in Mexico City, August 1975, on that topic. One volume will summarize the issues raised in five workshops, along with the case studies written by the participants and background papers. The second volume will include a critical review of the literature and an annotated bibliography, primarily of unpublished works. These two volumes will be published by the American Association for the Advancement of Science and distributed by the Overseas Development Council, 1717 Massachusetts Avenue, N.W., Washington, D.C. 20036.

REFERENCES

BARKOW, J. H. (1972) "Hausa women and Islam." Canadian Journal of African Studies 6, 2.

BOSERUP, E. (1970) Women's Role in Economic Development. London: George Allen & Unwin.

DIETER-EVERS, H. (n.d.) "The role of professionalism in social and political change." Singapore: University of Singapore, Department of Sociology, Working paper No. 24.

DOBERT, M. (1974) "The changing status of women in French speaking Africa; two examples: Dahomey and Guinea." (unpublished manuscript)

DODGE, N. T. (1974) "The role of industrial revolution and social revolution in the modernization of women: the Soviet case." Prepared for the Society for International Development, 14th annual conference, Abidjan, Ivory Coast, August.

EBIHARA, M. (1974) "Khmer village women in Cambodia: a happy balance," in C. J. Matthiasson (ed.) Our Many Sisters: Women in Cross-Cultural Perspective. New York: Free Press.

Economic Commission for Africa, UN Economic and Social Council (1974) "The data base for discussion on the interrealtions between the integration of women in development, their situation and population factors in Africa." Regional Seminar on the Integration of Women in Development with Special Reference to Population Factors, Addis Ababa. UN Document E/CN.14/SW/37.

EKWENSI, C. (1961) Jagua Nana. Greenwich, Conn.: Fawcett.

FORTAS, M. (1954) "A demographic field study in Ashanti," in F. Lorimer (ed.) Culture and Human Fertility. Switzerland: UNESCO.

GEERTZ, H. (1961) The Javanese Family. Glencoe, Ill.: Free Press.

GREEN, J. J. (1973) "Philippine women: towards a social structural theory of female status." Prepared for the Southwest Conference of the Association for Asian Studies, Denton, Texas, October 12-13.

GUGLER, J. (1972) "The second sex in town." Canadian Journal of African Studies 6, 2.

HAGEN, M. (1972) "Note on the public markets and the marketing system of Managua, Nicaragua." (unpublished manuscript)

HOFFER, C. P. (1972) "Mende and Sherbo women in high office." Canadian Journal of African Studies 6, 2.

HOSKINS, M. W. (n.d.) "Vietnamese women in a changing society." (unpublished manuscript)

JAQUETTE, J. S. (1973) "Literary archetypes and female role alternatives: the woman and the novel in Latin America," in A. Pescatello (ed.) Female and Male in Latin America: Essays. Pittsburgh: University of Pittsburgh Press.

KALLGREN, J. K. (1973) "Enhancing the role of women in developing countries." Prepared for Agency for International Development.

KAPUR, P. (1972) Marriage and the Working Woman in India. Delhi: Vikas.

LITTLE, K. (1973) African Women in Towns: An Aspect of Africa's Social Revolution. London: Cambridge University Press.

MEHTA, R. (1970) The Western Educated Hindu Woman. Bombay: Asia.

OCLOO, E. (1974) "The Ghanian market woman." Prepared for the Society for International Development, 14th World Conference, Abidjan, Ivory Coast, August.

OKEDIJI, O. (1974) "The cultural consequences of population change in Nigeria." Prepared for a seminar on the Cultural Consequences of Population Change, Bucharest, Romania, August.

OMVEDT, G. (1973) "Caste, class and women's liberation." Prepared for the annual meeting of the Association for Asian Studies.

Pan-African Women's Centre and African Women's Development Task Force (1974) "Memorandum."

PAPANEK, H. (1973) "Purdah: separate worlds and symbolic shelter." Comparative Studies in Society & History 15 (June): 289-325.

――― (1971) "Purdah in Pakistan: seclusion and modern occupations for women." Journal of Marriage and the Family.

PAULME, D. [ed.] (1971) Women in Tropical Africa. Berkeley: University of California Press.

PESCATELLO, A. [ed.] (1973) Female and Male in Latin America: Essays. Pittsburgh: University of Pittsburgh Press.

POOL, J. E. (1972) "A cross comparative study of aspects of conjugal behavior among women of three West African countries." Canadian Journal of African Studies 6, 2.

REINING, P. (1973) "Utilization of ERTS-1 imagery in cultivation and settlement site identification and carrying capacity estimates in Upper Volta and Niger." Springfield, Va.: National Technical Information Service.

REMY, D. (n.d.) "Underdevelopment and the experience of women: a Zaria case study," in R. Reiter (ed.) Towards an Anthropology of Women. New York: Monthly Review Press.

――― and J. WEEKS (1973) "Employment, occupation and inequality in a non-industrialized city," in K. Wohlmuth (ed.) Employment in Emerging Societies. New York: Praeger.

ROSALDO, M. and L. LAMPHERE (1974) Woman, Culture and Society. Stanford: Stanford University Press.

SIMMONS, E. B. (1974) "Cultural assumptions and women's roles in development." Prepared for the Society for International Development, 14th World Conference, Abidjan, Ivory Coast, August.

SMITH, M. F. (1973) "Domestic service as a channel of upward mobility for the lower-class woman: the Lima case," pp. 191-208 in A. Pescatello (ed.) Female and Male in Latin America: Essays. Pittsburgh: University of Pittsburgh Press.

——— (1954) Baba of Karo: A Woman of the Muslim Hausa. London: Faber & Faber.

SNYDER, M. and D. TESBA (1973) "Women and the national development in African countries: some profound contradictions." New York: Ford Foundation, Task Force on Women.

STACK, C. B. (1974) All Our Kin: Strategies for Survival in a Black Community. New York: Harper & Row.

STOLMAKER, C. (1971) "Examples of stability and change from Santa Maria Atzompa." Presented at the annual meeting of the Southwestern Anthropological Association, Tucson, Arizona.

SULLEROT, E. (1971) Women, Society and Change. New York: McGraw-Hill.

TINKER, I. (1974) "Women's place in development." Summary of papers presented to Society for International Development, 14th World Conference, Abidjan, Ivory Coast, August.

——— (1973) "What's Happened to Progress?" in N. Fitzroy (ed.) Career Guidance for Women Entering Engineering. New York: Engineering Foundation.

TRACER, S. B. (1973) "La Quisqueyana: the Dominican woman, 1940-1970," in A. Pescatello (ed.) Female and Male in Latin America: Essays. Pittsburgh: University of Pittsburgh Press.

UCHENDU, V. C. (1965) The Igbo of Southeast Nigeria. New York: Holt, Rinehart & Winston.

VAN ALLEN, J. (1972) "Sitting on a man: colonialism and the lost political institutions of Igbo women." Canadian Journal of African Studies 6, 2.

WARD, B. E. (1970) "Women and technology in developing countries." Impact of Science on Society 20, 1.

——— (1963) Women in the New Asia. New York: UNESCO.

WIPPER, A. (1972) "The roles of African women: past, present and future." Canadian Journal of African Studies 6, 2.

WITKE, R. (1974) "Women in the People's Republic of China: American perspectives." Delivered at the Wingspread Conference, June 25.

YOUSSEF, N. H. (1974) "Women's status and fertility in Muslim countries of the Middle East and Africa." Prepared for the Symposium on Women's Status and Fertility Around the World, at the annual meeting of the American Psychological Association, New Orleans, August 30-September 3.

5

POVERTY

Women and Children Last

HEATHER L. ROSS

There is **nothing in the nature** of economic progress which assures that all people will benefit equally. Indeed, one of the important functions of humane government policy is to correct major imbalances that occur when economic activity rewards some people much more than others. Those who concern themselves with this kind of public policy have been finding that, more and more, a key element determining who moves ahead in the economy and who does not is *family structure:* husband-wife families are making progress in the white community and in the black community as well, but female-headed families are falling behind in both communities.

THE POVERTY POPULATION, 1960-1972

We can see the effects of these divergent trends by looking at the dramatic changes in the composition of the poverty population over the last decade. In 1960, there were 40 million poor persons. By 1972, this number had fallen to 24.5 million poor persons. But, as Figure 1 shows, virtually the entire decline was accounted for by persons in male-headed families, while the number of poor persons in female-headed families rose by 867,000.

This substantial change in the composition of poor families can be seen in Figure 2. In 1960, 29% of poor families were female-headed. By 1972, 43% were female-headed. Focusing further on families with children, the shift is even more dramatic: more than half of these

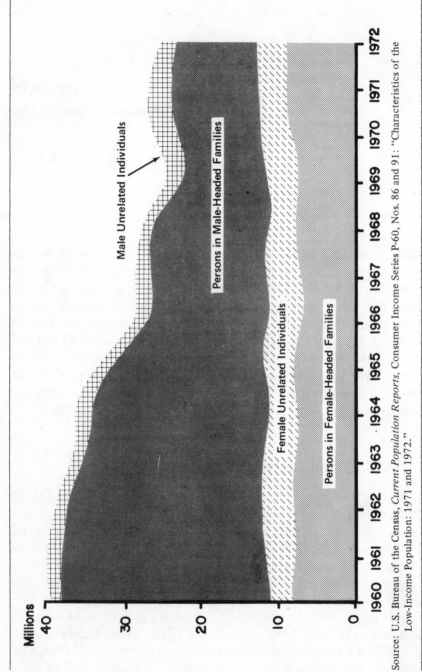

Source: U.S. Bureau of the Census, *Current Population Reports*, Consumer Income Series P-60, Nos. 86 and 91: "Characteristics of the Low-Income Population: 1971 and 1972."

FIGURE 1: Persons in Poverty, 1960-1972

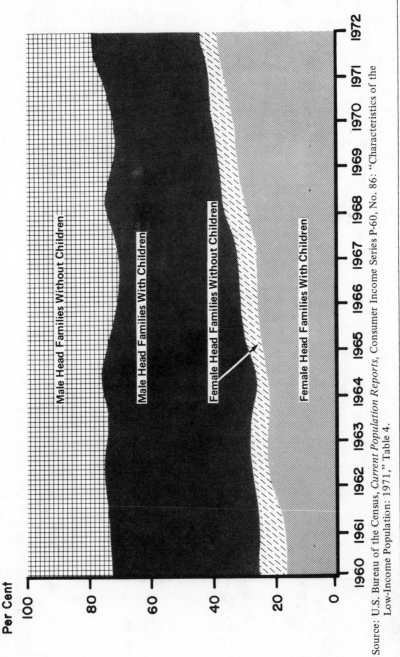

Per Cent

Male Head Families Without Children

Male Head Families With Children

Female Head Families Without Children

Female Head Families With Children

Source: U.S. Bureau of the Census, *Current Population Reports*, Consumer Income Series P-60, No. 86: "Characteristics of the Low-Income Population: 1971," Table 4.

FIGURE 2: Families in Poverty, 1960-1972

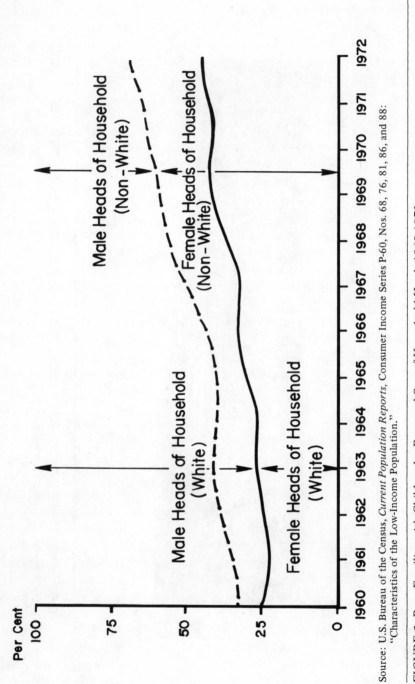

Source: U.S. Bureau of the Census, *Current Population Reports*, Consumer Income Series P-60, Nos. 68, 76, 81, 86, and 88: "Characteristics of the Low-Income Population."

FIGURE 3: Poor Families with Children by Race and Sex of Household Head, 1960-1972

poor families are now female-headed. And disaggregating further, by race, we find that 70% of nonwhite poor families with children are female-headed, while 43% of white poor families with children are female-headed. Thus, the trend toward female-headed families is more pronounced in the black community, but it is nevertheless well under way in the white community as well.

Figure 3 charts the changing relationship between poverty and sex of household head annually, from 1960-1972, for white families and non-white families separately. The lower line shows that about one-quarter of poor white families with children were female-headed in 1960 and three-fourths male-headed. Following the line upward over the 1960s, it is evident that the proportion of female-headed families increased steadily to 43% by 1972. For nonwhite families, about one-third of poor families with children were female-headed in 1960 and two-thirds male-headed, but by 1972 70% of these families were female-headed. Nonwhites have always had a higher proportion of poor, female-headed families with children, as can easily be seen in the figure. But the pace at which the population of poor families with children has been tipping toward female-headedness is almost as rapid for whites as for nonwhites. So the trend toward female-headed families at low income levels is not exclusively a black phenomenon—as many seem to have believed and as earlier treatments of the subject (for example, Moynihan, 1965b) implied.

Furthermore, the trend toward female-headed families is not solely a poverty-level phenomenon. Figure 4 shows poor female-headed family growth relative to total female-headed family growth. The bottom area of the figure shows the number of poor female-headed families with children. Their number moved irregularly during the decade, but started edging up significantly around 1969. The next band in the figure shows the number of near-poor female-headed families with children—that is, families with incomes between 100% and 125% of the poverty line. Their number remained fairly stable during the 1960s, but also began to increase at the end of the decade. The top line shows the total number of female-headed families with children at all income levels. It is evident that the top line of total female-headed families with children has been moving up much more rapidly than the bottom area of poor female-headed families with children. In fact, it has been moving up more than twice as fast, so that the great majority of new female-headed families with children formed in this era were nonpoor.

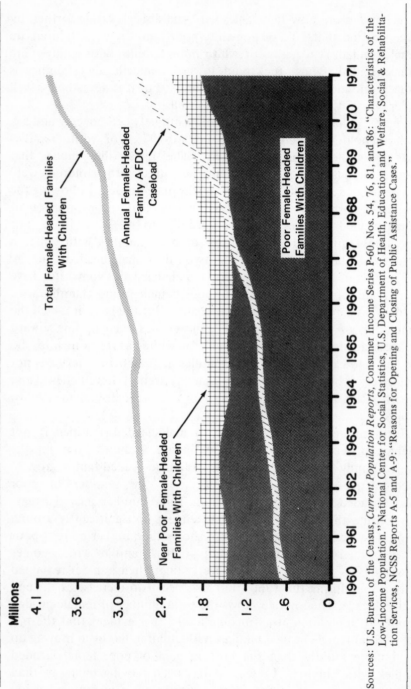

Millions

FIGURE 4: Trends in Poverty, Welfare, and Female Family Headship, 1960-1971

Sources: U.S. Bureau of the Census, *Current Population Reports*, Consumer Income Series P-60, Nos. 54, 76, 81, and 86: "Characteristics of the Low-Income Population." National Center for Social Statistics, U.S. Department of Health, Education and Welfare, Social & Rehabilitation Services, NCSS Reports A-5 and A-9: "Reasons for Opening and Closing of Public Assistance Cases."

The trend toward female-headed families has, nevertheless, af-fected the welfare caseload. Figure 4 shows the welfare caseload growth as measured by the number of female-headed families with children served each year by AFDC (Aid to Families with Dependent Children). In 1960 the annual caseload for such families represented less than half the poverty population, but steady growth brought it to total almost 70% of all female-headed families with children by 1971.

A few cautionary words are in order regarding this figure. First, the family unit definition for a welfare unit differs from that for a female-headed family unit as measured by the census, with the former being broader than the latter. Second, the use of an annual caseload figure for AFDC gives a much higher caseload total than the monthly figure usually reported, since the annual number of units served is much higher than any average monthly total due to high caseload turnover. Figure 4 does not indicate that all poor and near-poor female-headed families with children are presently re-ceiving welfare, nor does it mean that large numbers of relatively high-income, ineligible women are presently receiving it. What it does show is that the number of female-headed family units served by welfare over the period has risen dramatically, and that this number is now quite large relative to the total count of female-headed families measured by the Census Bureau.

Two major factors need to be cited in connection with this large welfare caseload growth. One is an increasing rate of participation in the welfare program. The probability that a female-headed family with children which is eligible for welfare will actually be receiving it at any point in time has grown significantly, especially since 1967. In 1967, 63% of eligible families were AFDC recipients, but in 1971, 94% were (Boland, 1973). This increase in the participation rate was the result of both higher applications by eligible families and an increasing acceptance rate on the part of welfare agencies.

The second major factor is the increasing number of eligible families. Part of this increasing coverage of female-headed families with children is due to raised income eligibility ceilings. As states have raised their welfare benefit levels over the 1960s, the incomes at which families can establish eligibility for welfare have gone up correspondingly, so that welfare coverage has extended higher and higher up the income distribution of female-headed families with children. From 1967 to 1971, the entry level—that is, the income level at which welfare eligibility could be established—rose by 25% nationwide (Lurie, 1973). Over the same period, the exit level—up to which families could earn and still retain welfare eligibility once established—grew by 85%. The other part of the explanation for the increasing pool of eligibles is simply increased formation of female-headed families with children at low income. And the issue here, to which we will return shortly, is what role, if any, welfare has played in the growth of this group.

To sum up, we find that female-headed families with children are on the increase at all income levels, with many more being formed who are nonpoor than are poor. But because the number of poor families who are male-headed has declined so significantly over the 1960s, the poverty population has come to be increasingly characterized by female-headed families. Christopher Jencks (1974), in an article entitled "The Poverty of Welfare," concluded that "there have been several million women with dependent children and inadequate incomes for at least a generation." What is so striking now is that they form such a large *share* of the poverty population. Furthermore, this tipping toward female-headedness is going on almost as rapidly in the poor white community as in the poor black community.

WHY ARE FEMALE-HEADED FAMILIES WITH CHILDREN INCREASING?

This is an important question and a difficult one to answer. One way to begin is to break down the growth of female-headed families with children by its various demographic components. Is it marital disruption, illegitimacy, or other social factors that are contributing to this growth?

The pie charts in Figure 5 show major components of growth which can be identified in published census data, and their relative importance in contributing to the growth of female-headed families with children over the decade 1960 to 1970 for nonwhites and whites separately. Female-headed families increased by 700,000 among whites from 1960-1970, and by 392,000 among blacks. Part of this increase was due to population growth. Adding more adult women to the total population would result in more women heading female-headed families with children even if the *proportion* of women heading such families had not changed. This component is shown as "population" in the chart. But the proportion of women heading families with children has changed for several reasons. One is marital disruption. With a significantly increasing divorce rate, the chances of a woman experiencing marital disruption have increased considerably. This tends to increase the number of female-headed families with children even if no other change occurs. This factor is shown as "marital disruption" in the chart.

But other changes are occurring. The probability that a woman who experiences marital disruption will have one or more children living with her has also increased considerably. This heightened probability reflects these statistical realities: there are more divorced women and fewer widows among the maritally disrupted population, divorced women are younger than in the past, childlessness has become rarer among the population as a whole. It is shown in the chart as "presence of children." Furthermore, the probability that a woman who has experienced marital disruption and has at least one child will set up her own household rather than doubling up with relatives has also increased. Unmarried women with children are also more likely to have their own household. The joint effect of these probabilities is shown as "living arrangements." It reflects women's increasing economic ability to establish independent households plus a trend away from extended family living patterns throughout society.

Finally, the probability that an unmarried woman will have a child living with her has grown, and this component is labelled "illegitimacy." It reflects the increasing illegitimacy rates for first births of both whites and nonwhites. The interaction wedge shows the residual growth that is not explained by any one factor independently, but rather by the joint effect of two or more factors operating in conjunction with one another.

Looking now at the actual values recorded for nonwhites and whites over the period 1960 to 1970, we see that the largest factors contributing to the formation of female-headed families for whites are population growth and marital disruption, with presence of children in disrupted marriages coming in a close third. Living arrangements and illegitimacy make only modest contributions to the total growth. These results on living arrangements run counter to arguments by other researchers that changed housing patterns are perhaps the most significant element in the recent growth of female-headed families with children (Cutright and Scanzoni, 1973).

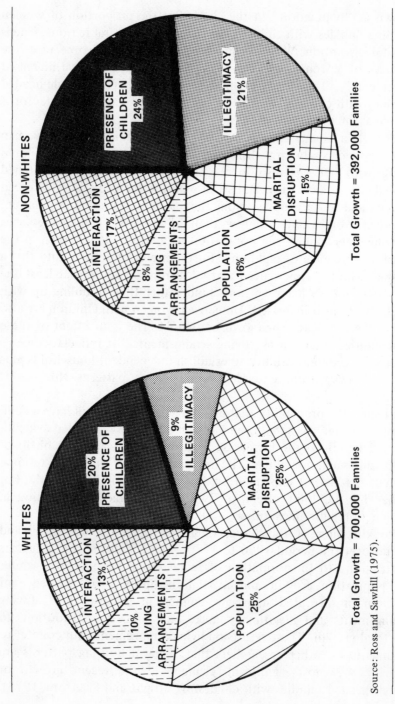

NON-WHITES

PRESENCE OF CHILDREN 24%

ILLEGITIMACY 21%

MARITAL DISRUPTION 15%

POPULATION 16%

LIVING ARRANGEMENTS 8%

INTERACTION 17%

Total Growth = 392,000 Families

WHITES

PRESENCE OF CHILDREN 20%

ILLEGITIMACY 9%

MARITAL DISRUPTION 25%

POPULATION 25%

LIVING ARRANGEMENTS 10%

INTERACTION 13%

Total Growth = 700,000 Families

Source: Ross and Sawhill (1975).

FIGURE 5: Components of Growth in Female-Headed Families with Children, 1960-1970

For nonwhites, it is the child-related components—illegitimacy or the presence of children in disrupted marriages—which account for the greatest share of growth.

Contrasting the behavioral differences of the two racial groups, it appears that the combination of marital disruption and presence of children in disrupted marriages accounts for a simialr percentage of growth for whites and nonwhites, but with a slight emphasis on disruption for whites and on presence of children for nonwhites. The major behavioral difference lies in the role of illegitimacy, with nonwhites showing a greater effect here, despite the fact that the nonwhite illegitimacy rate peaked in the middle 1960s and has declined since, while the white rate continues to climb. This is the result of illegitimacy declines for nonwhites being concentrated in other than first births, and of a greater probability that nonwhite women will keep their illegitimate children with them. Behavioral changes of all kinds have clearly been more important for nonwhites than for whites. Simple population growth accounts for considerably less nonwhite growth than white over the period, even though the total population growth for nonwhites far exceeded that for whites during those years.

ROLE OF THE WELFARE SYSTEM

The figures above provide a context for asking the important question of what role the welfare system has played in the growth of female-headed families with children. By restricting its benefits for the most part to these kinds of families, has welfare encouraged their formation? Has it done so through illegitimacy, through family-splitting, through undoubling of families, or how?

The first point to note is the magnitude of the financial incentive for women to head their families—that is, the dollar value associated with not living with the father of one's children and receiving welfare versus the value associated with living with him and forfeiting welfare. The tradeoff between what low-skilled men (or low-skilled working mothers) can provide and what welfare can provide has been tipping over the last decade in favor of welfare, especially when the value of benefits tied to welfare status, such as medicaid coverage, are included. It is relatively easy to calculate these tradeoffs for different state welfare programs and different local labor markets, and this has been done by a number of recent analysts.

But determining the behavioral response to these tradeoffs—that is, the way people actually act when confronted with these financial incentives—has proved to be very difficult. On illegitimacy, for example, no one has yet found statistical evidence that higher AFDC payments are related to higher illegitimate births, even though many people think this may be true.

On marital disruption the picture is also mixed. Some analysts have found that higher AFDC benefit levels mean higher proportions of ever-married women with children living as heads of households (Honig, 1974), and some have found that they do not (Cutright and Scanzoni, 1973). The bulk of the evidence supports the latter finding, but the most sophisticated recent work suggests the former.

It should be noted that in the case of both illegitimacy and marital disruption, welfare could contribute to the total number of female-headed families by *keeping* people in that status as well as by putting them there in the first place. This could occur if women failed to marry or to remarry due to concern for losing welfare benefits. This is a particularly interesting aspect of welfare effects on family organization now, because the eligibility rules in this area have recently been changed. In 1968 the Supreme Court invalidated the man-in-the-house rule, and in 1970 it further ruled that in the case of a man assuming the role of spouse, including a nonadopting stepfather, no presumption could be made that the man was contributing any of his resources to the support of children in the family. Documentation of an actual flow of resources from the man to the children would have to be made before any adjustment in benefits to the children could be carried out.

Thus, welfare no longer discriminates against married people: a woman can marry a man who is not the father of her children without necessarily losing their benefits. The potential for significant change in the living arrangements of welfare families is evident here. Women will be able to marry and continue welfare coverage of their children. If the poor are at all sensitive to financial incentives structured into government programs, one would expect some response to this rule change, and indeed this seems to have occurred. Stepfather cases in AFDC have grown appreciably since the court rulings, and they are currently increasing half again as fast as the overall caseload.

Finally, on the issue of living arrangements, it seems likely that welfare has contributed to the census count of female-headed families with children by providing recipient units with the resources needed to establish their own households, rather than doubling up with relatives. But again the empirical evidence to make this case, and to measure the magnitude of it, has not been assembled.

The message from this discussion of welfare effects on female-headed families with children is that not a lot is known conclusively, although there are considerable hints of several different influences that may be operating. Most of the work done in this area is recent and exploratory, but a start is being made (U.S. Congress . . . , 1973). There is a definite need for continued work to raise our level of understanding and to help in the design of improved social policy.

POLICY IMPLICATIONS

What can we say now, with the information we do have at hand, about how policy-makers should deal with the changing demography of poverty? Without waiting for more information, can we draw some conclusions about how public policy should respond to increasing numbers of poor female-headed families with children? Four potential strategies are outlined here.

Strategy 1

The first strategy I will call "broadened income maintenance eligibility." This could mean coverage of working poor families with children, broader coverage for families with or without children, or universal income maintenance for all low-income people. The major benefit of this policy would be aid to needy people who are making an effort at self-support, but who still lack adequate incomes. This would provide more equitable treatment of low-income people, with its incentive counterpart of removing the penalty against marrying and living together with one's own spouse and children. The goal here would be a neutral policy, thus removing the penalty of the present AFDC system against intact and childless families.

How to structure such a neutral program is a complex question. Different methods of defining a recipient unit and measuring its resources can have profound effects on the way people choose to group themselves. Considering people as individuals, as families, as households, or as groups of persons legally responsible for each other will affect the costs and distribution of benefits of an income maintenance system—and also the way people live or appear to live.

But the crucial question to address here is not whether or how a neutral definition might be established, but how much regrouping or staying together of families that neutral policy would buy. The answer to this is—probably not much. The trend toward marital instability is going forward in all segments of society. Among low-income people, where instability is still most pronounced, the existence of an income transfer program could operate to sustain, rather than retard, this trend. Consider, for example, a program like the Family Assistance Plan, in which the benefit reduction rate was 67%—that is, a 67-cent benefit loss would have been incurred for every dollar earned. Subtracting further the benefit reductions in other programs (such as food stamps, public housing, and medicaid) which accompany rising income, there was not much, economically, to be gained by a family having a man with earnings as part of their family unit. It would probably have been more attractive for him to stay outside the family and have some informal income-sharing arrangement which would be difficult to detect, much as under the present AFDC system. Also, results of the New Jersey income maintenance experiment, which paid welfare benefits to intact families with children, show that income maintenance did not lead to greater family stability among those getting benefits than among another group of similar people who were observed but not supported. The New Jersey results suggest that people do not use money to buy stability, but to buy personal independence and the opportunity to choose among different family relationships.

Welfare reform of this broadening sort is needed. But such a program is not likely to regroup families significantly, nor will such a program, by itself, lead to more income for women and children who are already covered by welfare.

Strategy 2

A second strategy is one suggested by Moynihan in his 1965 Labor Department report. Although no explicit policy recommendation appears in the published document, the text strongly implies that the key to dealing with female-headed families and poverty is improving the economic status of men, so that they will become better providers. This, too, is a good idea: increased capacity for self-support is the logical and humane road toward ending poverty. But the outcome of this goal for regrouping families or keeping them together is very uncertain. Divorce rates have increased over 60% since 1960, and reliance on men's earning power is no longer very reliable protection from poverty for women and children. Helping male teenagers to find work and earn a living wage has great value in its own right and may well encourage families to form, but it is no assurance that those families will stay together. And even if those males later form a new family, as the great majority of divorced men do, there will be a transitional period for women and children when an adequate income of their own is required. Again, this is a good and necessary policy recommendation, but it is not sufficient to the task of keeping women and children out of poverty.

Strategy 3

What might be termed the "income-by-right" strategy is also a welfare approach (as such, it resembles Strategy 1); but it emphasizes making benefits more adequate for those currently covered, rather than extending coverage to others. The argument here is that women have a right to their traditional roles of full-time homemaker and mother, and that they should not be denied those roles because they are poor or without a husband. In the case of illegitimacy or marital disruption, if the missing male parent does not provide adequate support, the rationale is that the state should step in and support women so they can stay home with their families.

This is an increasingly unpopular view, especially as women in the nonpoverty segment of society are moving more and more into the labor force, while the labor force participation of low-income women is dropping. The result is a growing rift between the poor and nonpoor. As the latter increase their labor force participation, the former go on welfare and reduce theirs. A comparison of the income distribution of female-headed families with children in 1967 to that in 1970 shows that between 1967 and 1970, while the total number of female-headed families with children increased by 16%, the number of female-headed families with children with no income other than public assistance increased by 39%—over twice as fast. Furthermore, for those with income other than public assistance in the $1,000-$5,000 range, the range of earnings which many of these women with few skills might expect to get from working full-time or part-time in the labor market actually declined.

This split in behavior is one of the elements leading to the increased unpopularity of the AFDC program. That program is inadequate now, judged by the fact that over half its female-headed family recipients are still poor after receiving benefits. Thus, many women and their families are not well provided for by welfare currently, but there is little hope that significantly increasing benefits to them alone is a politically feasible goal.

Strategy 4

Finally, there is Strategy 4—full economic independence for women. With the breakdown of traditional families wherein men supported women and children, women need the economic capability to support themselves and to contribute to the support costs of their children. Developing this capability would entail major changes. For one, it means a concerted attack on sex discrimination in the market: equal pay would be required for equal work. A five-year panel study by the University of Michigan found that if women who headed families in economic need had been paid wages equal to the wages paid men of comparable skills and experience, 55% would have been nonpoor.

Strategy 4 would also mean an end to the occupational discrimination which crowds women into low-paying jobs. There is a great irony here: women coming onto welfare rolls now are younger, healthier, have fewer children and a better education than any group before them, but the jobs they can get are being relegated more and more to the backwater of the economy. An example is clerical work, where many women are employed and where wages have risen much less rapidly than overall wages in the economy. It may be that women are opting for welfare, rather than work in this lagging, low-paid sector. Another aspect is equal access to education, training, and other institutions in our society—in contrast to the present priorities of the welfare-related Work Incentive Program which place men in training and employment first.

There are two final points to be made about this strategy. One is that some protection must be afforded to women for whom the rules of the game are being changed. They were raised to play a traditional role which is now slipping beyond their grasp, and they are ill-prepared for the new functions they must take on. This suggests the creation of a voluntary program which stresses opportunity in attracting women into the labor force, rather than a mandatory program which forces them to take the low-level jobs they are currently rejecting.

The second point is that we must recognize that these efforts will make female-headed status much less undesirable by increasing the resources available to families headed by women. Women and children are certainly paying a heavy penalty now for living in female-headed families, even with the financial help of AFDC. Is making these families more viable, and thus perhaps increasing their numbers, against the public interest? Some people have argued that it is. Here is Daniel Patrick Moynihan in a 1965 magazine article:

> From the wild Irish slums of the 19th century eastern seaboard to the riot torn suburbs of Los Angeles, there is one unmistakable lesson in American history: a community that allows a large number of young men to grow up in broken families, dominated by women, never acquiring any stable relationship to male authority, never acquiring any set of rational expectations about the future—that community asks for and gets chaos. Crime, violence, unrest, disorder—most particularly the furious unrestrained lashing out at the whole social structure—that is not only to be expected; it is very near to inevitable. And it is richly deserved.

It was perhaps easy in 1965 to blame urban riots on female-headed families. But careful research since then has shown this accusation to be false. In the first place, it is clear that female-headed families are not totally devoid of male influence. But the second, more important point is that it is not the lack of male influence or the limitation of having one versus two parents which is the problem, but the lack of economic resources of female-headed families with children. Moving to help women acquire these resources for themselves is the most direct solution to the problems which they face and which society faces with them. Once we have accomplished this, independent adults can choose to group in families for their own satisfaction and joint well-being and for the well-being of their children. This will be a good family policy.

So we have reached a conclusion. We have seen that female-headed family growth is proceeding in all segments of society. We have seen that there are strong forces at work here which have been in operation for many years. We have seen several strategies which could contribute toward solving the problems of female-headed families, and there are others (such as contraception, abortion, and increased efforts to get male parents to support children) which have not even been discussed here. But mostly what we have seen is that this is not an issue with a welfare solution. Welfare cannot bring families together or keep families together even if we wanted it to. It cannot provide adequate resources to women and children to keep them from falling behind the mainstream of progress in society. So the main chance for women, with or without children, is the same as for other disadvantaged people—improving their opportunity and capability to earn a decent living in the job market that has offered them so little for so long.

REFERENCES

BOLAND, B. (1973) "Participation in the Aid to Families with Dependent Children program (AFDC)." Washington, D.C.: Urban Institute Working Paper 971-02, August 1.

CUTRIGHT, P. and J. SCANZONI (1973) "Income supplements and the American family." Studies in Public Welfare Paper No. 12, prepared for the U.S. Congress, Joint Economic Committee, Subcommittee on Fiscal Policy, November. Washington, D.C.: Government Printing Office.

HONIG, M. (1974) "AFDC income, recipient rates, and family dissolution." Journal of Human Resources 9, 3 (Summer).

JENCKS, C. (1974) "The poverty of welfare." Working Papers 4: 5.

LURIE, I. (1973) "Legislative, administrative, and judicial changes in the AFDC program, 1967-71." Madison, Wis.: Institute for Research on Poverty Reprint 93.

MOYNIHAN, D. P. (1965a) The Negro Family: The Case for National Action. Washington, D.C.: U.S. Department of Labor, Office of Policy Planning and Research.

——— (1965b) "A family policy for the nation." America 113 (September): 280-283.

ROSS, H. L. and I. V. SAWHILL (1975) Time of Transition: The Growth of Families Headed by Women. Washington, D.C.: Urban Institute.

U.S. Congress, Joint Economic Committee, Subcommittee on Fiscal Policy (1973) "The family, poverty, and welfare programs: factors influencing family stability." Studies in Public Welfare Paper No. 12, November 4.

6

THE CONDITION OF WOMEN
IN BLUE-COLLAR JOBS

PAMELA ROBY

There has been a recent resurgence of interest in women in working-class jobs. Several influences—the rise of the blue-collar women's rights movement, women's liberation, and a national concern with the "blue-collar blues" which have resulted in declining productivity—have begun to generate new research on women in working-class jobs after 50 years of neglect.

Much useful research on the conditions of women in working-class jobs was conducted between 1900 and 1925. The books and articles of that era described blue-collar women's working conditions and the physical, psychological, and social problems which those conditions presented. The books were written for students, politicians, philanthropists, ministers, and other citizens who the authors felt might be induced to help the women through the provision of charity or the promulgation of social reforms. Most of the books were by upper-middle-class, white, Protestant women and were neither read nor prepared by working-class women themselves. The work was useful in that it made public the women's horrible working and living conditions. These studies, along with much agitation by working women and men and horrors such as the 1909 New York Triangle Shirtwaist Fire, led to the beginnings of reform legislation for working women.

AUTHOR'S NOTE: Portions of this chapter are excerpted and revised from the author's forthcoming monograph, *The Conditions of Women in Blue-Collar and Service Jobs: A Review of Research and Proposals for Research, Action and Policy* (New York: Russell Sage Foundation, Social Science Frontiers series).

Concern with blue-collar working women diminished with the advent of World War I and the general decline of urban social reform. Following 1925, the United States has experienced a notable lack of social science research focused on women in working-class jobs, slippage in many job conditions, and five decades of technological change in industrial conditions which have made previous research obsolete. In recent years not a single book has been devoted primarily to women employed in blue-collar industrial or service jobs. Recently, a few books have dealt with employed women, but have focused on professionals or executives.

Why should social science research be devoted to blue-collar employed women and their families? First, women in blue-collar industrial and service occupations are a large and growing part of the female labor force—40% in 1974. Research is needed to help policy-makers gain a better understanding of how to meet the needs of these women and their families. Research should precede policy-making; policy implications should be considered at every step of research; and evaluation research should accompany the implementation of social policies.

Due to the development and increasing sophistication of radical sociology and radical political economics over the past decade, researchers who pursue studies on the issues set forth later in this chapter are unlikely to be guilty of the "fallacy of the middle range," as were their predecessors. The early writers concentrated on specific problems confronting women in working-class jobs without relating the problems to their origins in the larger social, economic, and political system. Current policy-oriented research and reform efforts are likely to be directed toward obtaining fundamental as well as incremental change.

Most of the research recommendations presented here have been suggested by over 100 women in blue-collar jobs and by union, company, and organizational officials who make or are concerned with policies affecting women on these jobs. Others come from my own reflections following discussions with these individuals and tours through numerous factories and workplaces.

The research proposals fall into five categories relating to various aspects of the women's lives: (1) wages and working conditions; (2) opportunities for work, training, and upward mobility; (3) government, company, and union policies affecting conditions of living during off-the-job hours; (4) policies affecting the attitudes and "consciousness" of the women; and (5) unionization and union policies and practices.

WAGES AND WORKING CONDITIONS

Law Enforcement Processes

Since 1963, the federal and state governments have passed several laws prohibiting discrimination against women in the labor force —among them the Equal Pay Act and Title VII of the Civil Rights Act of 1964. Executive Order 11246, issued by President Lyndon B. Johnson in 1965 and amended in 1967 by Executive Order 11375, forbids discrimination against women in companies which hold federal government contracts. Most states also have fair employment laws which forbid sex discrimination in employment. The processes by which these laws are enforced and how the processes can be improved deserve extensive and careful study from a number of perspectives (U.S. Commission on Civil Rights, 1973: 124; Lyle, 1973; Adams, 1973). Evaluation research on how companies' progress toward their stated affirmative action goals is being monitored by the responsible federal offices is clearly needed. Which and how many industries are not meeting the federal affirmative action requirements? What is being done about them?

We should also study the processes by which complaints are filed and completed. What barriers prevent women from filing or carrying through on complaints under each of the laws? To what extent have unionized and nonunionized blue-collar women been made aware of the existence of the laws? What is involved in their filing a complaint—must they make long-distance phone calls or take time off from their jobs to file? To what extent do union stewards help women file complaints? What attitudes do government officials display toward the women who make complaints? Are the government offices open during the hours women can make complaints or only during their working hours? What additional staffing is needed in affirmative action compliance offices for them to have adequate outreach and compliance programs for blue-collar women? What follow-up has occurred after decisions have been made in favor of complainants?

It is also important to explore judges' knowledge of and attitudes toward the new laws on women's employment rights. What percentage of the judges and other officials who make decisions on female employees' complaints are women? Dorothy Haener, an international representative of the U.A.W. who has long been involved in women's issues, says that a book on court, Equal Employment Opportunity Commission, and wage-and-hour decisions regarding working women and affirmative action in-service training of employment service personnel, judges, court commissioners, and public prosecutors is very much needed.

Linda Tarr-Whelan, Deputy Director of Program Development of the American Federation of State, County and Municipal Employees (AFSCME) and National Secretary of the Coalition of Labor Union Women (CLUW), urges that we investigate what kind of legislation could restore the protections of the protective laws which have been rescinded over the last decade. We also should explore the extent to which equality of law has been achieved through abolishing protections for women rather than extending them to men.[1] A major question is to what extent women have been treated unequally by being given the heaviest or dirtiest jobs in their shops by foremen who resent their presence. The E.E.O.C. (1969) has ruled against this type of treatment, but a large-scale survey of women in blue-collar industrial and service jobs needs to be conducted to determine the pervasiveness of this type of treatment and means of coping with it.

High-quality muckraking research is needed to uncover and document the many sewing and other industrial operations which employ thousands of women outside of the law and make no effort whatsoever to obey minimum wage and other laws by exploiting poor, recently arrived immigrant women who know neither English nor minimal employment norms.

Breaking into Traditionally Male Jobs

There may always be a tendency for "men's jobs" to pay more than "women's jobs" as long as they remain segregated. In addition, some women are discovering that they prefer jobs traditionally held by men. Therefore, we must devote study to processes by which women may break more quickly and easily into jobs traditionally held by men.

Gloria Johnson (1974), Director of the Women's Department of the International Union of Electrical Workers (IUE), suggested that one might explore cases when men have supported women who have moved into traditionally male jobs. Women steelworkers, who have recently broken into jobs held only by men since World War II, have reported that black men—perhaps sensitized by their own experiences of fighting discrimination—have helped them learn their new jobs, while white men have often harassed them and refused to teach them even safety precautions. Harassment included foremen who made women (during their probationary period) carry excessive weights which tractors, rather than men, normally carry; male workers' refusing to teach women saftey precautions which they have always taught new men; men telling women, "You wanted the job, now you can cope with it;" and foremen refusing women normal breaks and giving them the jobs of two men to perform—all reported to me by women who have recently broken into jobs traditionally held by men. Some of this treatment resulted in physical injury; some resulted in women dropping out of the job or being fired; some was followed by women gritting their teeth, keeping their jobs, and later organizing other women or filing union complaints or law suits against the companies.

Opening apprenticeship opportunities for women in traditionally male jobs is one answer to these problems which will be discussed below. In addition, however, we need a study of the experience of women who are moving into traditionally male jobs so that we can learn what types of male attitudes and harassment other women breaking into new job areas will need to learn how to combat. A booklet should be published for women entering nontraditional jobs on how to best use unions and laws to cope with male chauvinism.

Stewards, foremen, and workers who actively assist women in breaking into new jobs should be rewarded with bonuses, just as they would be if they performed some other aspect of their job especially well. The young college-educated "blue jeans" women who have much confidence and choose to work in a plant rather than an office may be able to pioneer in the traditionally male jobs and help other women break into them, too. Careful evaluation research must accompany all the suggestions proposed above and be used as a guide for modifying and constructing new proposals to facilitate women's breaking into jobs traditionally closed to them.

Hours of Work

Historically, the length of the work day has been a major rallying issue for workers. Today both the number of hours people work per week and how these hours are scheduled are again matters of concern. State protective laws which were intended to protect women against long working hours have been repealed (Spokeswoman, 1974).[2] Now many blue-collar women as well as men must work ten-hour days and six-day weeks. The long days and weeks mean that workers must do shopping, laundry, and other housework on their seventh day, and that week in and week out they have no day for rest. Many of the negative effects of this schedule on the morale, physical and mental health, and family life of both male and female workers can easily be guessed. The hours and their effects need to be documented, widely publicized, and changed. Toward this end, the U.S. Department of Labor should routinely publish the number of hours women and men work weekly in its *Employment and Earnings.*

How to make work schedules maximally compatible with family life is a more complex question which should be given extensive attention. How do various work schedules affect blue-collar women and their families? At a time when the ten-hour day, four-day week is being considered, the effect of differing types of work schedules on various groups of women and their families (single women, married but childless women, married women with children, and single parents) should be given serious consideration. To date, although the four-day week has been widely debated, its potential impact on working women and their families has been left unexamined (Poors, 1970). Because many companies and governmental units have already shifted to the four-day, ten-hour week, we need only to interview women working under the new schedules in order to learn the benefits and difficulties which they present to family life. Similarly, we need to explore the impact of various existing mixes of night and day work schedules on workers and their families.

Part-time work and a shorter work week also deserve study because they could answer the needs of many mothers with young children. From 1963 to 1973, part-time employment of adult women grew by 54% compared to a 28% increase in full-time employment of adult women. In 1973, of the 30 million adult women in the civilian labor force, 6.7 million were either working part-time or seeking part-time employment (Greenwald, 1974). We should study union and employer attitudes concerning part-time work rewarded by pay and benefits proportionate to the time worked and follow up this study with experimental demonstration research projects which attempt to work around the problems raised. Industry-by-industry cost and productivity studies, including records of part-time workers' absenteeism, should be made. We ought also to investigate how part-time work at adequate wages for fathers as well as mothers of young children would be accepted by and affect blue-collar families (cf. Gronseth, 1972). Perhaps workers would prefer a shorter work week for all. Surveys should be conducted to determine the extent to which workers would support and work for a 35- or 30-hour work week. All research and social policy related to working hours should be informed by the fact that the vast majority of working women bear and raise children sometime during their lives.

Job Benefits

Benefits are often distributed more unequally than wages among workers and managers. A major national survey ought to be conducted on fringe benefits which accrue to women from industry to industry, job to job, and union to union. The findings of this study and the importance of fringe benefits should then be made known to women looking for jobs.

Historical, Demographic, and Ethnographic Research on Working Conditions

One must study history in order to understand today's social policies and working conditions. Trend analyses should be made to learn what accounted for historical shifts in women's wages and in the percentage of women working in various blue-collar, industrial, and service jobs. To what extent are women's wages, training opportunities, and job opportunities correlated with national economic conditions (e.g., recessions, government spending, foreign competition) and historical events (e.g., wars)? What can be done in the future to prevent these events from disproportionately affecting women?

Demographic as well as historical studies should be made to guide policy-makers and pressure groups. More local-level (county or city) census information on women's wages by occupation and ethnicity is required for local politicians and others to be adequately informed of the status of women in their communities. National census data should be mined in an effort to construct pictures of the work and living conditions of various groups of employed blue-collar women and to gain a better understanding of the types of social policies which are required to improve their lot. We need to combine census and participant observer workplace studies to learn the degree to which double discrimination is operating against Black, Chicano, Puerto Rican, Filipino, and Chinese women. Census data should also be used to document the extent to which the full-time "working poor" are *working women* and their children.

Policy-makers and social change agents also require ethnographic or descriptive studies on working-class women's occupations and lives in order to better understand their needs. The creation of paraprofessional jobs was accompanied by much political fanfare. New studies should be made of the wages, on-the-job training opportunities, and opportunities for promotion of educational, legal, police, and nurses aides. In addition, in-depth interview studies should be conducted with paraprofessionals and other blue-collar industrial and service workers to learn how they view their jobs—how do they see their mornings, their afternoons? How do they believe their jobs can be improved for themselves and their families? Finally, U.S. policy-makers should be enlightened by summary studies of the status of, and policies affecting, blue-collar employed women in other nations.

WORK, TRAINING, AND PROMOTION OPPORTUNITIES

The Right to Work

Presently many blue-collar women are worrying more about obtaining work, rather than about working conditions. Title VII of the U.S. Civil Rights Act, noted above, prohibits sex discrimination in the hiring, promotion, training, layoff and discharge policies of employers, employment agencies, unions, and hiring halls with 15 or more employees. Much research and action will be required before this prohibition becomes a reality.

A major question is how to change the attitudes and procedures of state and private employment officers across the nation as rapidly as possible, so that they will encourage rather than prevent women from applying for higher-paying, traditionally male jobs. This action research ought to be conducted on a continuing nationwide basis until no employment office keeps separate job files for men and women or in any other way discourages women from applying for traditionally male positions. Changes are also called for on the part of employers and armed service recruiters. Research is no longer needed to document the sexist attitudes of both. Rather, a concerted effort accompanied by evaluation research is needed to spread information concerning affirmative action laws among employers, recruiters, and women job applicants; to inform employers that many of their beliefs—such as the one that women's absenteeism rates are higher than men's—are incorrect; and to induce employers and defense recruiters to actively seek out women for traditionally male jobs and to help them learn and adjust to the jobs.

Unemployment data and other research show that minority women aged 16-19, women with large numbers of children, and older women who have been out of the labor force for a considerable length of time bearing and rearing children have the greatest difficulty in obtaining work. Experimental research on job subsidies, training programs similar to those for veterans, and other inducements should be conducted to determine by what means employers might be most effectively encouraged to hire, retain, and promote these women.

The whole area of government unemployment statistics, including procedures for counting and reporting on the unemployed, ought to be reexamined and restructured. Women who are currently not included among the unemployed are those who would like or need to work, but are unable to work because they have inadequate child-care; those who now work 10, 20, or 30 hours a week, but would like or need to work full-time; those who were unemployed for 10 or 11 months of the year, but are employed during the month of the employment count and would have liked to be employed year-round; and those who would like very much to work, but have looked for work so long that they have given up on actively doing so over the previous four weeks (Leggett and Cervinka, 1972). Bertram Gross and Stanley Moss (1972: 10) have "conservatively estimated" that 5 million housewives desire work and would work if suitable employment were available. None of the 5 million were counted in the U.S. Department of Labor's statistics on the unemployed.

Of course, lying behind the issue of developing accurate and complete unemployment statistics is the issue of the right to work. The guarantee of the right to work would be for both men and women, a major advancement beyond the right of people of different sexes, races, creeds, and nationalities to have an equal opportunity to *compete* for work. Much poverty, unhappiness, and mental illness from forced unemployment would be eliminated, and a more productive and richer nation would be created if the Murray-Wagner Full Employment Bill of 1945 (which aimed at a federal guarantee of regular, useful, and remunerative employment for all Americans able and willing to work) were passed and implemented today. The right to work should include the right to work part-time for those who wish it. Much research and action will be required for the passage and implementation of such a full employment bill.

The Right to Training

In the United States, lack of training or education has been overemphasized as a cause of unemployment and poverty (Wachtel, 1974; Miller and Roby, 1970). The extremely low unemployment rates of World War II testify to the fact that many of those who are considered "unemployable" due to lack of training and other factors in times of low labor force demand are indeed employable when the labor force demand is high enough. Nevertheless, individuals' right to training for work in which they are interested should not be overlooked. In an ideal tomorrow, when jobs are no longer sharply differentiated by prestige and pay, training will allow individuals to have variety in their work by enabling them to move from job to job. Today training represents a step toward a more interesting, prestigious, or better-paying job.

In most areas of education and training, research is no longer needed to document sex discrimination. The armed services' training programs for men and women is an exception. A major research project should investigate the degree to which each branch of the armed services advertises and provides training for women, as compared with men, for relatively high-paying skilled jobs, and the effectiveness with which each branch places women in high-paying jobs after they have been trained and leave the services.

Although federal laws forbid it, blatant sex discrimination has already been documented in civilian, government-sponsored education and training programs (U.S. Department of Labor, Manpower Administration, 1974: 1; Ellis, 1972a; and Ellis, 1972b: 80). In federal training programs such as the Job Corps and WIN, in vocational education, in public high schools, in apprenticeship training, in career education and in on-the-job training within companies women are primarily told about and trained for low-paying, traditionally female work such as secretarial and home-making jobs. Furthermore, counselors and teachers associated with these programs all too often misinform women students. They do so by allowing or encouraging students to believe that as wives and mothers they will not need to work when in fact their husbands are unlikely to be able to support a family alone, by neglecting discussion of current divorce rates and the high probability that women students as young adults will have to support themselves and their children, and by not informing students of occupational projections for the best job opportunities 10, 20, and 30 years hence.

Action projects accompanied by evaluation research should be undertaken throughout the country to bring vocational education, job training, and apprenticeship programs in line with the standards set by equal employment laws. Of the 6.4 million women and girls enrolled in public vocational programs in the United States in 1972, 50% were being trained in home economics and another 30% in office practices. While little effort is being made to guide women into higher-paying, less female-stereotyped occupations, the National Planning Association estimates that, by 1980, 20.1 million job openings will occur in primarily traditionally male occupations for which high schools offer vocational courses with entry-level preparation (U.S. Department of Labor, Women's Bureau, 1973).

The state of vocational education requires two simultaneous actions. The first, adapting its curriculum and counseling to updated labor force projections, will benefit both men and women. This action should not only gear training programs to jobs for which there will be a demand ten years hence, but should also establish a full-credit course in which students are taught about labor force projections and the range of jobs for which there will be considerable demand in the future. The second needed action is to involve women on an equal basis with men in every stage of vocational education —from student recruitment to career counseling and training to follow up on how they do on the job.

Apprenticeship programs must also be opened to women. Programs such as the Wisconsin Women in Apprenticeship Project which have proven successful in one locality should now be established in every city of the nation. The programs must be operated over a considerable duration, because eradicating barriers to women in apprenticeship requires several separate sequential actions. The Wisconsin Project found that in order to increase the numbers of women in apprenticeships and to expand the range of occupations for which women might apply and be accepted for apprenticeships, the Project had to (1) change the attitudes and practices of employers and unions; (2) motivate women; and (3) change the attitudes and procedures of those in government agencies, the educational system, and the legal regulatory system (U.S. Department of Labor, Manpower Administration, 1974: 3).[3] Because most blue-collar women do not realize until their late twenties or early thirties that they will have to work most of their lives, elimination of young age limits (usually 26) for apprenticeship programs was an important procedural change initiated by the Project.

In addition, Nancy Seifer (1973: 67), who has worked extensively with women in working-class neighborhoods, recommends mid-career grants for women workers which would provide for continuing education and/or training for women in new and expanding fields. She notes that many women after child-rearing are ready to and should have the right to make entirely new career decisions. For such continuing education for women to be successful, Joyce Kornbluh of the University of Michigan Institute for Industrial and Labor Relations has observed that special services must be provided. More weekend courses and centers for continuing education for women workers—including a lounge, library, tutorial help, scholarships, counseling, training for job interviews, child-care, brown bag lunches, and instruction on how to use the library—would make community colleges and universities more attractive and useful to blue-collar women. Research should be conducted at several colleges to discover additional ways in which blue-collar women could be assisted, and existing university degree programs for workers should be monitored for sexism. Retraining programs in England, West Germany, and France which offer any person who seeks it a one-year training stipend at nearly full salary provide excellent models for the United States (Striner, 1972).

For these affirmative action programs to be totally successful, attitudinal changes must begin with girls at an early age. They should be told stories in kindergarten, grade school, and Girl Scouts about women's move into traditionally male positions. Girls as well as boys should be encouraged to exercise not only to develop strength in order to qualify for more jobs, but also for their general health. For their mothers, the federal government should develop special advertising, placement services, and preferences for blue-collar "veterans of motherhood" as it has for veterans of foreign wars.

Promotion Opportunities

Many factors in addition to training affect the promotion of women. Basic research is needed for us to understand employers' promotion practices for women: an industry-by-industry study should be made, controlling for personal characteristics (age, race, education), industry, geographical location, and union.

We ought also to investigate the impact of different forms of job-posting on women and minorities. What forms of job-posting are most effective in various types of work situations? Related research which should be undertaken is a sweeping investigation of how various companies treat maternity leave in contract seniority provisions. The federal and state governments ought to develop a system of rewards to encourage industry to promote women, and industry in turn should create a system to encourage its management to promote women.

LIVING CONDITIONS

The off-the-job living conditions of blue-collar employed women are affected by a number of factors: company and union benefits, community services, and the actions and attitudes of spouses and other family members. In this section we will examine research and policy needs related to each of these factors.

Wages

For the purposes of organizing and political action, we ought to determine what the blue-collar woman's wages can buy. To what extent are the financial needs of the single mother, the single woman, and the wife met by these wages?

Company and Union Maternity Benefits

Coverage not only of maternity expenses and paid sick leave for the period of hospitalization, but also several months of parental and infant adjustment have long been part of Hungarian, Israeli and other national policies. Such policies are much needed by the rapidly increasing young female work force in the United States (cf. Ferge, 1973; Weiss, 1973). Ruth Weyand, Associate General Counsel of the International Union of Electrical, Radio and Machine Workers, stresses that Congress, when it passed Title VII of the Civil Rights Act, intended that *all* women employees be treated equally, not just those who promise never to bear children. Since most women bear children and 40% of women drop out of the labor force to do so, U.S. employment policies under the equal employment laws ought to protect women from discrimination because they are pregnant, might become pregnant or have young children, and ought to provide hospitalization and medical benefits for the birth of a child equal to those provided for other causes of hospitalization and medical treatment.

Many young women also need therapeutic abortions. Local 1199 of the National Union of Hospital and Health Care Employees now has its own insurance plan which pays for both therapeutic abortions and maternity benefits for pregnant members, whether or not they are married. Maternity also involves seniority issues. In companies which do not grant maternity leave, women must resign at the time of the birth of their child and thereby lose seniority rights important to promotion, pensions, and wages. Often the woman who is forced to resign is also prevented from returning to her job as early as she would like or is not rehired at all. Statistics, therefore, should be gathered on the maternity leave policies, seniority policies, maternity benefits, and abortion policies of major employers and unions. Linda Tarr-Whelan (1974) suggests that we should also gather cost estimates for employers, if they are to pay full maternity expenses of their employees. She notes that the cost of employee maternity expenses has been reduced by the lower birth rate; on the other hand, hospital maternity expenses have increased.

Child-Care

Following maternity leave, women workers are faced with child-care needs. We cannot assume that a woman has solved her child-care needs simply because she works. A survey by the National Council of Jewish Women (Keyserling, 1974) found that thousands of American children are grossly neglected, living ten hours a day on their own, staying day after day at their mothers' places of work because no other arrangements could be made for them, or somehow surviving in child-care centers or family day-care homes of such poor quality that the children may suffer lasting damage. The child-care needs of workers vary by their familial, company, and union situations. Members of the Amalgamated Clothing Workers (1972a; 1972b) are offered outstanding child-care by their union, the only union with this service. At the other extreme are thousands of postal, bank, maintenance, and factory workers who work at night and have neither child-care centers nor babysitters available to them.

Because extensive research has already documented the severe child-care needs of these and other workers, more research is not required on the need itself. Rather, child-care should be established for the millions who need it, and research should be conducted to guide policy-makers as to the types of child-care which should be established in various locales and for various workers (Roby, 1973a). The research should determine whether parents prefer child-center care or stipends for home or family care; whether they prefer centers near their homes or their workplaces; centers run by the community, union, or company. What forms of child-care do workers of various ethnic backgrounds want? What forms of care do parents want for infants and children of various ages? Evaluation research should also accompany the early development of the child-care programs.

Even parents who have solved their child-care problems are faced with the problem of caring for temporarily ill children. Some nations are giving parents extra days of sick leave for the care of their children (Cook, 1974). Although many parents might welcome this policy, it might lead to increased employer discrimination against parents. Sweden has experimented with a system of "child visitors" who care for sick children in their own home (Roby, 1973a: 306, 309). No conclusive research has been conducted on the effect on children of having a "child visitor," rather than their own parents, care for them while they are ill. It would be important to know the answer to this question, as well as how many days should be allowed for child sick leave, and what policies parents and employers would prefer for the care of temporarily ill children.

Flexible hours are also a critical factor for blue-collar employed mothers. They need the flexibility enjoyed by professionals who may leave the workplace to take themselves and their children to the dentist or doctor, to shop for clothes, or to visit a school play. Furthermore, the United States has on the whole ignored the long hours worked by employed mothers. Time budget studies should be conducted on the hours women spend on the job, commuting, and domestic work by industry and occupation, in order to acquaint the public and legislatures with their plight (Roby, 1973b; Walker, n.d.). In such a study, special attention should be devoted to the hours worked on the job, the transportation difficulties experienced by the women which could be ameliorated, and features of American living patterns which could be improved in order to reduce domestic working hours—for example, communal (i.e., for four to six families) washers and dryers which would free women from driving to and remaining at a laundromat, and communal play areas which would reduce the time parents spend watching over their own children.

Retirement

We do not know what economic and social problems a woman faces when she retires. Does she, like many men, have adjustment problems? Researchers undertaking this study should compare samples of married, widowed, divorced, and never married women and control for the number of years worked prior to retirement and union or company retirement groups. Even more important would be a study of the economic and pension situation of blue-collar women, including blue-collar wives. Because women live longer than men and inflation reduces the buying power of flat pensions, retired blue-collar women may experience greater economic hardships than blue-collar men. Many small unionized as well as nonunionized plants have no pension plans at all. We do not know what percentage of women are concentrated in these pensionless plants. Many workers need to be told of the importance of pensions since they will often be the first in their families to live beyond age 65.

POLICIES AFFECTING THE ATTITUDES OF
BLUE-COLLAR EMPLOYED WOMEN

Social Research, Inc., of Chicago (1973: 5, 9, 12) has found that a sample of working-class women drawn from eight cities was less home-bound and more active in the local community and more assertive within their homes in 1972 than a similar sample in 1959. Nearly all the sampled respondents also endorsed the principle of "equal pay for equal work," and most endorsed the idea of allowing any woman to hold any job for which she also has the necessary work skills and qualifications. As yet we do not know, however, what degree of awareness employed working-class women have of their legal employment rights, of the Coalition of Labor Union Women, or of union and/or company affirmative action efforts. Nor do we have information on what work means to women of various occupational and ethnic groups—the questionnaire from Harold Sheppard and Neal Herrick's study, *Where Have All the Robots Gone?* (1972), of white male union workers should be administered to women.

We do have informally gathered information about the attitudes of many blue-collar employed women. Those whom I have interviewed —who work closely with these women—have expressed many concerns. Ruth Weyand (1974) wonders how to get women in her union to recognize that income inequality between the sexes is unfair, so that they will ask her to make legal complaints on their behalf. She notes that the women are morally incensed about the lack of maternity benefits and maternity leave, but do not have the same feelings about income inequities.

West Coast organizers for the United Electrical Workers express heartache from hearing dozens of women electrical workers in their twenties echo their employers' suspicions: "I won't be working long—only until we pay for the washer and dryer (the car, our vacation, etc.)—I don't need to worry about how this job's treating me." The organizers know many women workers in their forties and fifties who held the same beliefs 20 years ago, and there is no reason to believe that these young women will not be working most or all of the next 30 years. Other activists lament the plight of women who have job-related grievances, but who have families to support and realistic fears of losing their jobs should they express their grievances.

Rose Beard (1974), President of the United Automobile Workers' Women's Committee for Regions I, IA, IB and IE and an inspector in the sewing division of the Ford Motor Company's Ypsilanti plant, is concerned that many rank-and-file women are less willing to work for forewomen than they are for foremen. She has also pointed out that women must be taught not only to make grievances so that they may move up to better jobs, but to refrain from working twice as hard in their new job as men in the job. For example, she notes that in her plant women were always excluded from clean-up, an "easy" men's job. Now that women have obtained clean-up jobs, they are exhausting themselves by cleaning the plant as if it were their home!

Numerous persons, employers as well as union representatives, asked me, "How do you give women the confidence to break into a job traditionally held by men when they know about the job and their legal rights to it, and they believe they can do the job?" Several union representatives asked, "How can we quickly wake women up to their own value so that they will have pride in being nurses' aides; so that they will realize that electronics work is really not unskilled?" They observe that women must have this pride in order to fight for equitable wages.

To say that these attitudes simply reflect "the way these women are" would be "blaming the victim" and ignoring much social-psychological literature (Ryan, 1971). We know that individuals' attitudes are shaped by their experiences, their families, schooling, friends, occupational role models, and the opportunity structure of their jobs (Long-Laws, 1972). We also have the finding of an internal study of the International Union of Electrical Workers, a union which has organized many women's conferences and has in numerous other ways worked diligently to raise women's awareness of their rights and to obtain rights for women: the union members report, "We now know our rights," and "men know we can do more than make sandwiches for the union" (Johnson, 1974).

The establishment of various policies could change women's attitudes which, among other factors, prevent them from advancing occupationally. However, before hastening to discuss these policies and policy experiments, let us note that many women have already begun to change their personalities. Some have been proud of the change; others have not liked it; and others have been confused or displeased with what it has done to their marriages (McCourt, 1974). These findings suggest that the initiation of demonstration research or social policies intended to change attitudes and behavior must be done very carefully and must devote attention to the project's impact on women's sense of self, marital situation, and friendships as well as her work attitudes.

If we are to embark on attitude change and behavior modification, there are a number of paths we might take. Consciousness-raising, like that now pursued by thousands of middle-class women might be tried in industrial plants, in working-class communities, or among chapters of the Coalition of Labor Union Women. It might even be tried as a first step in organizing nonunionized women. Successful consciousness-raising groups do have the advantage that they can support and help women to change all areas of their lives—familial, educational, religious, occupational.

Numerous other activities might supplement or be used instead of consciousness-raising in an effort to encourage blue-collar women to realize their own value and to bid for better-paying jobs. Women who enter traditionally male occupations should continue to be reported not only in union literature, but in women's magazines, in local and junior and senior high school newspapers, and on television, so that women will be informed that the occupational structure is changing. Employers concerned with affirmative action should also be interviewed about new opportunities for women in their companies and written up in similar literature. The stories of typical working women today should be developed and distributed to high school and working women so that they will become aware that they are likely to work the majority of their adult years and that it will be worth their while to seek equal pay and better jobs. The history of working women should also be developed and distributed so that women today will have a better understanding of their positions and be able to take greater pride in themselves.

Employers attempting to fulfill affirmative action goals should provide plant tours for women employees in low-paying jobs to show and describe to them better-paying positions within the plant. Short training programs should follow the tours to further demystify high-paying traditionally male jobs such as frame work in the telephone system. High school students should be given similar tours through several large plants in their community so that they will learn that in every plant there are better- and poorer-paying jobs (as well as better- and poorer-paying industries).

Insecurity based on a lack of experience, lack of skills, and lack of familiarity with the job market overcomes many women who have been away from the labor force bearing and raising children. Such psychological obstacles prevent some from even looking for jobs and others from looking further than the first job mentioned by a friend who has recently returned to employment, generally in low-paid work. In order to overcome these problems, the United States should adopt a policy similar to that of Sweden, where women who have spent several years at home raising their families have a right to government-subsidized training and a special training allowance to cover child-care and other expenses (Seifer, 1973: 66-67).

Television should not be overlooked as a means of informing women of better-paying job opportunities and helping them overcome insecurities which could prevent them from seeking the jobs. Nancy Seifer (1973: 78-79) has recommended that:

> Television and radio programs reflect the reality of working class women's lives, and present characters both who appeal to their aspirations and sense of dignity and with whom they can realistically and positively identify;

> Radio and television talk show discussions during both daytime and evening hours and articles in newspapers and magazines deal specifically with the changing roles of working class women;

> Newspaper and magazine articles discuss legislative gains affecting all women, changes in the labor force, and new career opportunities for women without college educations;

> "How-to" features be developed by all the media on continuing education programs and job training experiences, with concrete information on such programs' locations, eligibility requirements, costs and benefits;

> Historical programs spotlight working class women in leadership roles throughout the American experience, giving special attention to the struggles of immigrant and ethnic groups to affect societal and employment reforms.

UNIONS

In 1972, 12.5% of all women in the labor force were union members. Over three-quarters of these women were concentrated in 21 unions. Although unionization appears to improve women's wages, women are affected not only by policies which hinder unions and unionization generally, but also by sexist union practices and policies.

Let us look first at policies affecting unions and unionization. Labor union history is badly neglected in the public schools. Therefore, women and men working in unorganized plants usually do not realize the benefits they are missing by being ununionized, and many young women and men enter the labor movement knowing little about the history of labor. Readable elementary and high school texts are needed which explain the benefits of unionization to workers and which relate the history of labor's fight for social justice. Organizing of both women and men is hindered not only by the lack of public school labor education, but by the lack of U.S. laws similar to those of Japan and European industrial nations which limit the freedom of corporations to move their operations without consideration for the social impact of the move on the community in which they have resided. The lack of such laws permits some corporate employers to prevent unionization by threatening to move or by actually moving their plants when union organizing begins.

What is the position of women within unions? In 1972, women comprised nearly 22% of the total union membership in the United States, and only 33 women held positions of union leadership. How might a larger proportion of women be brought into local, regional and national positions of union leadership? First we need more precise information on women's participation in unions. Just as the U.S. Department of Labor develops a price index, it could develop for union use an index of women's participation as elected and appointed officers in unions at the local, regional, and national levels, suggests Gloria Johnson (1974). The unions' goals should be to make the percentage of women staff members and officers at all levels of the hierarchy compare favorably with the percentage of women in the unions at the local, regional, and national levels. Because information on the number of women in union locals by state is lacking, the Department of Labor should add sex to its state breakdown of negotiated contracts.

Second, demonstration research projects and new policies accompanied by evaluation research should be initiated to abolish union barriers to women's full participation in high-level local, regional and national union offices and matters, and to encourage women to become more active in their unions. Different unions and various locals within the unions, like different professional associations and their constituent parts, bar women from full participation in different types of ways. Therefore, studies similar to that by Wertheimer and Nelson (1975) for New York should be conducted among various unions and various ethnic groups in different parts of the nation. Following the studies, women's caucuses and the Coalition of Labor Union Women should monitor the union's progress in abolishing the barriers and fulfilling affirmative action goals.

Unions themselves should initiate change by increasing the percentage of women on their paid staffs. Unions should lead the way in job-posting and other affirmative action steps suggested above for corporate employers. Unions might also sponsor courses on affirmative action for all their local, regional, and national leaders. The courses should include instruction on how to file a sex discrimination grievance against a company on behalf of a union member. Unions could also help to change their members' attitudes concerning the role of women by greatly increasing the proportion of union newspaper and magazine articles devoted to women who are active in the union; explanation of recent affirmative action laws; national and local activities of the Coalition of Labor Union Women; concerns of women's caucuses within unions; suggestions for how the union might better attain its affirmative action goals; up-to-date accounts of court cases which will affect union women; and discussion of union leaders' stance on, and willingness to bargain for, benefits of concern to women such as child-care, maternity leave, and various forms of job-posting. The papers should also direct articles to union men on the importance of their wives' and female coworkers' active participation in the union.

An interesting historical research project would be to analyze past union discussions on union resolutions regarding women. The resolutions and discussions would reflect some of the basic attitudes, strengths, and problems in various union policy-makers' thinking concerning women—thinking which, while faulty, may be found to be ahead of legislators'.

To date no study has been conducted on sexism in the labor negotiation process. The U.S. Bureau of Labor Statistics keeps on file all contracts of union agreements covering 1,000 or more workers. These are available to the public and should be scrutinized for sexually discriminatory clauses. Researchers should also investigate the degree to which a sample of the contracts lived up to their provisions in matters pertaining to affirmative action issues, and examine the rulings which are being made in arbitration concerning sex. What are the bases for the rulings? Do the arbitration decisions take into account recent rulings by the Equal Employment Opportunity Commission? For all job areas, a demographic study utilizing Bureau of Labor Statistics data should be conducted on the impact of women's wages and benefits. The study should control for the percentage of union members who are women, occupation, and geographical location.

How can women be encouraged to play a more active, assertive role in their unions? Both union and state college or university-supported leadership training programs for women union members —including courses on public speaking, handling grievances, organizing, and collective bargaining—should be a high priority. Internship programs and other new forms of training should be established so that women may become expert at the more difficult skills of negotiating and handling grievances. Women's active history in union organizing and strikes ought to be told loudly to both men and women, in order to challenge the beliefs that women are harder to organize than men or that they contribute little to unions.

Although unions themselves practice sex discrimination, women who are union members are better off in terms of wages, benefits, and working conditions than the majority of women who are not. Therefore, increasing the percentage of women workers who are union members and have union benefits is important (Raphael, 1974: 7). Historically, unions have often attempted to organize plants which already have higher wages, plants which are likely to have few women, because the cost of organizing these plants will be rewarded with higher membership dues than can be obtained from lower-wage plants. Consequently, women have too often been left to organize themselves or remain unorganized. The first step, of course, as pointed out by the Coalition of Labor Union Women's statement of purpose, is for unions to devote increased effort to organizing women. Research can aid these organizing efforts. A key question is what are the best issues around which to organize unorganized women. This question must be researched industry by industry and community to community.

CONCLUSION

Basic changes will be required in the economy before the living conditions of blue-collar women greatly improve. These changes involve vast reduction of the inequality in the distribution of our resources among all people in our society[4] and adequate employment for all who are able and wish it.

While we work for these long-range changes, reform can and should be made in policies affecting the living conditions of women in working-class jobs. This paper has described many such policy changes and research projects which should be conducted relating to the conditions of these women and, in turn, their families. Foundations and government granting agencies now appear to be responding to the energy of the Women's Movement and the new blue-collar women's rights movement by seeking and funding projects relating to blue-collar employed women.

However, because this funding—no matter how plentiful—will be limited compared to the need, research priorities will have to be established. In this paper, I have discussed possible negative consequences, as well as benefits, which could result from the policies and research recommended. These factors plus

(1) the number of women whose conditions could be improved by the research or policy changes;

(2) the degree to which their conditions could be improved;

(3) the relative need of the prospective population;

(4) how quickly the improvement might be implemented;

(5) the researcher's connections with relevant change agents;

(6) the complexity of the proposed research; and

(7) the extent to which the research process might raise the consciousness of the target population about their general economic and social needs and the type of broad societal changes which would be required to meet them

should all be considered in the choice of a specific research project. Using these criteria, the following areas might be considered top priorities: research on occupational health conditions of blue-collar women (leading to the construction of additional guidelines under, or amendments to, the Occupational Safety and Health Act); and demonstration research in vocational education on how to track women into high-paying, traditionally male, skilled jobs (which could be incorporated into the guidelines of the Vocational Education Act).

Development, implementation, and dissemination of information concerning policy in line with the research findings are as important as the research itself. For this reason researchers who pursue studies suggested above should inform the Coalition of Labor Union Women and other advocates of blue-collar women, legislatures, and relevant company, government and union officials of their policy-relevant findings.

NOTES

1. The U.S. Equal Employment Opportunity Commission has ruled in the Potlatch decision that, in cases where states have minimum wage, overtime, rest period, weight-lifting, and other laws to protect women, the employer must obey both the state protective law and the federal Civil Rights Act by including men under the protective law. Employers dislike this ruling and are trying to chip away at it in California and other states.

2. In a 1974 ruling, instead of extending the requirement of overtime pay after eight hours of work per day to men, the California State Industrial Welfare Commission voted to require overtime pay only after ten hours of work per day for all employees, to eliminate scheduled rest periods and lounges, and to allow mandatory ten-hour working days. Between 1969 and 1973, 15 states repealed their maximum hours laws for women. In others, federal courts and a state supreme court have held that the state hours laws conflict with Title VII: a few have held that women *may work* beyond the maximum hours limitations but *may not be required* to do so. Only Nevada continues to enforce a law setting 12 hours a day and 56 hours a week as absolute maximums for women, and requiring overtime pay after 8 hours a day and 48 hours a week. See *Union Labor Report, Weekly Newsletter,* Bureau of National Affairs, June 20, 1974.

3. In April 1974 the Manpower Administration amended three of its apprenticeship outreach contracts to provide new opportunities for women. The Apprenticeship Outreach Program, since its inception in 1964, generally has been directed toward recruiting minority men into apprentice trades. The expanded program places special emphasis on recruiting young women, who will be given the necessary counseling and tutoring to prepare them to enter all apprenticeship occupations. Three organizations will operate pilot projects in six selected cities: the National Urban League will expand its programs in Atlanta, Chicago, and Los Angeles; the Mexican-American Foundation will conduct a second outreach program in Los Angeles; and the Recruitment and Training Program, Inc. (formerly, the Workers Defense League of the A. Philip Randolph Foundation) will expand its programs in Boston, Cleveland, and New York. See U.S. Department of Labor, Women's Bureau (1974: 7).

4. For a statement of the importance of equality, see Roby (1974: 18-21). For a description of existing inequalities, see Miller and Roby (1970).

REFERENCES

ADAMS, A. V. (1973) Toward Fair Employment and the EEOC: A Study of Compliance Procedures Under Title VII of the Civil Rights Act of 1964. Washington, D.C.: Government Printing Office (EEOC Contract 70-15).

Amalgamated Clothing Workers Union (1972a) The Union and the Day Care Center. New York: Amalgamated Clothing Workers Union.

——— (1972b) A Union-Sponsored Day Center. New York: Amalgamated Clothing Workers Union.

BEARD, R. (1974) Interview, January 20.

COOK, A. H. (1974) Interview, February 15.

ELLIS, M. (1972a) "Women in technical education." Technical Education News 21, 2 (April): 5-6.

——— (1972b) "Let's examine emerging changes in the labor force and adjust our educational programs for women's role as worker." Industrial Education (December).

Equal Employment Opportunity Commission (1969) Case No. YCHO-122, Decision No. 72-0561.

FERGE, S. (1973) "The development of the protection of mothers and children in Hungary after 1945," in P. Roby (ed.) Child Care—Who Cares? Foreign and Domestic Infant and Early Childhood Development Policies. New York: Basic Books.

GREENWALD, C. S. (1974) "Part-time work and flexible hours employment." Presented to the Workshop on Research Needed to Improve the Employment and Employability of Women, Washington, D.C., U.S. Department of Labor, June 7.

GRONSETH, E. (1972) "Work-sharing families: husband and wife both in part-time employment." Presented at the Gottlieb Buttweiler Institute, Ruschlikon by Zurich, June.

GROSS, B. and S. MOSES (1972) "Measuring the real work force: 25 million unemployed." Social Policy 3, 3 (September/October): 10.

JOHNSON, G. (1974) Interview, February 4.

KEYSERLING, M. D. (1974) Windows on Day Care: A Report on the Findings of the National Council of Jewish Women. New York: National Council of Jewish Women.

LEGGETT, J. C. and C. CERVINKA (1972) "Countdown: labor statistics revisited." Society 10, 1 (November/December): 99-103.

LONG-LAWS, J. (1972) "Causes and effects of sex discrimination in the Bell system." Testimony before the Federal Communications Commission, Docket No. 19143, Washington, D.C.

LYLE, J. R. (1973) Affirmative Action Programs for Women: A Survey of Innovative Programs. Washington, D.C.: Government Printing Office (EEOC Contract 71-45).

McCOURT, K. (1974) Interview, January 10.

MILLER, S. M. and P. ROBY (1970) The Future of Inequality. New York: Basic Books.

POOR, R. [ed.] (1970) 4 Days, 40 Hours: Reporting a Revolution in Work and Leisure. Cambridge: Bursk & Poor.

RAPHAEL, E. E. (1974) "Working women and their membership in labor unions." Monthly Labor Review 97, 5 (May): 26-33.

ROBY, P. [ed.] (1974) The Poverty Establishment. Englewood Cliffs, N.J.: Prentice-Hall.

——— [ed.] (1973a) Child Care—Who Cares? Foreign and Domestic Infant and Early Childhood Development Policies. New York: Basic Books.

——— [ed.] (1973b) "Parenting perspectives from other nations," in P. M. Markun (ed.) Parenting. Washington, D.C.: Association for Childhood Educational International.

RYAN, W. (1971) Blaming the Victim. New York: Random House.

SEIFER, N. (1973) Absent from the Majority: Working Class Women in America. New York: National Project on Ethnic America of the American Jewish Committee.

SHEPPARD, H. and N. Q. HERRICK (1972) Where Have All the Robots Gone? New York: Free Press.

Social Research, Inc. (1973) Working-Class Women in a Changing World. Chicago: Social Research, Inc. Prepared for Macfadden-Bartell Corporation, Study No. 287107.

The Spokeswoman (1974) "California's protective laws endangered." Vol. 4, 11 (May): 4.

STRINER, H. (1972) Continuing Education as a National Capital Investment. Washington, D.C.: W. E. Upjohn Institute for Employment Research.

TARR-WHELAN, L. (1974) Interview, February 1.

U.S. Commission on Civil Rights (1973) The Federal Civil Rights Enforcement Effort: A Reassessment. Washington, D.C.: Government Printing Office.

U.S. Department of Labor, Manpower Administration (1974) Women in Apprenticeship —Why Not? Washington, D.C.: Government Printing Office, Manpower Research Monograph 33.

U.S. Department of Labor, Women's Bureau (1974) "Steps to opening the skilled trades." June (mimeo).

——— (1973) "Issues in vocational training for women and girls." (mimeo)

WACHTEL, H. M. (1974) "Looking at poverty from radical, conservative and liberal perspectives," in P. Roby (ed.) The Poverty Establishment. Englewood Cliffs, N.J.: Prentice-Hall.

WALKER, K. (n.d.) "Time budget research on working women." Ithaca, N.Y.: Cornell University, Department of Consumer Economics and Public Policy. (mimeo)

WEISS, R. B. (1973) "Pre-school child care in Israel," in P. Roby (ed.) Child Care—Who Cares? Foreign and Domestic Infant and Early Childhood Development Policies. New York: Basic Books.

WERTHEIMER, B. M. and A. H. NELSON (1975) Trade Union Women: A Study of Their Participation in Seven New York City Locals. New York: Praeger.

WEYAND, R. (1974) Interview, January 29.

7

SEARCH FOR A PARTNERSHIP ROLE
Women in Labor Unions Today

BARBARA M. WERTHEIMER

Welcome sisters, to our number,
Welcome to our heart and hand.
At our post we will not slumber,
Strong in union we shall stand.

So sang women sewing machine operators at their union meetings back in 1865. More than 100 years later, union women singing "Solidarity forever, for the union makes us strong" are emerging as a new force to be reckoned with in labor unions. This chapter examines where women are in the work force and in trade unions today and focuses especially on the new momentum which recently culminated in the formation of the National Coalition of Labor Union Women (CLUW). A number of key questions which particularly concern union women are discussed in the concluding section.

WOMEN IN THE WORK FORCE

Today some 33 million women in the United States work outside their homes for pay. This is 49% of all women between the ages of 18 and 64. Since World War II, the number of women in the work force has increased 75%, while the number of men at work rose only 16%. Looked at another way, in 1920 only one in five women entered in the labor force, while 1972 figures show that close to two out of five are there. Projections for 1980 indicate an increase in women's labor force participation rate of 3.8%, while that of men will be almost static–0.3% increase (Meinkoth, 1972: 27).

WHO ARE THE WORKING WOMEN?

Half of the women at work are 38 years old or over, and close to three out of five are married. More than two out of five hold year-round, full-time jobs. The labor force participation rates for women by marital status and age are shown in Table 1, enabling the reader to compare those rates for the years 1950, 1960, and 1972. Note the steady increase in the numbers of married women in the work force. In 1950, while 50.5% of all single women were in the work force, only 23.8% of married women were. Twenty-two years later, the percentage of married women at work had almost doubled.

Increasingly, working women are mothers, and 40% of them have children under 18. Of the 12.7 million working mothers, 4.4 million have children under 6, and 2.4 million have children under 3 years of age. In spite of the fact that the total number of children in all U.S. families fell by one and a half million between 1970 and 1973, the number of children with working mothers rose by 650,000.

TABLE 1: Labor Force Participation Rates of Women by Marital Status and Age–1950, 1960, and 1972 (in percentages[1])

Marital status and year	Total	Age					
		Under 20 years	20–24 years	25–34 years	35–44 years	45–64 years	65 years and over
Single:							
1950	50.5	26.3	74.9	84.6	83.6	70.6	23.8
1960	44.1	25.3	73.4	79.9	79.7	75.1	21.6
1972	54.9	41.9	69.9	84.7	71.5	71.0	19.0
Married, husband present:							
1950	23.8	24.0	28.5	23.8	28.5	21.8	6.4
1960	30.5	25.3	30.0	27.7	36.2	34.2	5.9
1972	41.5	39.0	48.5	41.3	48.6	44.2	7.3
Widowed, divorced, or separated:							
1950	37.8	(²)	45.5	62.3	65.4	50.2	8.8
1960	40.0	37.3	54.6	55.5	67.4	58.3	11.0
1972	40.1	44.6	57.6	62.1	71.7	61.1	9.8

1. Labor force as percent of noninstitutional population in group specified.
2. Not available.

Note: Data relate to March of each year. Data for 1950 and 1960 are for women 14 years of age and over; data for 1972 are for women 16 years of age and over.

Source: Department of Labor, Bureau of Labor Statistics.

One in every six mothers raises her children alone. Nowhere in the country are there sufficient child-care facilities, and where working women gather, this is a problem that always comes up for discussion. For the 5.6 million children under the age of 6, the Women's Bureau of the Department of Labor reports that there were only 905,000 child-care slots in 1972—many of these in private, high-priced facilities.

WHERE DO WOMEN WORK?

The Bureau of the Census lists 250 distinct occupations, but half of all working women are found in 21 of these (while half of all men are found in 65). Twenty-eight percent of all women are in service jobs (6.8 million women), up from 20% in 1940. Some 60% of all working women hold white-collar posts. Nine out of every ten women in manufacturing hold unskilled, semi-skilled or white-collar clerical jobs. A startling 22% of all working women are on government payrolls, constituting 45% of the total number of government employees (federal, state, and local jobs). The U.S. Civil Service Commission reports that 77 out of every 100 women in federal employment are in the GS 1-6 ratings, compared to 44 of every 100 men. At the other end of the scale, three of every 100 women in civil service are in the GS 12 levels or higher, compared to 23 of every 100 men.

Women constitute 99% of all household workers, 73% of all clerical workers (but 96.6% of all secretaries and typists), 63% of all service workers, but only 4% of all skilled craftsmen and foremen. In fact, just one in every 60 working women is in a skilled trade. This occupational distribution, for 1968, is graphed in Figure 1.

Thus, workers still hold jobs that are to a large extent sex-segregated. In the occupations where most women work, experience does not add much to their ability to perform, and there are few opportunities for upgrading or advancement. The pay tends to be low.

EARNINGS OF WORKING WOMEN

Most women work because they need the money. While it is true that the higher the educational level of a woman, the more likely she is to be in the work force, by far the largest number of women work

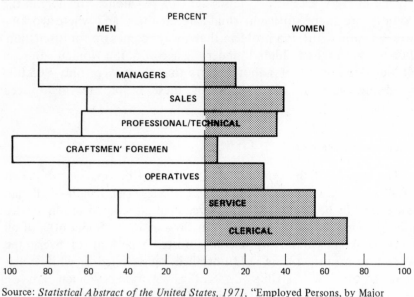

Source: *Statistical Abstract of the United States, 1971,* "Employed Persons, by Major
Occupation and Sex: 1950-1971," p. 222.

FIGURE 1: Occupational Distribution of Men and Women: 1968

to support families or to contribute their salaries to the family
income to lift it above the poverty level. The Bureau of Labor
Statistics presents this information graphically in Figure 2.

Knowing, then, that 66% of all working women are either single,
widowed, divorced, separated, or have husbands earning under
$7,000 a year, the earnings of women become of paramount
concern. And at every level, women earn less than men. For example,
average earnings for a worker in manufacturing in January 1973 were
$159 a week. But in manufacturing industries where women are
clustered, such as the garment trades (81% female), the average was
$93. Women employed in hospitals averaged $108; in hotels, $76. In
laundry and dry cleaning establishments, the figure was $87.
However, in construction, where women constitute only 6% of the
total work force, the average pay was $223 a week.

How do the overall earnings of women compare with those of
men? Table 2 indicates the 1970 earnings of full-time, year-round
workers, men and women, between 1955 and 1972.

The earnings gap between women and men seems to be getting
wider. In 1971 the annual median earnings for year-round, full-time

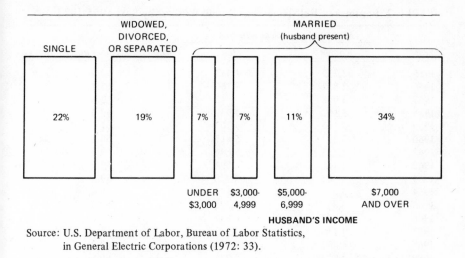

Source: U.S. Department of Labor, Bureau of Labor Statistics,
in General Electric Corporations (1972: 33).

FIGURE 2: Most Women Work Because of Economic Need (Women in Labor
Force in March, 1970)

women workers was $5,593 compared with $9,399 for men. In 1973
it was $5,903 for women and $10,202 for men. This means that for
every dollar a man earns, a woman earns 58 cents—down from 64
cents in 1957 (U.S. Department of Commerce, 1973). Adjusting this
for the intermittent work experience of many women—by assuming
that women worked the same number of hours each year for the
same number of years, with no time off for bearing children or
part-time work—they would still earn only 75% of what men earn.

WOMEN'S ROLE IN INDUSTRY

Why is this true? How does it happen that women are locked into
low-skill, low-paying jobs? There are several reasons, and a pattern
may be traced back into history for women have always worked. In
the preindustrial period of this country's development, men and
women living in a primarily rural economy shared the economic
responsibilities of family and farm. Women had an essential role as
producers of almost everything their families consumed or wore.
They shared the hardships of penetrating the wilderness, and no
aspect of the farm was unfamiliar to them. Many times circumstances
forced women to take over complete responsibility for crops,
livestock, and the family's safety in addition to the production of
household items for family use.

TABLE 2: Earnings of Full-Time Year-Round Workers by Sex, 1955-1972[1]

Year	Median Wage or Salary Income		Women's Earnings as % of Men's
	Women	Men	
1955	$2,719	$ 4,252	63.9
1956	2,827	4,466	63.3
1957	3,008	4,713	63.8
1958	3,102	4,927	63.0
1959	3,193	5,209	61.3
1960	3,293	5,417	60.8
1961	3,351	5,644	59.4
1962	3,446	5,794	59.5
1963	3,561	5,978	59.6
1964	3,690	6,195	59.6
1965	3,823	6,375	60.0
1966	3,973	6,848	58.0
1967[2]	4,150	7,182	57.8
1968	4,457	7,664	58.2
1969	4,977	8,227	60.5
1970	5,323	8,966	59.4
1972	5,903	10,202	57.9

1. Worked 35 hours or more a week for 50 to 52 weeks.
2. Data before 1967 are not strictly comparable with later years, since earnings of self-employed are not included.

Source: U.S. Department of Commerce, Bureau of the Census, *Current Population Reports*, P-60.

As industry developed and jobs drew families to the city, women, too, went into the factory. Most families could not manage on the earnings of one wage earner alone. The jobs to which women gravitated were extensions of work they had done at home: textiles and weaving, sewing, manufacture of hats, shoes, and buttons, laundering and cleaning, household work, and later, secretarial and clerical work. The supply of female labor was swelled by immigration, and "women's jobs" invariably were in labor-intensive industries where competition focused on which company could get the most workers for the least money and the longest hours. Women soon became entrenched in jobs which men often refused to fill.

But times have changes. Today women live longer (73 years compared with 45 years as recently as 1920), are healthier, better educated (7 in 10 have a high school education or better), and bear fewer children than ever before. Minimum wages are set by the government, and hours are shorter. With federal equal pay and equal employment legislation, with an Equal Employment Opportunities Commission actively prosecuting thousands of women's complaints, with strong trade unions on the scene, and with women moving into almost every occupational category, why do women's pay scales still compare so unfavorably to men's?

Economic pressures, aggravated by inflation and the demands of a higher standard of living, push women into the work force, but they are often not free to accept the best job at the best rate. Convenience of location limits their choice. So do the hours required. Women may have to accept jobs that do not require overtime, especially those 6.6 million women who head families for which they alone are responsible. They may not be able to try for promotions, since extra responsibilities may not fit in with family obligations. Women who still accept the traditional view of their own role, a socialization process that begins at birth, may not apply for jobs usually considered "male." Finally, discrimination is still a big factor both in the jobs that are offered to women and the job training and upgrading opportunities that are not.

This is underscored in a study analyzing the Wisconsin Apprentice program over a three-year period (Mapp, 1973). In 1970 some 280,000 men in the United States were in such programs but only 1,200 women—many of them studying hairdressing. The Wisconsin survey of 78 businesses in the Fox River Valley revealed that none had women apprentices. The reasons ranged from apologias that women could not take the harsh conditions under which men work (but women already held jobs in other plants under those same conditions) to inadequate posting of apprentice opportunities (for instance, in the men's rooms) to the age barrier women face where apprentice programs are restricted to young workers 18-24 years old. Women of this age group are often starting families, and hence are not in the work foce in these crucial years. The study reported that government administrators of job training seem unaware of the requirements of affirmative action programs, and vocational schools still discriminate in tracking girls toward female job slots.

However, there is progress. In the last two years women have risen from representation in only 47 of the 370 skilled job classifications listed by the Census Bureau to 170. In 1970, although there were only half a million women in skilled occupations, this constituted an 80% increase over 1960.

WOMEN AND UNEMPLOYMENT

Unemployment rates are another factor that must be considered: these have always been higher for women than for men. Minorities and women traditionally are the last hired and the first fired. Where union contracts protect workers through seniority clauses, it may be women, entering jobs after periods of absence for child-rearing, who have lowest seniority and are again the first laid off. Table 3 demonstrates the unemployment rates by sex and age for two years, 1972 and 1973. In every age group, for both years, women suffered greater unemployment than men.

Overall unemployment for white workers was 5.0% in 1972, and 4.3% in 1973, while that for minority workers was 10% and 8.9%,

TABLE 3: Unemployment Rates, by Age and Sex

	Annual Average	
Age and Sex	1972	1973
Total, 16 years and over	5.6	4.9
16 to 19 years	16.2	14.5
16 and 17 years	18.5	17.3
18 and 19 years	14.6	12.4
20 to 24 years	9.3	7.8
25 years and over	3.6	3.1
25 to 54 years	3.7	3.2
55 years and over	3.3	2.7
Male, 16 years and over	4.9	4.1
16 to 19 years	15.9	13.9
16 and 17 years	18.2	17.0
18 and 19 years	14.0	11.4
20 to 24 years	9.2	7.3
25 years and over	3.1	2.5
25 to 54 years	3.1	2.5
55 years and over	3.3	2.5
Female, 16 years and over	6.6	6.0
16 to 19 years	16.7	15.2
16 and 17 years	18.8	17.7
18 and 19 years	15.2	13.5
20 to 24 years	9.3	8.4
25 years and over	4.6	4.0
25 to 54 years	4.9	4.4
55 years and over	3.4	2.8

Note: Data adjusted to reflect seasonal experience through December 1973.

Source: Department of Labor, Bureau of Labor Statistics.

respectively, in those years. By far the highest unemployment is suffered by minority women between the ages of 16-19, but women in general show a higher unemployment rate than men at every age level but one: women over age 60 are found more frequently in the labor force than men at that age.

WOMEN IN LABOR UNIONS

Unionization has a positive effect on earnings of women workers. The bar graph in Figure 3 shows that both white and black women in unions benefit economically from the protection of a union contract, as do minority men. One might speculate that the reason white men do not seem to benefit as much is that salaried workers are included in the computation, and many more white males hold supervisory or nonunion white-collar jobs (for example, insurance salesmen) which skew the figures.

Some 5.3 million women are union and employee association members—16 out of every 100 women workers. This compares with about 28 out of every 100 male workers. Over the last 10 years, the proportion of women unionists in the female work force has dropped from 13.8% to 12.5%. Table 4 shows the trends in labor force participation and union membership for U.S. women between 1952 and 1972.

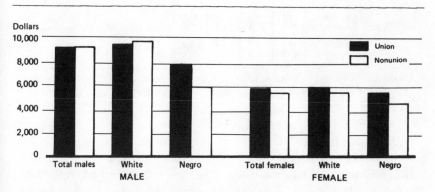

Source: U.S. Department of Labor, Bureau of Labor Statistics (1972: 4).

FIGURE 3: Median Earnings of Wage and Salary Workers, by Labor Union Membership, Sex, and Race, 1970 (year-round, full-time workers)

TABLE 4: Civilian Labor Force Participation and Union Membership of
U.S. Women, 1952-1972 (numbers in millions)

Year	Civilian labor force		Membership		Women as a percent of total civilian labor force	Women membership as a percent of—	
						All women in labor force	Total union membership in the United States
	Total	Women	Total	Women			
Unions and associations [1]							
1970_____	82.7	31.5	21.1	5.0	38.1	16.0	23.9
1972_____	86.5	33.3	21.5	5.3	38.5	16.0	24.9
Unions							
1952_____	62.1	19.3	16.0	2.9	31.0	15.1	18.1
1954_____	63.6	19.7	16.7	2.8	30.9	14.1	16.6
1956_____	66.6	21.5	17.2	3.2	32.2	14.9	18.5
1958_____	67.6	22.1	16.8	3.1	32.7	13.8	18.2
1960_____	69.6	23.2	16.9	3.1	33.4	13.3	18.3
1962_____	70.6	24.0	16.4	3.1	34.0	12.8	18.6
1964_____	73.1	25.4	16.7	3.2	34.8	12.5	19.1
1966_____	75.8	27.3	17.8	3.4	36.0	12.6	19.3
1968_____	78.7	29.2	18.8	3.7	37.1	12.5	19.5
1970_____	82.7	31.5	19.2	4.0	38.1	12.6	20.7
1972_____	86.5	33.3	19.3	4.2	38.5	12.6	21.7
Change— unions:							
1952–72							
Number____	24.4	14.0	3.3	1.3			
Percent_____	39.3	72.7	20.4	44.1			
1952–62							
Number____	8.5	4.7	.4	.2			
Percent_____	13.6	24.6	2.8	5.6			
1962–72							
Number____	15.9	9.3	2.8	1.1			
Percent_____	22.6	38.6	17.1	36.5			

1. Associations were first surveyed in 1970. That survey covered 23 associations while the
1972 study covered 35. The number of unions covered in 1952 was 215; in 1962, 181; in
1970, 185; and in 1972, 177.
Source: Berquist (1974: 4).

More than half of the women members of labor organizations
belong to 12 trade unions; three-quarters of all women unionists
belong to just 21 labor unions. The 1971 *Directory of National
Unions and Employee Associations,* compiled and published by the
Bureau of Labor Statistics, provides a wealth of data based on
returns from 208 unions and professional and employee associations.
These cover 22.6 million workers, up 542,000 since 1968. Union
membership gains do not match the increase in the numbers of

workers in the labor force, but one-half of all new union members are women—although in total they constitute less than 25% of the 16-million member American Federation of Labor-Congress of Industrial Organizations (AFL-CIO).

Leading all unions in both number and percentage of women members are the two largest garment unions: the International Ladies Garment Workers and the Amalgamated Clothing Workers of America. Together they have some 700,000 members, over 80% of them women. The 10 other unions with the largest numbers of women members are the International Brotherhood of Electrical Workers; Communications Workers of America; International Brotherhood of Teamsters; United Automobile Workers; Service Employees International Union; American Federation of State, County and Municipal Employees; United Steel Workers of America; International Union of Electrical Workers; Retail Clerks International Association; and Hotel and Restaurant Workers.

In spite of the fact that some unions are making notable progress in organizing, there are whole segments of the work force not yet unionized, especially in industries and occupations predominantly female. Twenty-five million women workers are not in unions: only one in every 12 hospital workers is organized, just 17% of all government employees, just one-fifth of all service workers. Outside the largest cities, even apparel workers are without a union. The two large garment unions, by their own estimates, could triple their memberships if they could complete the organization of their jurisdictions. Office and sales workers, bank clerks, farm workers, household workers—all are major unorganized groups. Figure 4 indicates the extent of union organization, by sex and race, in the United States as of 1970.

While women constitute 20.7% of all union members, including independent unions and employee associations, they hold few top elective or appointive offices in their international unions—less than 5%. Only one national AFL-CIO union, the American Guild of Variety Artists, has a woman president. No woman sits on the Executive Council of the AFL-CIO, and only one department head, the librarian, is female. On the organizing field staff of this federation there were, as of May 1974, no women. Table 5 indicates selected union and association offices held by women in 1952, 1962, 1970, and 1972. The changes, particularly among unions, do not alter the picture substantially. Thus, union power on a national level

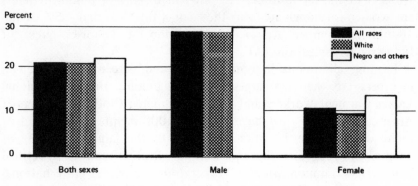

Source: U.S. Department of Labor, Bureau of Labor Statistics (1972: 4).

FIGURE 4: Percent of Wage and Salary Workers in Labor Unions, 1970

is by and large in the hands of male leaders on whom female members must depend to represent their interests.

Examination of individual national and international unions, however, reveals some changes in recent years. Increasingly, unions elect women to their top executive boards, although not yet in numbers proportional to their female memberships. Union conventions pass strong resolutions on increasing attention to women's needs in collective bargaining, recruiting and promoting more female staff members at every level, and job upgrading and promotion opportunities for women.

In May 1974, for example, the Retail, Wholesale and Department Store Union convention adopted unanimously a resolution urging the union "to pursue aggressively efforts to organize unorganized women, encourage women to play a more active role in their unions and encourage the various regions and locals to actively seek out and employ women from the rank and file for full time positions." The issue of the *United Storeworker* (1974: 1) that carried this story ran two other items that illustrate areas of activity and progress. One item reported the changeover to straight-commission earnings of three ready-to-wear departments in a store where women had for years worked on salary plus one-half of 1% commission. (Traditionally in sales work it is men who hold the high-commission jobs in furniture, appliances, rugs, shoes, and so forth.) The second item told of the first woman to take on a furniture sales job in the Bridgeport, Connecticut, branch of a major department store.

Local unions—the smallest and most basic self-governing unit in

TABLE 5: Selected Union and Association Offices Held by Women, 1952, 1962, 1970, 1972[1]

Position	Unions				Associations[2]	
	1952	1962	1970	1972	1970	1972
Total positions held by women.........	31	28	37	37	31	44
Total women.......................	30	24	34	33	30	41
ELECTIVE OFFICES						
President..........................	2	0	1	2	2	6
Secretary-treasurer.................	9	7	10	13	18	17
APPOINTIVE POSITIONS						
Director of organizing activities.........	([3])	1	1	0	0	2
Research director....................	10	3	7	3	0	3
Research and education director........	1	3	0	0	0	0
Education director...................	2	2	2	3	0	0
Director of social insurance...........	([3])	5	7	6	0	1
Editor............................	6	6	4	3	5	5
Legal activities.....................	([3])	1	1	1	0	1
Legislative activities.................	([3])	([3])	2	3	0	0
Public relations activities.............	([3])	([3])	2	3	1	1
Other[4]	1	0	0	0	5	8

1. In 1952, 215 unions were surveyed; in 1962, 181; in 1970, 185; and in 1972, 177. In 1970, 23 associations were surveyed; in 1972, 35.
2. Associations were first surveyed in 1970.
3. Not surveyed.
4. Appointive positions surveyed for unions and associations varied somewhat. Appointive positions included in the category "other" for associations are: executive director, collective bargaining director, and government relations director. In 1952, the union position included in the category "other" is executive secretary.

Source: Berquist (1974: 8).

labor organization structure—relate to regional and national trade unions much as cities and towns relate to the states and the federal government. Women hold increasing numbers of posts on the local level as stewards, committeewomen, and officers, though more tend to be secretaries and trustees than presidents.

Women's grievances are taken quite seriously these days. A good example (Stessin, 1973) is the case of a pregnant cashier who, armed with a doctor's note attesting to her health and ability to work, asked the manager about the maternity leave policy of the supermarket where she worked. When the manager learned that she was not married, she was fired because her "continued employment would hurt the company's image with the community." The worker went to her shop steward, who processed the grievance; when the union could not succeed in settling it in her favor, it went to arbitration, as provided in the union contract. The arbitrator's ruling makes delightful reading:

I doubt that the public holds an employer answerable for the morals of his employees after working hours. I find the company has failed to show that Miss X's condition as a pregnant unmarried woman would have the kind of harmful effects suggested. Her condition cannot be considered industrial misconduct. She should be reinstated immediately, assuming she is physically able to resume her job duties.

Without a collective bargaining agreement, grievance procedure, and and alert union, this story might have had a very different ending. A. F. Grespiron (quoted in Stone, 1973: v), President of the Oil, Chemical and Atomic Workers International Union, sees it this way:

> A revolution is taking place . . . in the relationships between men and women in their places of employment. In organized labor, we like to believe that we have common sense enough to adjust to change . . . adjustment to the new revolution in women's rights and roles is the most difficult we have to face, and by "we" I mean both men and women. But adjust we must. Equal rights and opportunities for women must and will develop.

WOMEN IN LABOR HISTORY

It would be a mistake, however, to view women's role in unions as a new one. When the early struggle to organize and build unions was going on, women were there. As early as 1824, some 200 women struck with the men in a Pawtucket mill against a wage cut (and won). The United Tailoresses of New York struck in 1825; Dover, New Hampshire, was the scene of the first industrial strike (or "turn out," as it was then called) of women alone in 1828. In the famous Lowell, Massachusetts, strike of 1826, 2,500 women turned out against a raise in their board charges in company-owned rooming houses. It was women who launched the first trade union press with publications such as *Voice of Industry,* reporting conditions in the New England mill towns.

While history books do not record much about these women, their names were once household words, some locally, some nationally. There was Sarah Bagley, organizer and labor orator, who later became the country's first telegrapher. Augusta Lewis organized Women's International Typographical Union Number 1. Dynamic Kate Mullaney of the Troy Collar Workers Union became Assistant Secretary and National Organizer for Women for the National Labor Union in 1868.

A number of Irish women, fiery and energetic, became active in the 1870s and 1880s: Leonora Barry, Mary Stirling, Mary Elizabeth Lease of the Grange (who told farmers to raise less corn and more hell), and Mary Kenny, the bindery worker who in 1893 became the first paid woman labor organizer of the AFL. Sara Agnes McLaughlin, carpet weaver, was the first woman to hold an elective post of influence in the American labor movement; she became Secretary-Treasurer for the United Textile Workers. Not many history books record the death of Fannie Sellins, a United Mine Workers organizer, who was shot and killed during a strike, or Ella May Wiggins, a textile strike leader killed by an armed mob (including a company official) on June 7, 1929.

There was a time when labor organizer Mother Jones seemed to be everywhere at once. "My address is like my shoes," she said, "it travels with me." Agnes Nestor, glove worker, was the first woman union president in the AFL. Labor organizer and eloquent speaker Leonora O'Reilly began her union life by being carried to meetings in her mother's arms: Winifred O'Reilly was an active shirtwaist worker. Maggie Condon and Hannah O'Day, packinghouse workers, organized Local 183 of the Amalgamated Meatcutters. In spite of disastrous strikes, their words ring out: "Girls, we ought to organize for them that comes after us."

It was young Bessie Abramowitz who in 1910 led 13 women out of a Chicago clothing factory, a walkout that mushroomed into a bitter 14-week strike involving 45,000 clothing workers and is credited as the event responsible for the birth of the organization that was to become the Amalgamated Clothing Workers of America. Clara Lemlich, young and very beautiful, called for a general strike in 1909 that brought on the citywide walkout of 20,000 New York shirtwaist workers against inhuman sweatshop conditions, long hours, and constant wage cuts. During 13 cold winter weeks, with police clubbings and arrests, the women chanted: "We strike for justice." One judge answered them in court: "You are on strike against God." When Fabian George Bernard Shaw heard this story he cabled across the Atlantic: "Delightful. Medieval America always in intimate personal confidence of the Almighty." The women emerged from this strike singing:

> In the black of the winter of nineteen-nine,
> When we froze and bled on the picket line,
> We showed the world that women could fight,
> And we rose and won with women's might.

And we gave new courage to the men
Who carried on in nineteen-ten,
And shoulder to shoulder we'll win through
Led by the I L G W U.

During World War I, women entered factory and clerical jobs in larger numbers than ever before; this trend was even more pronounced in World War II. The view that certain jobs cannot be performed by women is dropped whenever their labor is in keen demand. In fact, during the World War II campaign to draw more women into war jobs, the U.S. Department of Labor stated: "It can hardly be said that any occupation is absolutely unsuitable for women."

Following the war the decline in women's labor force participation reflected their loss of jobs to returning servicemen. Three million women left the work force, although most would have preferred to stay. Sheila Tobias, Associate Provost of Wesleyan University, studied what actually happened to "Rosie the Riveter" after the war (Tobias and Anderson, 1973). The myth is that she happily returned to her kitchen to let a veteran have her job. With the cooperation of the United Automobile Workers, Tobias examined grievances, letters, tapes, and other original sources, and found that, in fact, eight out of ten Rosies had been working *before* the war, but in lower-paying nonmanufacturing jobs. During the war they moved into factories and unions, many for the first time. Following the war they did not go back to their kitchens so much as they did to lower-paid, traditionally female jobs. By 1950 the number of women in the work force had returned to its wartime peak.

The key union issue for women during the immediate postwar period was seniority, particularly in rehiring. A number of unions tried to protect their women members, but in most cases layoffs affected anywhere from 50 to 100% of their women members. Rehiring was a problem because of veterans' preference; when women were recalled, it was often to lower-paying, less skilled jobs. Women found they had difficulty collecting unemployment compensation, particularly if they refused lower-rated work. Compensation boards declared them too choosy and denied their benefits.

It was in the 1950s and 1960s that many of the women unionists who are coming to the forefront today got their start, in unions such as the Packinghouse Workers, Farm Workers, AFSCME, Communication Workers, the International Union of Electrical Workers and others. (This is not to say that there have not been women leaders at all times in unions, particularly in the two leading apparel unions, where women such as Pauline Newman, Fania Cohn, Gladys Dickason, Rose Pesotta, Dorothy Bellanca, Bessie Hillman, Dolly Lowther, and others carried major responsibilities, often sitting on general Executive Boards at one time or another.) But in the 1960s a groundswell began, and in the 1970s it has gained so much momentum that it commands attention and recognition from unions large and small, from the press, and more important, from union women all across the country.

THE NEW MOMENTUM

To assess the significance of this new momentum, it is worthwhile to examine several studies—one, a year-long research project aimed at learning about the participation of women in their labor unions and what barriers keep them from leadership roles.

UNION SELF-STUDIES

Perhaps the first self-study by a union that looked at this question was done by the 1.5 million-member United Automobile Workers in 1962. In a survey of its 150,000 women members, it found that only 800 held an elective office, although literally thousands were active as elected or appointed committee members on political action, community services, recreation, grievance and negotiating committees.

Two years later the United Packinghouse Workers undertook a similar survey of its 15,557 women members (21% of the total union membership). Some 542 women held local union offices. Of this number, only 24 were local presidents, while 102 were recording secretaries, 198 were executive board members, and 95 women were trustees.

In 1967 the American Bakery and Confectionary Workers International Union queried its locals and found that of 136 reporting, 58 had a total of 115 women holding some office. Thirty of the 115 women were recording secretaries; three were local presidents.

Two surveys were completed by the International Union of Electrical Workers (30% women members). The first study, in 1967, was followed by a second two years later to assess the effectiveness of the union's Social Action and Women's Activities Committees in stimulating the participation of women members. In 1967, for example, the union found that 890 women held key union positions in their locals; in 1969 there were 1,467 holding such posts, a substantial increase. Forty percent of the total membership was covered by the survey, but the assumption must be made that it was the most interested locals that reported. Seventeen women were local presidents, 76 were secretaries, 130 were trustees, and 391 were executive board members.

The pattern revealed by these studies is that relatively few union women are in leadership roles, but those who are office-holders are most frequently on executive boards, with the major elected office being either secretary or trustee.

BARRIERS TO THE PARTICIPATION OF WOMEN IN UNIONS

Why are women underrepresented in union leadership positions? With a grant from the Ford Foundation, Wertheimer and Nelson (1975) proposed to investigate what stood in the way of women's participation at every level of union activity.[1] What led some women to accept responsibility and to compete for union leadership posts, while others held back? How do women see themselves in relation to their unions, and how do officers and male rank-and-file workers view their absence from most decision-making levels?

This year-long research endeavor was an outgrowth of courses and conferences that the Metropolitan Office of Cornell's School of Industrial and Labor Relations had been conducting for several years with blue-collar and working women. It received the cooperation of the New York City Central Labor Council (AFL-CIO) and involved the intensive participation of seven New York City local unions who were interested in learning more about their women members.

A survey of 108 New York City local unions having substantial numbers of women members constituted the first of three parts in this study of the barriers to the participation of women in labor unions. Union leaders, responding to a questionnaire, indicated that the overwhelming majority of their women members held semi-skilled or unskilled jobs with little opportunity for advancement. The survey covered unions representing some 541,336 unionists, of whom 284,189 were women. It found that women often seemed reluctant to compete against men in running for union office and were more likely to run for office where there were large numbers of women in the union—although in 10% of all the locals where women were in a majority there were no women on the local's executive board. Elected offices most frequently held by women were secretary and trustee.

Focusing on seven local unions that represented a cross-section of New York blue-collar workers and one white-collar sales local, the second part of the study hypothesized the barriers to participation of women in unions as being (1) socio-cultural-personal; (2) job-related; and (3) union-related. Rank-and-file members in these seven locals were surveyed. In the socio-cultural-personal category, it was important to learn how the attitude of her husband affected a woman's union participation, the role played by her family respon-sibilities, by the fear of going out at night, or by a woman's self-esteem. In the job-related area, to what extent was the experience gap of women returning to work a factor, or holding a dead-end job, or fear of male supervisors? Possible union-related barriers included lack of encouragement to run for office, lack of openings, male competition for posts, lack of female role models, or lack of leadership training opportunities.

This portion of the study revealed that participation of women in their labor organizations is handicapped by a lack of information and experience, rather than by any lack of interest. In the socio-cultural-personal category, both women and men declared family responsi-bilities a major barrier to further participation, although from 15% to 20% of the members in each union saw no barrier to their further participation. This constitutes a sizeable reservoir of potential union activists. Second to family responsibilities as a barrier, unionists stated, was a lack of information about the union.

The greatest job-related barrier was a feeling that supervisors are hard on active unionists, a problem which training in handling such situations and the concomitant increased self-confidence could go far toward solving.

In the union-related category, findings point up the strong desire of women members for education programs and courses in leadership skills. Thus, the barriers respondents indicate as key in each category can be seen to overlap. An increase in skills and self-confidence through education and leadership training is precisely what would assist in dealing with the major job-related problems, and would provide the added information which members requested in the socio-cultural-personal area. Additionally, both men and women indicated a need for union recognition and encouragement of their efforts, and for learning why it is important to the union to have them participate further.

The final portion of this year-long study focused on interviews with top leaders as well as with rank-and-file women leaders of the seven local unions. These provided a close-up of leaders' views of women members and how women rank-and-file leaders see themselves and their union roles. The sacrifices women make to attend meetings and take an active part in the union are recognized and appreciated by the leaders, who view women as being as interested in the union as are the men.

Rank-and-file women leaders tend to see activity in the union as a way of helping others, and give this as the reason they most want to participate. However, they view the union as hierarchical and feel themselves closed out of decision-making. They are eager for recognition and to move ahead in the union. Once involved in union activity, they almost always continue and even increase their commitment. There is a strong feeling among them that more women should run for union office.

This study of women's participation in unions shows a rising self-awareness among women unionists, coupled with a sense of inadequacy and a reluctance to compete against men for key union posts. In seeking ways to encourage labor union women and to provide education and training in some of the areas where they indicate a need, a pilot Trade Union Women's Studies program was designed. Funded by the Ford Foundation, it is conducted through the New York office of Cornell's School of Industrial and Labor Relations to provide a range of labor studies and leadership training programs for union women. Through a longitudinal study, the value of this training to participants and to their unions will be assessed. In addition, periodic conferences for labor leaders, union staff, and labor educators are built into the program.

UNION WOMEN: MOBILIZING FOR ACTION

That labor union women are increasingly eager to act in concert to meet their needs through their unions is illustrated by the First New

York Trade Union Women's Conference, held in that city January 19, 1974. On an icy winter Saturday, over 500 union women gathered to discuss some of their special concerns: organizing unorganized women, upgrading women and promoting affirmative action on the job and in unions, achieving more of their goals through the mechanism of collective bargaining, and increasing the participation of women in their unions.

This conference grew out of a series of monthly meetings where union women leaders and staff, under the auspices of Cornell's trade union women's program, discussed particular problems of women in the work force and in unions. The decision of this group was to sponsor a conference that would bring together as many unions and union women as possible. A total of 140 women representing local, national, or international unions were involved in one way or another in planning and executing this event, in itself the best method of leadership training.

There was powerful oratory at the First New York Trade Union Women's Conference, on a scale that was to be repeated two months later at the founding convention of the Coalition of Labor Union Women (CLUW). Keynote speaker Addie Wyatt, Director of the Women's Division of the Amalgamated Meatcutters and Butcher Workmen, and rapidly gaining a reputation as the Martin Luther King, Jr., of the labor movement, fired the group with her words. "We will no longer wait for others to focus in on our needs," she said. Speaking of her early experiences packing Army stew during the war, she recounted: "I had one strike against me because I was a worker, two strikes against me being black, and three strikes against me being female. I needed as much union as I could get." Emphasizing that women did not want to take any brother's place in the labor movement, she spoke of commitment and a partnership role:

> Together we can share our experiences, find ways to fulfill our commitment to the union and get the union to fulfill its commitment to us. The union is pledged to make this a better way of life for all workers, regardless of race, color, creed, or sex. I am inspired, and I hope you are, by what unions have already done and by what the labor movement must and can do in the future [Kopelov, 1974: 19].

The massive and emotionally stirring founding convention of CLUW in March of 1974 brought together 3,200 women unionists from 58 national and international unions to establish a new organization. Dedicated to unifying "all union women in a viable organization to determine, first, our common problems and concerns and, second, to develop action programs within the framework of our unions to deal effectively with our objectives" (Coalition of Labor Women, 1974: 3), membership in the national coalition is open only to unionists. The plan is to work primarily through chapters set up around the country. These CLUW chapters are expected to be concerned about organizing unorganized workers, affirmative action in the work place, working toward political involvement and legislative goals, and increasing the participation of women within their unions. These four areas of concern to union women are discussed below.

1. Increasing Union Action on Problems of Women Workers

"For so long women have settled for so little," Addie Wyatt once said. Today union women are prepared to ask for more, and unions are responding when women make themselves heard.

Affirmative action: Under the law, both companies and unions are responsible in cases involving discrimination. Some unions move aggressively to support women and minority members. According to Electrical Workers (IUE) general counsel Winn Newman (Union Labor Reports/Weekly Newsletter, 1973: 2), many company affirmative programs are a "sham" and a "cover-up," and the IUE has directed every local to review its contracts for violation of equal pay or other legislation. Where these are found, immediate corrective action is recommended—action ranging from use of union grievance procedure all the way to the EEOC and the courts. Checklists on what constitutes race and sex discrimination are furnished as a guide. The IUE is not the only union aggressively pursuing equality on the job, but the more union women mobilize, the sooner all unions will move in this area.

Women's divisions or departments: A number of unions have women's divisions. These have varying degrees of influence with the union's top leadership. In no case, as yet, is a woman director of such a department, an elected top officer, or executive board member of the union. Where the union is already committed to increasing the involvement of its female membership, the women's division can expect wide support. Some unions believe a separate department concerned with women's interests is not a good idea: women members, they feel, should be integrated into every aspect of union life, not separated. Other unions view such departments as the way to offer women auxiliary channels for leadership experience: they may be closed out of local leadership posts if these are already filled by men or have small chance of election where men are in a majority. A women's division has the potential for increasing the self-awareness of women, providing them with role models, and bringing the special concerns of women members to the attention of union executives. The chances of having such a department in a union would seem strongest where women do not constitute a majority of the union's membership, and where an argument can be made that the needs of women members may be slighted without such special focus.

Labor education: The year-long Cornell study, described above, indicated the eagerness of union women to learn, study, make up for lost time, acquire leadership skills and use them to work more effectively through their unions. Twenty-two states and Puerto Rico have university labor education programs which unions utilize for conducting classes and conferences. Labor unions and state federations of labor hold conferences and workshops, some initiated by the union's national or regional education department, some by state labor federations, and some by union women themselves. Universities and unions alike are sensitive to pressure. There is no reason why labor educators should not respond to the educational needs of this expanding new "market."

Negotiating for union women's needs: Traditionally, union women on negotiating and bargaining committees take a somewhat silent seat. This is not altogether related to sex. The union has a spokesperson or two, just as does the company, and there is agreement ahead of time on recessing to caucus, rather than confusing the bargaining process with too many participants. Since most top union leaders are men, at bargaining time it is men who do the talking. The place where women can make an immediate impact is in the formulation of bargaining demands.

Some of the union contract areas of special interest to women include paid maternity leave; plantwide seniority so women can move across job lines; parental leave days for child-care (taking children to doctor, conferences with children's teachers); child-care center allowances; experimental flexible work hours; tuition refund and released time for education; training programs for upgrading and promotion; contract terminology changes so contracts do not always refer to "he;" increased hospitalization for maternity (most plans pay a small, flat amount which does not cover costs); and examination of pension programs for equity.

2. Organizing Unorganized Women

No one presumes to have the answer to this dilemma, but its urgency is understood by union women across the land. First, women enter the work force where the jobs are increasingly in the clerical and service areas—two areas largely unorganized and low-paid. Second, women still seem to be used to replace men in nonunion plants and are paid lower wages. "Low-Paid Women Big Threat to Jobs of Union Printers" is not a nineteenth-century headline but from page 1 of the March 2, 1972, issue of the *ITU Review* (International Typographical Union). The article asserts that

> It isn't women members of the ITU, who receive equal pay for equal work, who are the threat; it's the women who will work any hours, short or long, at almost any time of the day or night for half the union wages, who are the danger to unionized workers, both men and women.

Reporting a survey conducted by Kansas State College, the article states that 92% of 450 employers who returned questionnaires admitted that women are hired in production jobs equal to those of men, but are paid less for their work. The union paper goes on to point out that the threat to union wages stems from the number of large nonunion printing plants, where work is transferred from unionized operations. Thus, organizing remains a prime concern for all unions, and for men as well as women.

Third, unless the labor movement can expand—and presently it is static in growth, but losing ground when its numbers are compared with the rise in the total work force—there will not be much improvement in the number of union leadership posts available for rank and filers moving up. However, if the labor movement expands, particularly through the organizing of women workers, new posts will become necessary, and women will be there and ready to fill them.

Finally, as women unionists review the organizing record of unions, they feel they would like to test whether women can organize other women more successfully than men have done. It is time, they say, for unions to give financial and staff support to a major organizing effort.

3. Legislative Action

Some problems are best solved in ways other than through collective bargaining. Adequate child-care is an example of such an issue. Only rarely, as in those centers established by the Amalgamated Clothing Workers of America, are factory-based facilities financed largely through employer contributions practicable. But healthy children are society's responsibility, not alone that of the parents. Federally funded, round-the-clock child-care is one of the key concerns of union women, especially as the number of working mothers increases. They will look for ways to increase union support for such legislation. This may well culminate in a nationwide campaign not only for the legislation itself, but for the kind of congressional backing that will make it veto-proof.

Women unionists would like to see laws that protect *all* workers. A particular weight is not too heavy for a woman, they argue, it is too heavy only for a person who cannot lift it. Rest periods, as well, are important for all workers. Both men and women need the right to voluntary overtime.

4. Changing Attitudes Toward Women

Attitude changes usually follow behavior change. A man who feels a woman should not do his job will change his mind when he has worked next to a woman doing that job and finds she is not so bad at it after all. But how do you change the behavior and attitude of a business representative for the union who goes into a plant and says "Hi, girls!" to the women, while going to the men to discuss serious union business? How do you change the behavior and attitude of rank-and-file male members who, at union meetings, talk, hoot, or make open remarks such as "Oh boy, here come the women," when a woman seeks to speak from the floor? What is the best way to reach rank-and-file women who vote time after time for men for union office because "Men are better at that sort of thing"? How do you change foremen who pat women on the back as they move down the line, and suggest women stewards need "a good lay" when they are militant in settling a grievance? Part of the answer lies in making education and leadership training programs available to numbers of union women, thereby increasing their self-confidence and their competence in coping with negative plant and union hall attitudes.

IMPLICATIONS

In examining the four problem areas of particular concern to today's trade union women, an interesting conclusion emerges: these problems are by no means unsolvable. They call for dedicated, active union women who can combine experience with a judicious use of strategy, tact, and political know-how, and endless amounts of time and patience. If women do not get the kind of basic experience they need through their own unions, CLUW will undoubtedly provide a substitute training ground.

Because labor unions are organizations with both social and bread-and-butter goals, they have a constant need for good leadership. Fact: it *is* easier for women in those unions where there are many women members. Fact: because of the gains made by the women's movement, because of equal rights legislation and its enforcement, because of the changing image (to some extent) of women in the public media, women have new opportunities to participate and to succeed.

Fact: women will not turn back. As increasing numbers of mothers enter the labor force, so increasing numbers of children have a working mother as a role model. Studies indicate the girls of working mothers tend themselves to work outside the home as adults. The long-range effect of this should not be underestimated.

Fact: women are increasingly visible on the job and in their labor unions. They are more vocal than ever before and better prepared to participate. New women leaders have emerged, opening the door a little wider for countless others who will follow. The Addie Wyatts and Doris Turners, the Lillian Roberts and Gloria Johnsons, the Dolores Huertas and Diana Nunes are only a few of the many who are coming forward. As the list unfolds, the names of many minority women are among them, for a great many of the strong emerging women leaders are not white.

Union women seek a partnership role in the labor movement. They bring to the task of achieving this an enthusiasm reminiscent of the organizing days of the 1930s. No one has ventured to say how long it will take to achieve this role, but no union woman believes that it cannot be done.

NOTE

1. See also Wertheimer and Nelson (1974) for a fuller account of the study than space permits here.

REFERENCES

BERQUIST, V. A. (1974) "Women's participation in labor organizations." Monthly Labor Review 97 (October).

Coalition of Labor Union Women (1974) "Statement of purpose, structure and guidelines." Adopted at the founding conference, Chicago, March 23-24.

Council of Economic Advisors (1973) "The economic role of women," reprinted from the Economic Report of the President. Washington, D.C.: U.S. Department of Laobr, Women's Bureau.

General Electric Corporation (1972) "Women and business: agenda for the seventies." Business Environment Studies (March).

ITU Review (1972) "Low-paid women big threat to jobs of union printers." March 2.

KOPELOV, C. [ed.] (1974) Proceedings, First New York Trade Union Women's Conference. New York: Cornell University, New York State School of Industrial and Labor Relations, Trade Union Women's Studies, May.

MAPP, P. (1973) "Women in apprenticeship—why not?" Report prepared for U.S. Department of Labor, Manpower Administration. Madison, Wis.: State of Wisconsin, Department of Industry, Labor and Human Relations, Division of Apprenticeship and Training, August.

MEINKOTH, M. (n.d.) "Women, a source of labor supply in 1980." Philadelphia: Temple University, unpublished manuscript. (Quoted in General Electric Corporation [1972].)

STESSIN, L. (1973) "Women are breaking the blue collar barrier." New York Times (August 26).

STONE, K. (1973) Handbook for OCAW Women. Oil, Chemical and Atomic Workers International Union.

TOBIAS, S. and L. ANDERSON (1973) "What really happened to Rosie the Riveter: demobilization and the female labor force, 1945-1947." Delivered at the Berkshire Conference of Women Historians, March 2.

Union Labor Reports/Weekly Newsletter (1973) September 27.

U.S. Department of Commerce (1973) Quoted in U.S. News and World Report (October 8).

U.S. Department of Labor, Bureau of Labor Statistics (1972) "Selected earnings and demographic characteristics of union members, 1970." Washington, D.C.: U.S. Department of Labor Report No. 417.

WERTHEIMER, B. M. and A. H. NELSON (1975) Trade Union Women: A Study of Their Participation in New York City Locals. New York: Praeger.

——— (1974) "The American woman at work." Personnel Management (March).

8

STRUCTURAL CHANGE IN THE OCCUPATIONAL
COMPOSITION OF THE FEMALE LABOR FORCE

E T H E L   L .   V A T T E R

Women have been entering the paid labor force in increasing numbers during the past several decades, as can be seen in Figure 1, which shows not only increasing levels of participation over the life cycle, but also a changed pattern of participation between 1940 and 1950 to 1970. Current expansion is notable among married women, as can be seen in Figure 2. Married women with husbands present show the most pronounced change in participation rates between 1940 and 1970. What began as a change rate of 7.8% for 1940-1950 accelerated to 10.2% for 1960-1970. Increased participation occurred in every age subgroup.

One could speculate on the reasons for increased participation of married women with husbands—obviously, the major group available for additions to the aggregate supply of labor—and treat participation as a function of freedom of the married female to make choices as to whether and when she will enter the paid labor market and how long she will remain in it. The major factor keeping married women's participation rates lower than those of single women is, of course, the responsibility for "serving" families, including the bearing and rearing of children. Figure 1 depicts the dramatic changes that took place in female labor force participation after 1940.

AUTHOR'S NOTE: This research was supported by the Cornell University Agricultural Experiment Station, the College of Human Ecology, and the Department of Consumer Economics and Public Policy. The writer is indebted to John Miller, candidate for the M.S. degree in Social and Economic Statistics, and to Frederick W. Telling, candidate for the Ph.D. in Welfare Economics and Public Policy, for help in preparing the indices discussed in this chapter.

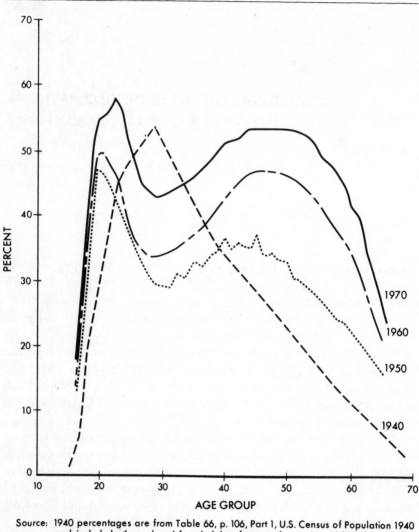

Source: 1940 percentages are from Table 66, p. 106, Part 1, U.S. Census of Population 1940
and include both employed female labor force and experienced female workers
seeking work; 1950, 1960, and 1970 data are from unpublished paper by Larry E.
Suter, Census Bureau, U.S. Department of Commerce, entitled "Occupation, Employment, and Lifetime Experience of Women."

FIGURE 1: Percentage of Women in Labor Force by Age, 1940-1970

Note that in 1970, for the 25-29 and 30-34 age groups, married
women with husbands present had below-average participation rates
of 38.4% and 40.2%, whereas single women in these corresponding
age groups had their highest participation rates of 82.5% and 72.2%,

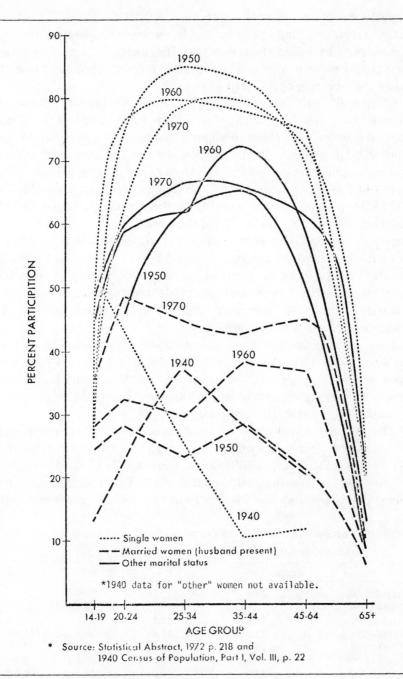

FIGURE 2: Labor Force Participation Rates of Women by Age and
        Marital Status, 1940-1970

respectively. However, looking at the 1960-1970 change in participation rates, one finds that the family-serving, child-bearing/rearing
factors may be losing their strength. The increases in participation
for married women with husband present were greatest for those of
prime child-bearing ages—20 to 35.

Of special significance has been the entry into the labor force of
women with small children: "in March 1970, one-fourth of all
married women with children under 3 years of age were part of the
American labor force. The proportion was one-third for those whose
youngest children were 3 to 5, and one-half for those whose children
were old enough to be in school" (Waldman and Young, 1971). By
1972, the percentages for working mothers with children under 3
had increased to 28, and to 32 for those with children under 6. Two
questions can be raised at the outset: (1) why are wives and mothers
in increasing numbers entering the paid labor force;[1] and (2) what
changes, if any, have occurred in the status of women in the paid
labor force, given their increasing participation? Although this
research is primarily concerned with the latter question, a quick
response to the first is in order.

Data on the contribution that working wives make to family
income (Table 1) lend credence to the hypothesis that *need* is the
main goad at low-income levels, *want* at middle-income levels, and
desire for self-actualization at high-income levels, although these
concepts are not mutually exclusive.

The median contribution to family income is highest at the two
extremes of family income. As family income increases, the
percentage contribution shifts away from the less-than-5% contribution and greater-than-50% contribution extremes toward the
moderate 5-30% and 30-50% contributions. Need is most certainly

TABLE 1: Distribution of Wives by Selected Percentages of Family Income
Accounted for by Earnings

Family Income	Median Contribution	Less than 5.0%	30-50%	Over 50%
Under $2,000	28.4	22.4	11.9	36.6
2,000-2,999	21.8	15.6	13.9	24.7
3,000-4,999	24.8	13.4	17.2	25.2
5,000-6,999	22.8	15.3	19.7	21.8
7,000-9,999	23.9	13.8	26.2	14.1
10,000-14,999	27.6	10.2	36.1	9.7
15,000 and over	27.9	7.8	28.1	7.0

Source: Adapted from U.S. Department of Labor (1971).

the primary factor at the under-$2,000 family income level. Self-actualization may be a major factor for income levels greater than $15,000 when one considers that most occuptions in which females make over 30% of $15,000 (i.e., over $4,500) require some skills, and work may indeed satisfy the desire to utilize them. The want to improve the real level of living probably functions for women at both middle and higher family income levels.

The concepts of need, self-actualization, and want to increase real level of living present an interesting mix of economic and psychological factors—now that aspirations and educational levels are rising, along with unemployment and prices! Since we may expect these trends to continue, we may also expect that women will less and less regard themselves as secondary, supplementary, or peripheral workers and more and more be concerned with their labor force status.

To answer the question of whether or not women's status has worsened, improved, or remained unchanged in the United States from 1940-1970, we now turn our attention to a number of indices based on the application to census data of a variety of assumptions.[2] They are discussed briefly below and in Appendix C.

The first index is expressed as follows:

$$a = \text{a gross measure of relative status, of } \frac{\bar{f}}{\frac{F}{L}} \text{ where } \bar{f} = \frac{\sum \frac{f_1}{1_i}}{N}$$

Here, a is deemed to be an inadequate measure because it is computed as if each occupational group contained the same number of women, and are of equal importance (status); $a' = [\Sigma(f_i/1_i)SES_i]/ [\Sigma(F/L)\ SES_i]$ seeks to avoid the failure to account for importance by using SES (socioeconomic status) scores of occupations.[3] In this case, a' is weighted measure of bias. The weight is the SES group number (the numbers range from 1 to 99 for approximately 500 occupational categories). The percentage of women in each occupation is multiplied by the SES number for that occupation. These are summed, and the total is divided by the sum of the percentage contribution of women to the total labor force times the SES group numbers. Thus, the SES group numbers (1-99) act as weights, and deviations from F/L in higher SES occupations are given, proportionately, greater weight.

Does $a' = x$ actually represent what it purports to represent? Can we conclude that the relative status of women in 1970 is about 66% of that of men in 1970? Here, there are at least two considerations: (1) a' may not actually measure the relative position of women, in which case another measure must be developed; and (2) even if the measure does reasonably reflect the extent to which women have less percentages in occupational groups than they contribute to the labor force, the fact remains that men have correspondingly greater percentages in occupational groups because their overall participation in the labor force is so much higher than women's, and a' does not measure women versus men, but rather women versus a given norm. It may be argued that the relative position of women versus men would be lower than the relative position of women versus a given norm, that men are favored to the same degree that women are disfavored, and that a credible measure might be expressed as follows:

$1 + (1 - a)$ = the ideal index on the assumption that the bias against women is equal to a bias in favor of men.

And, therefore,

$a'' = a'/1 + (1 - a')$ = measure of status of women relative to men (the figure for 1970 is 0.49).

Here, although a'' is a quick and easy index to prepare, it is rather arbitrary in construction and suffers from some other faults—mainly, a discontinuity when $a' = 2$.

A more appropriate method of measuring female/male status would be to construct an index of men's status (b') relative to some ideal norm analogous in construction to the a' index with the use of $m_i/1_i$ in place of $f_i/1_i$ and M/L in place of F/L, and to form an index of status of women to men as $c' = a'/b'$.

When dealing with groups of occupations less than the total labor force in size, one can consider the "participation rate"[4] for that group in the total labor force. One can construct an index which takes into account the distribution of women throughout the group of occupations (in part a function of the a' index) as well as the participation rate. This index can be written as follows:

$$a''' = \sum_k (f_i/1_i)\, SES_i \,/\, [\sum_k (F/L)\, SES_i] .$$

$\sum_k$ signifies summing overall occupations in the kth occupational group and F/L, the proportion of women in the total labor force rather than for the kth group (as would be the case if we were constructing an a' index for the kth group).[5] As was done for the a' index, one can also construct a $b' ''$ index in similar fashion and denote the ratio $a' ''/b' ''$ as $c' ''$.

We can go a step further in the development of an index of female occupational status by trying to construct an index which also takes into account the criticism of not considering the total number of persons in each occupational category. One way to construct such an index using a function of the number of persons in any occupational category is to use the standard deviation of $f_i/1_i$. (See Appendix C for a complete explanation.) The larger the standard deviation, the less important is the deviation of $f_i/1_i$ from F/L. Therefore, in computing an index using the standard deviation of $f_i/1_i$, one weights each component of the sum of the numerators as computed in a' by the inverse of the standard deviation. The inverse of the standard deviation varies in magnitude as the importance of the deviation of $f_i/1_i$ from F/L varies in magnitude. The new index is written as follows:

$$A' = [(\Sigma [(F/L)(1 - F/L)(1 - 1_i/L)/1_i]^{-\frac{1}{2}}(f_i/1_i)SES_i)/$$
$$(\Sigma [(F/L)(1 - F/L)(1 - 1_i/L)/1_i]^{-\frac{1}{2}}(F/L)SES_i)]$$

$$A' = \Sigma SQRT[(1_i/(1 - 1_i/L))(f_i 1_i)SES_i/\Sigma SQRT(1_i/(1 - 1_i/L))(F/L)SES_i]$$

Again, this A' index is a measure of female status relative to some ideal status. One may construct a B' index for men's employment status analogous to the construction of A' with the use of $m_i/1_i$ in place of $f_i/1_i$ and M/L in place of F/L. $C' = A'/B'$ is an index of women's employment status relative to men and is analogous to the construction of C'.

It is a simple step to the construction of $A' ''$, $B' ''$, and $C' ''$. They are similar in construction to their lower-case counterparts except for the added weighting by the $SQRT[(1_i/(1 - 1_i/L_k))]$, a function of occupational size for each occupation i and the size of the kth group of occupations. Their construction is identical to that of A', B', and C' except that the summation in both numerator and denominator is over some group of occupations, while the F/L and M/L proportions are for the total labor force. The triple prime indices here, as for their lower-case counterparts, combine both a measure of fairness and participation rate.

The indices just constructed are all measures of status in the work force. Construction of all indices is summarized in Appendix C, with the aim of easing interpretation. Capital letter and small letter indices measure similar categories, but the capital letter indices compensate for varying sizes of occupational groups. Because of the adjustment for group size, the capital letter indices will be more reliable estimators of women's status, we believe.

Using these measures, we shall now examine the question of whether or not the status of women in the labor force has improved, worsened, or remained constant between 1940 and 1970.[6]

Indices were constructed for the census years identified above for all occupations, 99 SES categories, and the following occupational subcategories: professionals, managers, clerical workers, craftsmen, operatives, service workers, and laborers. Changes in these measures over time are presented in Tables 2 and 3 and in Appendix A.

C' and c' (see Table 2) for all U.S. occupations and for the 99 SES groups moved in the same directions: up slightly in 1950 from 1940, down in 1960, and up again in 1970 to a level higher than for any previous decade. These movements undoubtedly reflect, respectively, the increased participation of women in more skilled (and better paid) occupations during World War II, their exodus from these ranks after the war was over (see Tobias, 1973), and their return to the paid labor force in increasing numbers, but into lower occupational levels (primarily white-collar, however), during the 1960s.

There is little difference in the changing status of women as measured for "all occupations" and for the 99 "SES groups," suggesting the feasibility of drastically reducing data input by use of SES weighting when trend comparison is of concern. More significantly, both measures show remarkable—perhaps the word should be deplorable—status stability over time, particularly in light of the

TABLE 2: Total Labor Force—Selected Index Values

		1940	1950	1960	1970
c' Index					
	U.S. All[1]	0.51[2]	0.54	0.48	0.54
	SES	0.58	0.60	0.53	0.58
C' Index					
	U.S. All	0.68	0.70	0.65	0.73
	SES	0.75	0.77	0.69	0.79

1. All = overall individual occupations; SES = overall SES groups.
2. Farm workers not included.

growing participation of women in the paid labor force. As the French say, "The more things change, the more they remain the same."

An interesting comparison with New York State can be made for the 1960-1970 decade (earlier data are not comparable). Between April 1960 and April 1970, the number of employed women 14 years and older in the state increased by 22%; that for men, only 2% (N.Y. State Department of Commerce, 1974). During this same period the relative status of women as measured by C' over all occupations increased slightly from 0.72 to 0.75, while C' over all SES groups remained constant at 0.79. This contrasts with index changes for the United States where C' over all occupations increased from 0.65 to 0.73, and C' for SES groups increased from 0.69 to 0.79—suggesting the importance of regional differences in the employment status of women.

Comparison with the corresponding c' indices portrays the same situation. U.S. indices show increase in status for women; N.Y. indices show stable or decreasing status. These differences between New York and the United States may be attributed to the following factors:

(1) By 1970, manufacturing had been replaced by services as the topmost employer in the state. Besides services, New York State had larger shares than the United States of employment in wholesale trade; finance, insurance and real estate; and in transportation, communications, and public utilities. (Overall, women made up 39% of the state's labor force in 1970, a figure approximately the same as that for the country.)

(2) Employed women in New York State in 1970 filled about 70% of the clerical jobs, 44% of the service jobs (except in private households where the rate is much higher), and 39% of professional and technical positions.

The lack of significant changes in the New York indices shown in Table 2 can be explained by the interaction between factors (1) and (2). Although women are entering the labor force much faster, they are entering more lower SES-ranked occupations in New York than in the United States. Factor (1) defines the growth of service, clerical, and sales-related jobs, and Factor (2) defines the participation of women in these jobs. Since the indices used here are formed to give status relative to the proportion of females in the labor force, they will decrease if females entering the labor force go into low SES-ranked occupations.

In addition to factors (1) and (2), the following is relevant to the contrast between New York and the United States:

(3) N.Y. women's "participation rate" in professional, technical, and kindred occupations, a wide-ranging category that employs almost one out of every six employed women (437,000) and has high SES rank, dropped from 104 to 101, despite the fact that in April 1960 there was a 54% increase in the total number of women in this category. Thus, in spite of their increased employment, they were barely holding their own in terms of status, as measured by the foregoing index. (Later, we will note that U.S. women professionals fared even worse than New York women professionals.) Specific examples in professional, technical and kindred workers include the following:

   (a) During the same period, female participation in noncollege teaching, which represented 40% of all professional women in 1970, fell from 204 to 171. Although their participation in college and university teaching is rising slowly, by 1970 it had reached only 77.

   (b) Another important group of women—in the medical and health fields—revealed trends meaningful for our analysis: participation rates among nurses and clinical laboratory technologists and technicians declined between 1960 and 1970. During the same period among physicians, dentists, and related practitioners, the female participation rate increases slightly, from 7% to 10% (N.Y. State Department of Labor, 1973: 1-5).

Appendix B includes charts that graph the values the various indices take on for seven major U.S. occupational groupings. Table 3 and Figures 3, 4, and 5 present the C' and C''' indices for these groups.

The C' index measures status of women within each occupational grouping. Looking at the figures, we see that the C' index behaves erratically for laborers, and craftsmen and foremen groups in the U.S. This may be due to the extremely low rate of participation of females in these occupational groups (less than 10% for laborers and less than 3% for craftsmen and foremen in 1970), since any addition of new females to the work group could significantly affect the status quo. Less erratic in their behavior are the C' indices for Service Workers and Managers and Officials. The indices for the remaining three groups seem almost stable in comparison. We look at the behavior of the C' indices proceeding from most to least erratic.

Women's status among laborers seems to be declining steadily throughout the 1940-1970 time period with a sharp decline from

TABLE 3: C′ and C′ ″ Measures of Female Occupational Mobility in Major
Occupational Groups—U.S. and New York

Occupational Group*	C′				C′ ″			
U.S.	1940	1950	1960	1970	1940	1950	1960	1970
1	0.59	0.67	0.70	0.70	1.05	0.99	0.83	0.72
2	0.94	0.96	1.00	1.18	0.29	0.33	0.33	0.37
3	0.85	0.81	0.77	0.80	1.61	1.99	1.98	2.21
4	1.25	1.35	1.46	1.25	0.07	0.10	0.08	0.10
5	0.86	0.86	0.81	0.82	0.72	0.71	0.59	0.57
6	0.48	0.57	0.59	1.01	1.89	1.74	1.92	2.42
7	1.94	1.58	1.55	1.16	0.14	0.14	0.11	0.15
N.Y.								
1	**	**	0.74	0.74	**	**	0.76	0.79
2	**	**	1.11	1.15	**	**	0.35	0.37
3	**	**	0.84	0.89	**	**	1.91	1.93
4	**	**	0.96	0.93	**	**	0.06	0.07
5	**	**	0.70	0.73	**	**	0.68	0.59
6	**	**	0.87	1.11	**	**	1.59	1.72
7	**	**	1.27	1.12	**	**	0.15	0.14

*1 = Professional and technical, 2 = managers and officials, 3 = sales and clerical,
4 = craftsmen and foremen, 5 = operatives, 6 = service workers, 7 = laborers.
**No comparable data for New York.

1940-1950, a slight one between 1950 and 1960, and again a sharp
one between 1960 and 1970. Even so, it seems that among laborers,
women are still better off than men (as of 1970) with a C′ index
value of 1.16. The New York index also shows a decline, but not
quite so sharp as for the United States. The status of women among
laborers was lower in New York at 1.12, but this may be because
New York C′ index for laborers is closer to the end of the steady
decline of women's status among laborers than we witness for the
United States.

This high (though declining) status of females among laborers has
little significance when one considers the small percentage of women
in laborer occupations or the status of women laborers relative to the
proportion of women in the labor force. The C′ ″ index for laborers
in the U.S. shows the almost hopelessly low status of women in this
group relative to participation in the total labor force. Women's
laborer status as measured by C′ ″ in the U.S. remained almost
steady throughout 1940-1960—dropping slightly in 1950-1960 and
reaching a new "low-high" of 0.15 in 1970. In New York the status
of women laborers as measured by C′ ″ is almost the same as for the
United States—decreasing in 1960-1970 from 0.15 to 0.14.

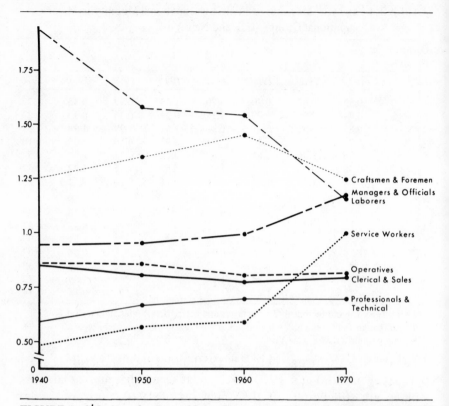

Craftsmen & Foremen
Managers & Officials
Laborers

Service Workers

Operatives
Clerical & Sales

Professionals & Technical

FIGURE 3: C′ Indices for Seven Major Occupational Groupings, U.S. 1940-1970

Going back to the C′ index, we look at the peculiar behavior of the index for the craftsmen and foremen group. There is a steady increase in status of women among craftsmen and foremen throughout 1940-1960. However in 1960-1970, there is a complete reversal in trend with the C′ index going back to its 1940 value of 1.25. The New York index shows a similar, though not so sharp, decline for the 1960-1970 period from 0.96 to 0.93, both far below the status of women for that group in the United States.

Again, we may note that the erratic behavior of this index, as in the case of laborers, becomes less significant when the extremely low participation rate of women in the craftsmen and foremen group is considered. The C′ ″ index of women's status in the craftsmen and foremen group relative to their participation in the labor force has been almost stable through 1940-1970 reaching a "low-high" for this period of 0.10. The C′ ″ index at 0.06 and 0.07 for New York was even more stable (almost static) between 1960 and 1970.

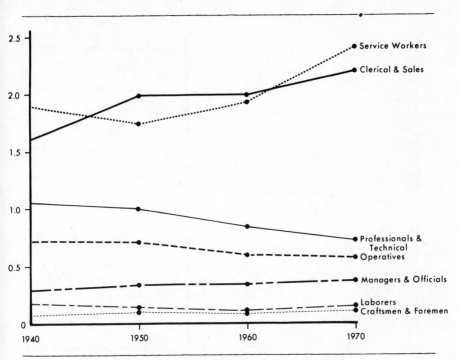

FIGURE 4: C′ ″ Indices for Seven Major Occupational Groupings,
U.S. 1940-1970

U.S. women's status among service workers has been improving steadily throughout 1940-1970 with a sharp increase in C′ to 1.01 in 1960-1970. The New York index showed a similar sharp increase in 1960-1970, taking on a value of 1.11. The C′ ″ index of women's status in service workers relative to their participation in the total work force behaves somewhat erratically throughout 1940-1970. C′ ″ declines in 1940-1950, increases in 1950-1960, and increases sharply in 1960-1970 to 2.42. The C′ ″ index for service workers in New York behaves in similar fashion to the U.S. index in 1960-1970, but reaches a lower level of 1.72. Given the increasing and high values of both the C′ and C′ ″ indices, we may conclude that women are entering higher SES-ranked service occupations.

U.S. women among managers and officials have shown a continuous improvement in their status, with sharp improvement in 1960-1970 to a C′ value of 1.18. New York women do not show such a sharp improvement, but are on par in standing with U.S. women with a C′ value of 1.15 in 1970. However, U.S. women's

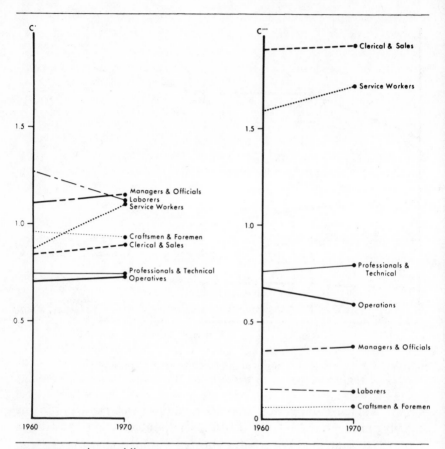

FIGURE 5: C' and C''' Indices for Seven Major Occupational Groupings,
N.Y. 1960-1970

status relative to female participation in the total work force remains
low for this group. The C''' index for U.S. has remained almost
stable throughout the 1940-1970 period, showing slight improvement to 0.37 in 1970. The New York index behavior for 1960-1970
is almost the same as for the United States, the New York C''' of
women's work status in managers and officials relative to total work
force participation reaching 0.37 in 1970. Although women are
improving their status among managers and officials, their increased
participation in the group is not enough to outweigh the increased
participation of women in the total labor force.

The remaining three C' indices for the United States are stable and
near static throughout 1940-1970. Women among professionals and

technical workers improved their status at a decelerating rate through 1940-1970, with C' reaching a value of 0.70 in 1960 and remaining there through 1970. The $C'\,''$ index for the professional and technical workers group relative to female participation in the total work force declined throughout 1940-1970, from 1.05 to 0.72. In contrast to this U.S. pattern, the New York index shows a slight increase in 1960-1970 reaching 0.79 from 0.76. Although the status of U.S. women among professional and technical workers has improved somewhat, this improvement was not enough to make up for the slow increases of occupations relative to total labor force participation rates.

The status of women among clerical and sales workers has been somewhat stable, declining in 1940-1960 and improving slightly in 1960-1970, at which point C' takes on the value 0.80. The status of women among this group is slightly higher in New York, with C' moving up to 0.89 in 1970. The $C'\,''$ index for clerical and sales workers is less stable and similar to that index for service workers. The participation of women in sales and clerical work is higher than their participation in the total labor force. Status of women relative to participation in the total labor force has been increasing, with $C'\,''$ reaching a value of 2.21. New York also shows a high value of 1.93 in 1970. Women seem to be entering sales and clerical jobs at the same low-ranked occupations as they have all along (C' has not changed much), although their participation in sheer numbers has greatly increased.

The U.S. C' index for operatives behaves much like the index for clerical and sales workers, with C' equal to 0.82 in 1970. The New York index shows the same slow growth between 1960 and 1970 as the U.S. index, but at lower values: C' for New York in 1970 is equal to 0.73. Looking, however, at the $C'\,''$ for operatives in the United States, one finds no resemblance in behavior to the clerical and sales index. The status of U.S. female operatives relative to participation in the work force is low and slowly decreasing throughout 1940-1970, reaching 0.57 in 1970. The New York $C'\,''$ index for operatives shows a decrease in 1960-1970 from 0.68 to 0.57. Among operatives, for the United States and in New York State, women seem to be losing ground.

This concludes the summary of status-index behavior. The 1960-1970 period seems to be a changing decade for women's status within occupational groups as evidenced by the rather drastic changes in four of the seven C' indices. Indices for New York did not parallel those for the United States, and we cannot see as clearly whether big changes are taking place. However, over the 1960-1970 period, we can compare the slopes of C' for the various occupations and note that most slopes for C' in New York occupations are all less in magnitude than those for the United States.

Status of women in occupations with respect to total labor force participation as measured by C' '' is much more stable than for status within groups. Women's position in sales, clerical, and service work is getting better, whereas status of female laborers and craftsmen and foremen (traditionally, very male occupations) relative to participation in the total labor force remains low.

U.S. status, as measured by C' '' women operatives, has declined and for managers has increased slightly, and in professional and technical occupations, it has declined. Quite disturbing is the performance of C' '' index for the professional and technical workers: women fared well in 1940, but lost out in 1950-1970; the index dropped from 0.99 in 1950 to 0.72 in 1970. Perhaps schools are not admitting as many qualified females as would be fair. Perhaps women do not enroll in certain fields in proportion to total school enrollment. More likely it is some combination of these factors, plus the family responsibility factor and discrimination, that are allowing women's status in the professional and technical groupings relative to participation in the total labor force to decline, and conversely causing the status of women in service, sales, and clerical groups, relative to total labor force participation, to improve.

By contrast, the status of New York State women during the 1960s in these same seven categories was relatively unchanged, except for the increase in C' for service workers from 0.87 to 1.11 and the decline in C' '' for operatives from 0.68 to 0.59.

Keeping in mind that our indices assume parity, or 1, as an ideal goal and that we have prepared a variety of measures but recommend C' (one that evaluates the changing status of women relative to that of men but adjusts for group size), we may conclude that:

(1) When all occupations are indexed, U.S. female status in 1970 was 0.73% of male status in 1970, up from 0.68% in 1940.

(2) These figures increase to 0.79 and 0.75%, respectively, when the 500+ occupations are squeezed into 99 SES categories, indicating that the procedure is viable for a social-indicator approach to female occupational-status mobility.

(3) For New York State, for the period 1960-1970, movement was in the same direction for all occupations, up from 0.72 to 0.75%, but female status relative to males remained unchanged by SES categories at 0.79%.

(4) Unadjusted for group size, the c' index for the U.S. moved in essentially the same direction for both sets of occupations (up in 1950, down in 1960, and up in 1970), but at substantially lower levels of parity.

(5) Unadjusted for group size, the c' index for New York State is unchanged for "all occupations" at 0.52% of parity, but drops from 0.58 to 0.54% for SES categories.

DISCUSSION

The above presentation traces the path of female occupational-status mobility for women from the decade of the 1940s, when they drastically altered their pattern of participation in the paid labor force (see Figure 1). A variety of indices were prepared to measure carefully any improvement that might have taken place. These indices took into account variations in income and education, the changed distribution of occupations, and changing labor market participation rates for both men and women. The results indicate that between 1940 and 1970 the status of women compared to men, as measured by indices that consider the overall distribution of occupations as well as their distribution within selected categories of occupations arranged hierarchically, has changed very little.

Other researchers have presented various economic models to explain this low status of women relative to men. Barbara Bergmann (1971), Valerie Oppenheimer (1970), and Juanita Kreps (1971) have suggested what I term the "demand-supply" model. It documents the fact that large numbers of women responded to the demand for workers during World War II and thereafter, particularly for white-collar workers. The smaller number that entered blue-collar occupations mainly withdrew during the 1950s, for reasons that have not yet been adequately studied. Barriers to training and entry into the higher professional and managerial ranks continued into the 1960s, despite efforts of many women's organizations to alter the existing occupational structure. The effects of legislation and governmental policy that forbid sex discrimination have not yet permeated throughout the labor market for a variety of reasons, including lax enforcement and feminine reluctance to claim equal rights. Implicit in this model are the notions that women are peripheral, secondary wage-earners who enter the labor market upon demand, preferably into part-time, low-level jobs that require reduced commitment and responsibility, and who willingly leave the labor market when demand declines or change jobs when the primary wage-earner must relocate.

Another viewpoint, that of the so-called "dual labor market" has been explicated by Peter Doeringer and Michael Piore (1971). Though elaborated to explain the lowly status of minority groups in the occupational structure, many feel that the dual market concept applies equally well to women. Its main thesis is that minorities seek and find jobs in that segment of the labor market where pay is low and unemployment and job turnover are high. (Bergmann also attributes the lesser status of women to their tendency to "crowd" into certain occupations such as teaching at the elementary and secondary level, clerical and sales work, health services, and so on.)

A recent economic study of discrimination against women in the United States (Tsuchegane and Dodge, 1973) concludes that male-female earnings differentials are caused by (1) market discrimination, curable in the short run; (2) social and cultural conditioning adverse to developing female capabilities, curable in the long run; and (3) physiological or psychological differences that may never be eliminated. (Meanwhile, sociological interest has moved from the concept of a "dual" to that of a "shared" role for women.) At a time when prices and unemployment are rising along with an increase in broken marriages and in the number of households headed by females,[7] women must articulate desired and desirable social and economic policy pertaining to their search for identity and independence.

In the short run, it must be recognized that women, even more than men, have a special interest in an economy where jobs are expanding. Despite the current bleak outlook, the service sector has growth and productivity potential, particularly in those occupations concerned with the refinement and extension of human capacities (education, medical care, research, and recreation) as distinguished from those that facilitate and effectuate the division of labor (transport, communication, finance, administration, wholesale and retail trade, and so forth). Ladders and lattices must be developed within emerging and merging occupations so that all workers can move vertically and/or horizontally, dependent upon motivation and capability rather than upon sex stereotyping. Counseling, training, and retraining will be of crucial importance to women, but not unimportant to men who currently average eight jobs during a 40-year work life. Especially important to working wives and mothers will be the provision of child-care facilities, at the workplace or in the community, integrated with work schedules that may differ for different occupational groups and priced so that the net return from work for pay is maximized. Improvements in the provision of other household services such as cooking, cleaning, marketing, laundry, and so on could also be made, and that would be particularly helpful to single-parented families.

Next in importance is the provision of part-time jobs for those women (and men) who may choose a combination of unpaid work in the household with paid work in the labor force, both of which contribute to the well-being of families and individuals and therefore have economic value not calculated in our national income estimates. Since the possibility for job development along nontraditional lines will be greatest in newly emerging occupations, counseling and training for potential employers is also in order.

Because activities of "liberated" women (and men) in the short run will determine long-run outcomes, a continuing high level of economic, social, and cultural pressure will be necessary for the evolution of a society in which all can freely choose from a variety of life styles. Only then can we decide whether differences are "sexually significant."

NOTES

1. Numerous studies show that U.S. women work mainly for the following reasons: to support themselves, to contribute to family living expenses, to help buy a house, and to contribute to children's education. In Canada, in 1964, in response to the question—"What are your reasons for wanting to work for pay?"—answers were distributed as follows:

Develop new interest	15%
Likes work environment	16
Sole support	18
Decreased family responsibilities	8
Develop new skills for future use	2
Keep skills up-to-date	3
Specific purchase	3
Education for family	4
Use skills	4
Supplement family income	27

2. For alternative assessments, see Gross (1955), Duncan and Duncan (1955), and Economic Report of the President (1973: 155-159).

3. See U.S. Department of Commerce (1963) for details of the methodology involved in arriving at these scores. Income and education are the primary inputs.

4. This is defined as a ratio of the percentage of women found in a particular occupation to the percentage of women in all occupations combined, for a given census year.

5. When the kth occupational group is the whole labor force, then there is no difference between the participation in the kth group and in the total labor force, a''' becomes only a measure of distribution and is equal to a'.

6. The 99 socioeconomic rankings had been tested for both 1950 and 1960 and found to have suitable stability for moving backward to 1940 and forward to 1970, for the U.S. data.

7. By March 1973, there were 1.5 million fewer children in families because of a steep decline in birthrates, but 650,000 more children had working mothers. See Waldman and Whitmore (1974).

REFERENCES

BERGMANN, B. (1971) "Occupational segregation: wages and profits when employers discriminate by race or sex." College Park: University of Maryland, Project on the Economics of Discrimination. (mimeo)

DOERINGER, P. and M. PIORE (1971) The Internal Labor Market. Lexington, Mass.: D. C. Heath.

DUNCAN, O. D. and B. DUNCAN (1955) "Index of dissimilarity." American Sociological Review 20 (April): 210-217.

Economic Report of the President (1973) January.

GROSS, E. (1955) "Plus ca change . . . ?" Social Problems 16: 198-208.

KREPS, J. (1971) Sex in the Marketplace. Baltimore: Johns Hopkins Press.

N.Y. State Department of Commerce (1974) New York Business Fact Book, Part 2.

N.Y. State Department of Labor (1973) Trends in Women's Occupations, New York State, 1960 to 1970. Labor Research Report No. 18, October.

OPPENHEIMER, V. (1970) The Female Labor Force in the United States. Berkeley: University of California, Population Monograph Series No. 5.

TOBIAS, S. (1973) "Whatever happened to Rosie the Riveter?" New York: MSS Information Corp., Module 9.

TSUCHEGANE, R. and N. DODGE (1973) Economic Discrimination Against Women. Lexington, Mass.: D. C. Heath.

U.S. Department of Commerce (1963) "Methodology and scores of socioeconomic status (SES)." Washington, D.C.: Working Paper No. 15.

U.S. Department of Labor (1971) "Marital and family characteristics of workers." Washington, D.C.: Special Labor Force Report No. 144, March.

WALDMAN, E. and R. WHITMORE (1974) "Children of working mothers." Monthly Labor Review (May): 50-57.

WALDMAN, E. and A. M. YOUNG (1971) "Marital and family characteristics of workers, March 1970." Monthly Labor Review (March).

APPENDIX A

Twelve Measures of Female/Male Occupational Mobility: United States—1940, 1950, 1960, and 1970[1]

		a'	$a''^{\,'2}$	b'	$b''^{\,'}$	c'	$c''^{\,'}$
1940	All	0.59	0.59	1.16	1.16	0.51	0.51
	SES	0.65	0.65	1.14	1.14	0.58	0.58
	1	0.56	0.82	1.31	1.06	0.43	0.77
	2	0.97	0.37	1.00	1.23	0.96	0.30
	3	0.68	1.02	1.25	0.99	0.54	1.03
	4	1.52	0.12	0.99	1.30	1.54	0.09
	5	0.78	0.69	1.07	1.11	0.73	0.62
	6	0.52	1.12	1.75	0.95	0.30	1.18
	7	2.58	0.24	0.96	1.26	2.70	0.19
1950	All	0.63	0.63	1.17	1.17	0.54	0.54
	SES	0.68	0.68	1.14	1.14	0.60	0.60
	1	0.66	0.85	1.23	1.08	0.54	0.79
	2	0.99	0.43	1.00	1.26	0.99	0.34
	3	0.65	1.11	1.38	0.96	0.47	1.16
	4	1.66	0.17	0.98	1.42	1.70	0.12
	5	0.80	0.70	1.07	1.13	0.75	0.62
	6	0.60	1.12	1.57	0.94	0.39	1.19
	7	2.07	0.25	0.96	1.32	2.16	0.19
1960	All	0.59	0.59	1.21	1.21	0.48	0.48
	SES	0.63	0.63	1.19	1.19	0.53	0.53
	1	0.68	0.77	1.19	1.13	0.57	0.68
	2	1.01	0.43	1.00	1.30	1.01	0.33
	3	0.71	1.19	1.38	0.91	0.51	1.31
	4	1.79	0.15	0.98	1.50	1.83	0.10
	5	0.75	0.60	1.09	1.20	0.69	0.50
	6	0.73	1.35	1.45	0.82	0.50	1.65
	7	1.97	0.20	0.96	1.33	2.04	0.15
1970	All	0.66	0.66	1.22	1.22	0.54	0.54
	SES	0.69	0.69	1.19	1.19	0.58	0.58
	1	0.68	0.70	1.21	1.19	0.56	0.59
	2	1.22	0.52	0.96	1.33	1.28	0.39
	3	0.80	1.31	1.35	0.80	0.60	1.64
	4	1.50	0.19	0.97	1.58	1.54	0.12
	5	0.79	0.63	1.09	1.26	0.73	0.50
	6	0.98	1.52	1.03	0.67	0.96	2.28
	7	1.09	0.22	0.99	1.47	1.10	0.15

Appendix A (continued)

		A'	$A''{}'^{3}$	B'	$B''{}'$	C'	$C''{}'$
1940	All	0.75	0.75	1.10	1.10	0.68	0.68
	SES	0.80	0.80	1.08	1.08	0.75	0.75
	1	0.71	1.04	1.20	0.99	0.59	1.05
	2	0.94	0.36	1.01	1.26	0.94	0.29
	3	0.91	1.37	1.07	0.85	0.85	1.61
	4	1.24	0.10	0.99	1.36	1.25	0.07
	5	0.89	0.79	1.04	1.09	0.86	0.72
	6	0.70	1.51	1.46	0.80	0.48	1.89
	7	1.89	0.18	0.98	1.33	1.94	0.14
1950	All	0.77	0.77	1.10	1.10	0.70	0.70
	SES	0.83	0.83	1.07	1.07	0.77	0.77
	1	0.77	1.00	1.15	0.99	0.67	0.99
	2	0.97	0.42	1.01	1.26	0.96	0.33
	3	0.90	1.53	1.11	0.77	0.81	1.99
	4	1.33	0.13	0.99	1.38	1.35	0.10
	5	0.90	0.78	1.04	1.10	0.86	0.71
	6	0.76	1.42	1.32	0.82	0.57	1.74
	7	1.54	0.19	0.98	1.36	1.58	0.14
1960	All	0.74	0.74	1.13	1.13	0.65	0.65
	SES	0.77	0.77	1.12	1.12	0.69	0.69
	1	0.79	0.88	1.13	1.06	0.70	0.83
	2	1.00	0.42	1.00	1.30	1.00	0.33
	3	0.89	1.48	1.15	0.75	0.77	1.98
	4	1.44	0.12	0.99	1.46	1.46	0.08
	5	0.86	0.69	1.05	1.16	0.81	0.59
	6	0.79	1.46	1.35	0.76	0.59	1.92
	7	1.52	0.16	0.98	1.43	1.55	0.11
1970	All	0.82	0.82	1.12	1.12	0.73	0.73
	SES	0.86	0.86	1.08	1.08	0.79	0.79
	1	0.79	0.81	1.14	1.12	0.70	0.72
	2	1.15	0.49	0.97	1.33	1.18	0.37
	3	0.92	1.50	1.15	0.68	0.80	2.21
	4	1.24	0.15	0.99	1.54	1.25	0.10
	5	0.87	0.68	1.06	1.20	0.82	0.57
	6	1.01	1.55	0.99	0.64	1.01	2.42
	7	1.14	0.23	0.99	1.49	1.16	0.15

1. Key to subheadings: All = overall individual occupations excluding farm workers, SES = overall groups of occupations—grouping by SES score, 1 = professional and technical, 2 = managers and officials, 3 = clerical and sales, 4 = craftsmen and foremen, 5 = operatives, 6 = service workers, 7 = laborers.

2. Formulae for a' and $a''{}'$, b' and $b''{}'$, and c' and $c''{}'$ yield identical results when taken over all of labor force.

3. Formulae for A' and $A''{}'$, B' and $B''{}'$, and C' and $C''{}'$ yield identical results when taken over all of labor force.

APPENDIX B

Graphical Presentation of Indices

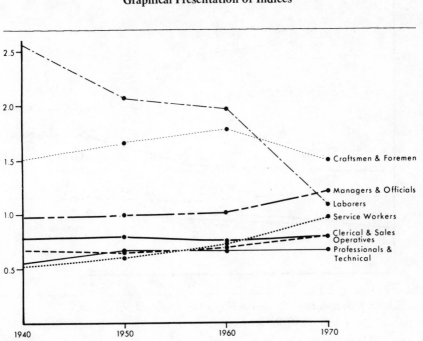

FIGURE B-1: a′ Indices for Seven Major Occupational Groupings,
U.S. 1940-1970

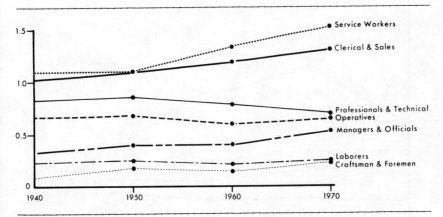

FIGURE B-2: a′′′ Indices for Seven Major Occupational Groupings,
U.S. 1940-1970

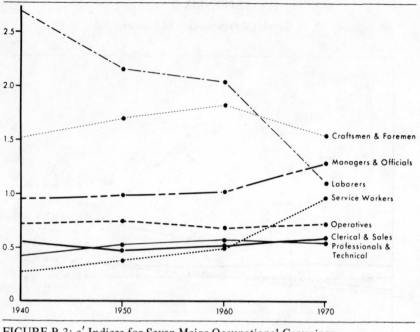

FIGURE B-3: c′ Indices for Seven Major Occupational Groupings,
            U.S. 1940-1970

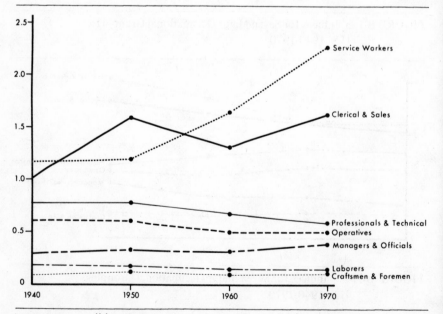

FIGURE B-4: c″′ Indices for Seven Major Occupational Groupings,
            U.S. 1940-1970

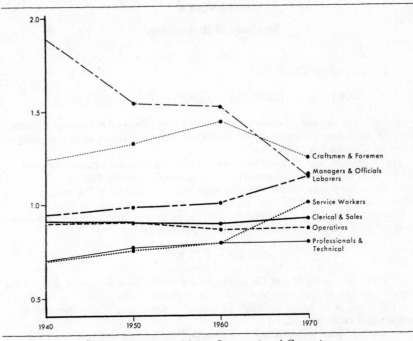

FIGURE B-5: A′ Indices for Seven Major Occupational Groupings,
U.S. 1940-1970

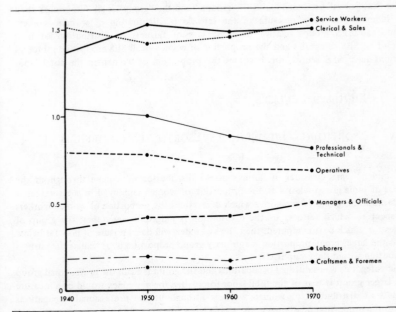

FIGURE B-6: A″′ Indices for Seven Major Occupational Groupings,
U.S. 1940-1970

APPENDIX C
Summary of Methodology

$$a' = \Sigma(f_i/1_i) \cdot SES/(\Sigma(F/L)SES_i)$$

$$A' = \Sigma SQRT[(1_i/(1 - 1_i/L))(f_i/1_i)SES_i/\Sigma SQRT(1_i/(1 - 1_i/L))(F/L)SES_i]$$

A' and a' are measures of fairness of the distribution of women throughout a selected group of job categories relative to the proportion of women employed in the group of categories for which it is computed.

The "categories" can be individual occupations, some grouping of occupations by an SES score, or some grouping of occupations by a major characteristic. The "group" can be a major occupational type, or even the total labor force. For example, if the "categories" are individual occupations and the "group" is all professional occupations, the a' index would be a measure of the fairness of distribution of women workers throughout the professional occupations relative to the proportion of women professionals.

$$a'' = a'/1 + (1 - a')$$

a'' is a measure of fairness of the distribution of women throughout some group of job categories relative to the proportion of women employed in the group of categories for which a'' is computed and to a measure of fairness of distribution of men throughout the same group of categories.

Because this index is constructed in a "shortcut" method it does not always result in a "good" measure of fairness of male distribution. This in turn causes the a'' measure to not always be a "good" measure of fairness of distribution.

If the "categories" are individual SES "groups" and the "group" is all SES groups, then the a'' index would be a measure of the fairness of distribution of women workers throughout all SES groups relative to a measure of fairness of distribution of men throughout all SES categories and the proportion of women in all SES groups (i.e., since all occupations have SES scores, this becomes the proportion of women in the total labor force).

$$a''' = \Sigma(f_i/1_i)SES_i/\Sigma(F/L)SES_i$$
$${}_k {}_k$$

$$A''' = \Sigma SQRT[(1_i/(1 - 1_i/L_k))(f_i/1_i)SES_i/\Sigma SQRT(1_i/(1 - 1_i/L_k))(F/L)SES_i]$$
$${}_k {}_k$$

A''' and a''' are measures of fairness of the distribution of women throughout the categories of some group relative to the proportion of women employed in the total labor force. Because the group of categories which determines the proportion of women workers with respect to which fairness of the distribution is judged is larger than the group of categories for which a' is computed, then the a''' index will be a measure of how far below or above the larger group proportion the primary group proportion is, as well as the fairness of distribution within the group itself.

If the categories are individual occupations and the group is again the professional group and the larger group is that of the total labor force, then the a''' index would be a measure of fairness of distribution of women workers throughout the professional occupations relative to the proportion of women in the whole labor force.

$$b' = \Sigma(m_i/1_i) \cdot SES_i/\Sigma(M/L)SES_i$$

$$B' = \Sigma SQRT[(1_i/(1 - 1_i/L))(m_i/1_i)SES_i/\Sigma SQRT(1_i/(1 - 1_i/L))(M/L)SES_i]$$

B' and b' are measures of fairness of the distribution of men throughout the categories of some group relative to the proportion of men employed in the group of categories.

All upper-case indices take into account the importance of occupational size.

$$b''' = \Sigma(m_i/1_i)SES_i/\Sigma(M/L)SES_i$$
$$kk$$

$$B''' = [\Sigma SQRT(1_i/(1 - 1_i/L_k)(m_i/1_i)SES_i/\Sigma SQRT(1_i/(1 - 1_i/L))(M/L)SES_i]$$
$$kk$$

B''' and b''' are measures of fairness of the distribution of men throughout the categories of some group relative to the proportion of men employed in the total labor force.

$$c' = a'/b'$$

$$C' = A'/B'$$

C' and c' are measures of fairness of the distribution of women throughout the categories of some group relative to measure of fairness of distribution of men throughout the categories used in computing c' and to the proportion of women employed in the group of categories for which c' and C' are computed. C' is superior to c' because it accounts for occupational size.

$$c''' = a'''/b'''$$

$$C''' = A'''/B'''$$

C''' and c''' are measures of fairness of the distribution of women throughout the categories of some group relative to a measure of fairness of the distribution of men throughout the categories of the group used in computing c''' and to the proportion of women employed in the total labor force. (The measure of fairness of distribution of men was computed relative to the proportion of men in the total labor force.)

If the "categories" are individual occupations and the "group" is the sales and clerical occupations, then the c''' and C''' indices would be measures of fairness of distribution of women workers throughout the sales and clerical occupations relative to a measure of fairness of the distribution of men workers and to the proportion of women in the whole labor force.

All measures theoretically range between 0 and infinity, with the exception of a'' which ranges between minus and plus infinity. The usual range is between 0 and 2 with indices occasionally taking on values beyond 2.

9

WORKING WIVES AND
FAMILY INCOME

CAROLYN SHAW BELL

References to the increasing number of women in the labor force abound these days, and more and more attention has been focused on the growing number of married women and married mothers who work in paid jobs. Yet little analysis has been devoted to the impact of these women's employment on their families' income. Most of the discussion has dealt with family structure: whether or not children are being neglected, whether women have two obligations (one to the job and the other to the home), whether the nuclear family is breaking up or the role of the husband/father is changing. The economic analysis which does exist has been directed to the occupational distribution of the new group of working women, and to various measures of occupational and income differences which might indicate economic discrimination. Very few calculations of the income earned by these women, or of its distribution, exist.[1]

This is a matter of some surprise, actually, for normally when a significant group of people become earners their purchasing power is avidly sought by producers and sellers looking for new markets.[2] Some market analysts may have calculated the rise in total family income without realizing the extent to which that increase stems from the earnings of married women. Other market researchers, depending on the family as the unit of analysis, may have ignored the nature of individual contributions to total family income in favor of inquiries as to the disposition of that income.

THE AVAILABLE DATA

To the question "How much do married women earn?" one answer recurs: about one-quarter of total family income. Nor has this fraction changed very much over time. Occasionally one finds some amplification, as in the following Bureau of Labor Statistics (1972: 8) statement:

> The overall relative contribution a working wife made to family income did not change and was about the same as it has been for at least a decade. In 1970, the median proportion of income contributed by the wife's earnings was 27%, ranging from 39% for wives who had worked full time all year to 16% for those who had worked less than a full year or all year at part-time jobs. About half of all working wives supplied between 20 and 50% of their family's income, while only 2% supplied 75% or more. Median family income in 1970 was about $9,175 when the wife did not work, $11,940 if she worked at all, and $13,960 if she worked all year at a full time job.

But a quotation like this raises more questions than can be answered with the existing data. Table 1 shows the frequency distribution summarized in this description; what other inferences can be drawn from this set of figures besides those given in the quotation? First, the averages do not reflect the significance of the wife's contribution, better seen by comparing median incomes for families with and without working wives. For example, although women who held some employment contributed only 16% of total family income, median income for these families was 23% higher

TABLE 1: Share of Family Income Accounted for by Working Wives' Earnings, 1970

Contribution to Family Income	Distribution of Working Wives*	
	Total, incl. Part-time	Year-round Full-time
Under 10%	20.8%	1.9%
10-20%	17.1	5.7
20-30%	18.2	18.2
30-40%	18.4	28.1
40-50%	13.4	24.6
50-75%	9.8	17.5
75% and over	2.4	4.1

*Number of wives with work experience totals 100%.

Source: U.S. Department of Labor, Bureau of Labor Statistics, *Special Labor Force Report* 130, "Marital and Family Characteristics of Workers, March 1970."

than in families with nonworking wives. Again, although full-time working wives provided 39% of total family income, the impact of this contribution on the total can be sizeable. In fact, families in which the wife has a full-time job enjoy a median income more than 50% higher than those where the wife is not employed outside the home.

Finally, some families of working wives depend substantially on their earnings. The quotation above refers to the fact that "only 2% supplied 75%" of total family income. But this 2% represents over 400,000 families. Two and one-half million *more* families get over half their total income from women's earnings. And these figures exclude the six million families lacking an adult male, where the working woman is solely responsible for the economic support of others.

The Department of Labor quotation also prompts the question as to the meaningfulness of *any* average calculation of this sort. How useful is either the median or mean as an abbreviation of the frequency distribution it represents?[3] The complete answer requires a close look at two income distributions, not one.

First, the distribution of families according to income levels obviously makes a given figure—say, 27% of family income—take on new meaning. Table 2 presents the data from which the averages in Table 1 were drawn. It shows, for example, that one out of five working wives earned between 20 and 30% of their family's total income. (They were also in the median income class.) But it also shows that a *higher* proportion of wives contributed this proportion of total family income among those with incomes over $15,000. Such working wives number almost one out of four.

Women whose employment provides over half the total family income also required detailed attention. Only one out of ten working women falls into this classification, but they are far more numerous at low-income levels. Over one out of four families with incomes below $5,000 relies on the earnings of a wife for over half the total family income. That a given percentage or dollar sum counts for more at low-income levels than at high ones has long been common knowledge to economists. It enables them to describe certain taxes as "regressive" because they take a larger share of income from low-income people than from high-income people. The same reasoning suggests that an extra dollar of income provides a larger percentage increase to low-income families than to high-income

TABLE 2: Earnings of Married Women (Husband Present) as a Percentage of Family Income in 1969[a]

Total Wives With Work Experience / Family Income	Median Percent Family Income Accounted for by Wife's Earnings	Percent distribution of wives by percent of family income accounted for by wife's earnings								
		Total	Less than 5.0	5.0 to 9.9	10. to 19.9	20. to 29.9	30. to 39.9	40. to 49.9	50. to 74.9	75.0 & over
Total		100	10.6	9.8	17.1	19.0	18.8	12.8	9.4	2.4
Under $2000	21.9	100	22.5	9.1	15.8	13.4	9.1	3.3	8.6	18.2
$2000–2999	24.6	100	13.7	14.1	16.0	13.4	12.4	6.9	11.8	11.8
$3000–4999	26.3	100	11.0	12.4	18.1	13.7	10.3	8.6	14.8	11.2
$5000–6999	24.2	100	12.7	13.1	18.4	13.6	10.2	11.4	15.4	5.2
$7000–9999	23.8	100	13.0	11.8	18.9	16.3	13.9	12.8	10.7	2.5
$10,000–14,999	28.2	100	9.6	8.5	15.7	19.6	22.4	15.1	8.4	.6
$15,000 and over	26.9	100	8.5	7.6	17.0	24.4	24.2	12.0	5.8	.4
Median Family Income	—	$11,482	$10,265	$10,006	$11,125	$12,629	$12,948	$11,824	$9,611	$5,643

[a]Data relate to the civilian non institutional population and include only those families in which the wife had paid work experience. Therefore, they are not comparable with data published in earlier years.

Source: U.S. Department of Labor, Bureau of Labor Statistics, Special Labor Force Report 130, "Marital and Family Characteristics of Workers, March 1970," U.S. Government Printing Office, 1971; Table U, p. A-24.

families. Thus, a given sum earned by a working wife represents a more significant contribution to families at low-income levels than at high.

Table 2 does not complete the picture, however, for it lacks any frequency distribution of the amounts married women earn. Often quoted is the median earnings of $3,000. Like the 27% average, the figure carries little meaning. To a family with total income of $6,000, $3,000 represents quite a different sum than to a family whose income totals $60,000. And to say that half the working wives earn more than $3,000 and half less than this amount conveys very little information about their economic contribution. For example, among married men earning between $4,000 and $7,000 in 1971, one out of five had a working wife. The median earnings of these women lay between $2,000 and $3,000. This represents not 27% of the total family income, but one-third. The wife earned 50% of what the husband did. Five percent of the wives earned *more* than their husbands did. Clearly, the distribution of income needs to be compared to the distribution of wives' earnings.

A complete analysis requires four cross-classified distributions, with various ratios calculated: (1) the set of earnings of working wives by total family income; (2) earnings of husbands by total family income; (3) income of the wife by total family income; and (4) income of the husband by total family income. Such figures would make it possible to verify two widely held assumptions—that "most of" total family income comes from wages, and that the husband is the breadwinner, i.e., that his earnings represent "most of" total family income.

To say that wages make up most of family income describes two well-known characteristics of the American economy. Labor income, or earnings from work, constitutes four-fifths of total national income. (The official statistics would combine "Compensation of Employees" and "Proprietors and Rental Income," because the latter partially represents labor earnings rather than any return to capital or to management.) This fraction has fluctuated between 75 and 80% since the first year for which data are available, not because of structural changes altering the share of income going to labor, but because of cyclical changes affecting profits and property income.

It is also true that 90% of all families receive labor income. The census data supporting this statement (U.S. Bureau of Census, 1972: 94-95) classify earnings into wages and salaries and self-employment

TABLE 3: Source of Family Income, by Income Decile and Race,[a] 1966
(percentage distribution of dollars received by families in each decile)

Total Family Income Deciles	Earnings[b]						Income from Capital[c]		Mixed Labor-Capital[d]		Transfer Payments[e]	
	of Head		of Wife		of Other Members							
	Negro	Non-Negro	Negro	Non-Negro	Negro	Non-Negro	Negro	Non-Negro	Negro	Non-Negro	Negro	Non-Negro
All	66	62	13	9	5	4	2	6	2	11	12	8
Lowest tenth	45	14	2	4	2	2	*	10	1	−5	50	75
Second tenth	57	27	6	4	3	1	1	8	2	10	31	50
Third tenth	68	45	8	5	3	3	4	11	2	7	15	29
Fourth tenth	71	58	6	6	6	3	1	5	2	10	14	18
Fifth tenth	68	67	15	8	6	2	1	4	3	9	7	10
Sixth tenth	72	71	15	9	3	3	1	4	1	7	8	6
Seventh tenth	70	69	14	9	9	5	2	4	1	6	4	7
Eighth tenth		66		13		5		4		8		4
Ninth tenth	63	68	25	13	6	5	3	3	2	8	1	3
Highest tenth		58		8		5		11		17		1

a "Non-Negro" includes approximately 2 per cent nonwhite non-Negro.
b Includes wage, salary, professional, and other self-employment income.
c Includes income from rent, interest, dividends, and trust funds.
d Includes farm income, unincorporated business income, and income from roomers and boarders.
e Includes Social Security, unemployment compensation, public welfare, veteran's benefits and other transfer income.

Source: Katona, George and James N. Morgan, Jay Schmiedeskamp, and John A. Sonquist, 1967 Survey of Consumer Finances, Survey Research Center, Institute for Social Research, University of Michigan, 1968, pp. 13–14.

income, which is further classified as nonfarm and farm. Of some 53 million families in 1971, 4,939,000 had no current earnings. Of 16,311,000 "unrelated individuals" only 6 million had no earned income. Most people receiving so-called "unearned income" have retired from the labor force and live on social security or pension benefits or on public assistance. Very few rentiers live in the United States.

Finally, for most families labor income (earned income) makes up the preponderance of total income. The *1967 Survey of Consumer Finances* (Katona et al., 1968) provides data on the percentage distribution of family income by sources. Table 3 reproduces these findings for families classified by income deciles; some differences appear, by income and by race. Among Negro families, earned income plays a much more important role than among whites, for whom transfer payments in the lowest income deciles and property income at all income levels provide substantial contributions to total family income. However, earned income amounted to over half the total for all families, except for those Negroes in the lowest income decile and the whites in the two lowest classes.

Hence, it is correct to say that in this country most family income comes from what people earn. Wages loom large in any global total: family incomes, families, or sources of income. Is it equally correct to say that husbands' income (which now becomes tantamount to husbands' earnings) represents "most of" the family income? This notion, unqualified, justifies the prevalent terms of "breadwinner," "primary earner," "the man with a family to support," and defining the man as the "head" of any household. To verify the statement that husbands earn "most of" the family income requires aggregate calculations corresponding to comparisons made earlier between labor income and total income.

First, what proportions of national income and personal income go to men? Only the Census Bureau reports income received by sex, and the data refer to persons 14 years old and over so that the total falls somewhat short of either personal income or national income. In 1971 (U.S. Bureau of the Census, 1972), 119,000,000 persons reported income; the mean was $5,878. Some 66,000,000 men, or approximately 56%, received income, with a mean of $7,892. The total income accruing to men, therefore, represented at least three-quarters of all income received by persons.

The second question, how many *families* receive income from men, is easier. In 88% of the cases, a man is the head of the household.[4] Only about one out of ten such men provide no earnings. The third aggregate question, what percentage of families receive the major share of income from men's earnings, will be discussed in more detail below. But clearly all three calculations support the statement that "most families" depend on the man of the family for "most income."

It does not follow, however, that the *significance* of women's earnings, particularly the earnings of married women, can be sufficiently expressed by such statements. No one knows the number of families for whom the wife's earnings are in some sense crucial. To count these families is impossible because of the personal circumstances involved.

A moderately well-off family, supported entirely by the husband and father, may face a sudden financial crisis due to emergency medical care, uninsured loss, or other unexpected catastrophes. If the amount involved can be met entirely or substantially by the wife's earnings, to designate the dollar sum she contributes as "only a fraction of total family income" disguises its economic significance. Likewise, if a man supporting his family suddenly finds himself unemployed, his wife's earnings may not consist of merely a minor share of the year's income. If she can support the family for any length of time, her husband will have that period to use in seeking better employment opportunities or in considering alternative jobs without the immediate pressure to take the first offer. The economic contribution of the wife in such cases cannot be measured by a simple ratio of her dollar earnings to total family earnings or total family income.

These examples remain anecdotal; no evidence exists to indicate their prevalence among the 53 million American families. Instead, the significance of the wife's earnings has been commonly measured by gross figures of the percentage of total income or total earnings provided. It is possible, however, to improve the average, so often cited, that only 27% of family income is contributed by working wives. A sharper insight comes from several distributions of family income which reveal the varying importance of women's contributions.

Any move from the microeconomic analysis of income to aggregate figures requires looking at the distribution of income. In attempting to analyze the *sources* of family income, figures on distribution become critical. But an immediate problem arises because of the different distributions of income that exist. Income is earned by individuals, but most individuals live in families. Thus, two units of analysis coexist: the individual and the family.

Most of the ambiguity and ignorance about women's earnings, women's contributions to the economy, and, for that matter, the economic status of women stem from the automatic identification of a woman as a wife and mother—that is, as the female adult of a family. Women have been generally defined in terms of belonging to a family, the single woman being usually regarded as the exception, the oddity, the abnormal. No such approach to men exists. Most data and their analysis refer to men in their own right as individuals, and much material about men in families has never been gathered. The family unit as a unit of economic analysis requires thoughtful reconsideration, but this chapter will not undertake the task.

We will, however, look closely at how the Bureau of the Census (1972: 9) defines a family, since the data to be presented come from that office—specifically, its *Current Population Reports:*

> The term called "family" as used in this report, refers to a group of two or more persons related by blood, marriage, or adoption and residing together: all such persons are considered as members of the same family. Thus if the son of the head of the household and the son's wife are in the household, they are treated as part of the head's family. On the other hand, a lodger and his wife, not related to the head of the household or an unrelated servant and his wife are considered as additional families, and not as part of the household head's family.

It is such groups of people who form the basic units of many income tabulations. What each individual family member contributes to total family income nowhere appears, although some figures exist on the number of earners and their relation to the head of the family. Other income tabulations refer to the individual worker as the basic unit, but there is no link between these individuals and their families. Both these deficiencies serve to perpetuate the picture of family resources discussed above. The Census Bureau itself displays some entertaining misconceptions.

The *Current Population Reports* series on consumer income (U.S. Bureau of the Census, 1972: 3) contains the following statement: "Since most families derive their income entirely or largely from the employment of the family head, *his* employment situation and work experience, and occupation are important factors in determining the level of family income" (italics added). Table 30 in that same report lists the number of earners in 1971 with their relationships to the head of the family. Of the 53 million families, only 17.8 million (37%) "derive their income entirely" from the earnings of the head of the family. This number is not equivalent to "most families." Contrary to the text, the data show that most families do *not* derive their income entirely from the family head. Using the masculine pronoun, furthermore, reinforces the notion that this person, the head of the family, is a man. The entire sentence lends credence to the concept of the man as primary earner, the breadwinner, the family supporter, and so on. The reference to families who derive their income "largely" from the employment of the family head may possibly be accurate, depending on the definition of "largely." The text offers neither details nor explanation.

Two methods exist, however, to evaluate the contribution of the earnings of working wives to their families' well-being. Scattered data on the earnings of husbands and wives enable the wife's earnings to be calculated as a percentage of total husband-wife earnings, by levels of family earnings. Other data provide figures on wives' earnings as a percentage of family income (which of course differs from husband-wife total earnings). To demolish the myth that "most families depend entirely or primarily on" the earnings of the man of the house, four different tables follow which show the diversity of family income sources.

Table 4 lists working wives by five occupational groups and provides figures on year-round and less than year-round employment. It should be emphasized that the data refer only to working *wives.* In 1971, 31 million *women* earned income; Table 4 includes only the 20 million of these who belonged to families where both husband and wife earned income. Perhaps most unfamiliar, but certainly most significant, is the fact that year-round employment is the norm for women as for men. Of all working wives, 52% worked 50 to 52 weeks in 1971. Year-round workers outnumbered part-year workers in each of the four occupational groups listed, although professional women tended to work year-round more than women in any other kind of job. That manufacturing includes many highly seasonal jobs helps explain for women (as it does for men) the higher rate of part-time employment among craftsmen and operatives. The category of "service workers" contains a large number of private domestic or household employees whose work also tends to be

TABLE 4: Weeks Worked in 1971 by Wife (for Families in which Both Husband and Wife Had Earnings), by Occupation of Wife

Work Experience of Wife	U.S. Total	Current Occupation Group of Wife				
		Profess. & Managerial Workers	Clerical & Sales Workers	Craftsmen & Operatives	Service	Others
Number (1,000's)	20,353	3,447	6,667	2,724	3,038	4,447
Total	100.00	100.00	100.00	100.00	100.00	100.00
50 to 52 Weeks	10,652.62	2,672.33	4,390.70	1,461.96	1,583.95	735.06
As % of Total	52.34	76.86	65.86	53.67	52.14	16.53
27 to 49 Weeks	4,253.78	540.53	1,277.27	751.02	727.22	939.80
As % of Total	20.90	15.55	19.16	27.57	24.60	21.13
1 to 26 Weeks	5,446.60	459.31	999.03	510.75	706.84	2,768.02
As % of Total	26.76	13.21	14.98	18.75	23.27	62.24

Source: Calculated from Table 68, *Current Population Reports*, Series P-60, No. 85; December 1972—Consumer Income.

highly seasonal or consists of temporary jobs. Year-round workers in "clerical" and "sales" positions number two-thirds of the total, well above the percentage for manufacturing and service workers, but below that for "professional" and "managerial" employees.

The data suggest that most families with working wives expect such women to contribute regularly, with 52 paychecks a year, and that those expectations are fulfilled. These facts do not support the claim that most women have a much less strong "attachment" to the labor force than men, and separation rates provide additional data on this point (U.S. Department of Labor, 1972: 182-183). Of the people who had quit a job in the previous 12 months, 51% of the women, but 40% of the men, gave "school or home responsibilities" as their reason. Some may find the difference between the two groups unexpectedly small. The pressure of economic conditions weighed more heavily on the women: over 20% of them reported slack work and seasonal or temporary unemployment as reasons for leaving their jobs, while only 17% of the men were so affected. Such figures round out the findings of unemployment surveys (U.S. Department of Labor, 1972: 37) that four out of five women seek full-time and year-round work.

The permanent income hypothesis suggests further implications of the possibility that wives' earnings provide a dependable or regular source of income. If one family earner receives sporadic payments, family spending patterns may be stabilized by the presence of such "regular" income. Examples include a real estate broker married to a school teacher, an artist married to a sales clerk, a lawyer with an independent practice married to a corporation lawyer. Data to verify this hypothesis or to measure the size of the "regular" earnings contributed to family income by working wives do not exist, but some approximation can be drawn from figures on wives' earnings and family income. Table 5 presents data by age of husband, Table 6 by occupation, and Table 7 by weeks worked during the year.

First, Table 5 shows clearly that families supported only by the husband's earnings are in the minority. At every age below 65 families with both partners employed outnumber those dependent solely on the man, although among younger couples the difference is slight. But it is in the younger age group that the percentage of working wives is growing most rapidly, so that ten years from now the picture may differ. More black families than white contain two working partners, and the income of such families exceeds that of those supported solely by the husband by a wider margin than for whites. The earnings of wives form a significant contribution to median family income at all ages. It may not be unreasonable to infer that these earnings, as a share of the total, appear sufficiently important for the majority of wives in all husband-wife families to work at least until the age of 65.

Table 6 shows the contribution of working wives classified by occupations. The 20 million families shown combine the two racial groups of Table 5, but include only those families where both husband and wife are employed. This is the same group that was analyzed in Table 4. As in almost every detailed set of figures, the

TABLE 5: Number of Families and Median Income by Earnings Status in 1971 of Husband and Wife, by Age and Race of Husband

	Husband-Wife Families							
	White				Negro			
	Husband Only Earner		Husband, Wife Both Earners		Husband Only Earner		Husband, Wife Both Earners	
Age of Husband	Number of Families	Median Income	Number of Families	Median Income	Number of Families	Median Income	Number of Families	Median Income
Total	14,468	$ 9,900	18,549	$13,025	831	$6,742	1,804	$10,374
Under 35 years	5,308	9,411	6,656	10,819	314	6,986	637	9,740
35 to 44 years	3,062	11,601	4,016	14,073	152	7,234	458	10,763
45 to 54 years	2,239	10,549	4,459	15,551	158	7,279	427	11,646
55 to 64 years	2,458	9,968	2,852	14,254	129	6,329	218	9,950
65 years & over	1,401	6,205	593	9,821	78	3,078	64	*

Source: Tables 65, 66, *Current Population Reports*, Series P-60, No. 85, December 1972, Consumer Income.
  *Base too small to be reliable.

TABLE 6: Mean Family Income and Mean Earnings of Wife, 1971 (for Husband-Wife Families in which Both Had Earnings), by Wife's Occupation

Current Occupation Group of Wife	Number (1,000's)	Mean Family Income	Mean Earnings of Wife	Earnings As % of Family Income
U.S. Total	20,353	$13,910.91	$3,657.78	26.30
White Collar Workers	10,144	16,004.83	5,932.08	37.76
Professional & Managerial Workers	3,477	17,825.57	6,018.25	33.76
Clerical & Sales Workers	6,667	15,055.63	4,174.18	27.72
Craftsmen & Operatives	2,724	12,447.10	3,182.65	30.63
Service Workers	3,038	11,292.03	2,473.59	21.91
Other	4,447	11,820.21	3,939.26	33.33

Source: Calculated from *Current Population Reports;* Series P-60, No. 85; December 1972—Consumer Income.

data fail to substantiate the widespread use of "one-quarter" or "27%" as the average contribution of working wives to family income. First, the mean amount of earnings by the working wife correlates with mean family income within occupational categories varying from roughly $2,500 to $6,000 over an income range of $11,000 to $18,000. The share of family income represented by these earnings, however, varies significantly between occupations. The highest percentage contribution comes from 3.5 million professional and managerial workers averaging $6,000 a year, who provide about 38% of the total family income. The lowest contribution (averaging $2,500 and about 22% of family income) came from service workers, who number just over 3 million. The ratios shown here may be deceptive; in fact, few families may exist in which a married woman craft worker earns 30% of the family total, or in which a saleswoman provides 28% of her family's income. But the data clearly warn that overall percentages can be ambiguous. The smallest contribution, 22% and $2,500, probably weighs far more importantly than the largest because it is part of a much smaller total income figure.

Table 7, which again incorporates the racial variable, reinforces these findings. Whether or not these percentages reflect any existing family, they deserve careful perusal. The conventional myth refers to working wives as part-time, peripheral employees; but the data show

TABLE 7: Percentage of Families, Mean Family Income, and Mean Earnings in 1971 of Wives in Husband-Wife Families (Both Earners), by Race of Husband, and Weeks Worked by Wife in 1971

Work Experience of Wife	White				Negro			
	Percent of Families*	Mean Family Income	Wife's Earnings	Percent of Income	Percent of Families*	Mean Family Income	Wife's Earnings	Percent of Income
Total	100	$14,184	$3,667	26	100	$11,103	$3,563	32
50 to 52 Weeks	52.1	15,962	5,270	33	54.8	12,629	4,872	39
27 to 49 Weeks	20.9	13,266	3,047	23	20.9	10,514	2,849	27
1 to 26 Weeks	27.0	11,462	1,052	9	24.3	8,176	1,232	15

*Twenty million: see Table IV, V, and VI.

Source: Tables 68, 69, 70, *Current Population Reports*, Series P-60, No. 85, December 1972, Consumer Income.

that over half these women, who are employed year-round, earn one-third of the family income. One out of five working wives contributes about one quarter of the family income, with only one in four earning less than 10%. Over a longer period, the percentage would be smaller, for Table 7 picks up data for *one year* from a group of families who—as far as the work experience of wives is concerned—represent a shifting population. Given the growth of women's participation in the labor force, and the rapidity with which this has occurred, a larger proportion of women than of men will be in the group reporting "worked 1 to 26 weeks." This does not mean that those same individuals will be in that group next year.

Table 7 also provides a useful exercise in evaluating the significance of mean income figures. For 18 million white families, mean family income amounted to $14,184; mean earnings for wives, $3,667. But dispersion around the mean (the extent to which these figures do *not* represent the total distribution) is far greater for wives' earnings than for total family income. The range from highest to lowest is 115% of mean earnings of wives and only 31% of mean family income. It follows that any ratio of the two numbers is also highly unrepresentative.

Differences between white and Negro families are apparent, as in previous tabulations. The median earnings of working wives provided a larger share of income to Negro families than to whites: 32% for the former group, 25% for the latter, with the differential larger at lower income levels. Median income figures of families in which women worked only part of the year fell well below those of families

TABLE 8A: Earnings of Husband in Husband-Wife Families by Wife's Earnings, 1971

| | | | Earnings of Husband | | | | | | | |
| | | | Percent Distribution | | | | | | | |
Earnings of Wife	Total Families (000's)	Total With Earnings	Less than $2000	$2000 –3900	$4000 –6999	$7000 –9999	$10,000 –14,999	$15,000 –24,999	$25,000; & over	Percent
None	23,980	20,094	7.9	6.4	16.8	23.5	27.3	13.5	4.7	100
1–$999 or loss	4,720	4,470	8.3	10.3	20.2	25.1	24.4	9.3	2.4	100
$1000 –1999	2,908	2,736	8.1	11.1	21.8	26.5	22.9	7.9	1.6	100
$2000 –2999	2,436	2,304	5.8	11.0	25.0	27.5	21.1	7.6	2.2	100
$3000 –4999	5,059	4,750	5.7	7.5	25.6	31.3	23.2	5.7	1.0	100
$5000 –6999	3,651	3,487	5.5	5.4	20.0	32.5	26.2	8.8	1.4	100
$7000 –9999	2,228	2,084	5.1	5.0	15.2	29.1	31.7	11.5	2.3	100
$10,000 & over	769	720	4.2	2.0	10.6	21.3	36.8	20.6	4.6	100
Median Earnings of Wife		$3,322	$2,418	$2,092	$3,196	$3,597	$3,686	$3,081	$2,941	

Source: Calculated from Table 31, p. 81, "Money Income in 1971 of Families and Persons in the United States," U.S. Bureau of the Census, Current Population Reports, Consumer Income, Series P-60, No. 85, December 1972.

with year-round employment for wives, for both races. But although wives working less than half a year averaged only about $1,000 in earnings, this represented almost 10% of total family income for whites and over 15% for Negroes.

Tables 8A and 8B compare wives' and husbands' earnings to provide different views of the significance of women's contribution to family income. Unlike the previous tables, this includes all husband-wife families, not merely those where both partners have some earnings. There were 45 million husband-wife families in 1971: in 4.5 million of them, husbands provided no earned income and 20 million of them lacked earnings by the wife. About 3.4 million families reported no earnings by either husband or wife; presumably, they have retired to live on social security and pension income or, at the opposite end of the age span, they may be students receiving financial aid or stipends.

Part A of Table 8 classifies the earnings of husbands by the earnings of wives. Thus, husbands among the five million families where the wives earned between three and five thousand dollars

TABLE 8B: Earnings of Wife in Husband-Wife Families by Husband's Earnings, 1971

Earnings of Husband	Earnings of Wife									Total with Earnings (000's)
	Percent Distribution									
	None	$1–$999 or loss	$1000 –1999	$2000 –2999	$3000 –4999	$5000 –6999	$7000 –9999	$10,000 and over	Percent	
Less than $2000	54.0	13.0	7.6	4.6	9.3	6.6	3.6	1.0	100	2,886
$2000 –3999	43.0	15.5	10.2	8.5	12.0	6.4	3.5	.5	100	2,967
$4000 –6999	44.0	11.6	7.7	7.4	15.7	9.0	4.1	1.0	100	7,763
$7000 –9999	44.6	10.6	6.9	6.0	14.1	10.7	5.7	1.4	100	10,568
$10,000 –14,999	51.6	10.3	5.9	4.6	10.4	8.6	6.2	2.5	100	10,649
$15,000 –24,999	60.5	9.3	4.8	3.9	6.0	6.8	5.3	3.3	100	4,471
$25,000 & over	71.3	8.1	3.3	3.8	3.6	3.7	3.6	2.5	100	1,341
Median Earnings of Husband	$9,408	$8,289	$7,963	$7,777	$7,915	$8,702	$9,563	$11,643		$8,858

Source: Calculated from Table 31, p. 81, "Money Income in 1971 of Families and Persons in the United States," U.S. Bureau of the Census, Current Population Reports, *Consumer Income*, Series P-60, No. 85, December 1972.

earned *less* than this amount in 13% of the cases. Averages also appear: among families where husbands earned between ten and fifteen thousand dollars, the median earnings for working wives was $3,686. The figures can be used to approximate total family income, although for complete accuracy nonlabor income from property and pensions would also be needed.

Part B of Table 8 reverses the classification to present figures for wifely earnings among families classified by the size of the husbands' earned income. Thus, women who earn three to four thousand dollars live in families at all income levels; the median earnings of the *husbands* of such women was $7,915.

Both tables reiterate, each in a different way, that working wives predominate in almost every income bracket. Not only do over half the couples in this country consist of two working partners, but they appear in both the lower and the upper segment of the income distribution. In families where the husband earns over $15,000 (about 13% of the total), their wives are employed in 40% of the cases. Even in the small top-income group (men earning over $25,000 represent only 3% of the total, but there are almost two million of them), working wives are not uncommon; they appear in one out of four of these highest-income families. The amount of wives' earnings also appears significant in every income class. One-fourth of all the married women earning over $10,000 have husbands earning over $15,000; clearly many families classified in the upper income brackets would not be there without the contribution of working wives.

The tables can be used to derive figures on the number of women who earn wages and salaries equal to, or exceeding, the sums earned by their husbands; in such cases both working partners may be equally responsible for total family income. From Table 8B, three million families exist in which the husband earns less than $2,000, and over one-half of their working wives earn *more* than $2,000. These women number almost one million; they must provide the chief financial support of their families, whether or not the Bureau of the Census chooses to identify their husbands as household heads. In the second lowest earnings classification for husbands—between $2,000 and $4,000—57% of the wives work; about one out of four earns more than her husband. Among families where the men earn between $4,000 and $7,000, over half a million contain wives who bring in more than $7,000 from their jobs and almost as many more match their husbands in earnings. Of husbands earning between $7,000 and $10,000, 7% are married to women who earn at least $7,000, and 150,000 of them earn more than $10,000. And so on. At least 2,300,000 working wives contribute more to family income than do their husbands. These cases account for 5% of all husband-wife families.

Other useful data can be drawn from these tabulations. For example, most working wives are married to men who earn between $4,000 and $15,000. Thus, most dual earning couples are middle-income couples. On the other hand, a wife is most *likely* to work if her husband has an income below $10,000 but above $2,000. This is the stuff of market analysis: these women have buying habits shaped by their employment as well as by the amount of income they have available to spend.

The distribution of working wives shows median earnings between $2,000 and $5,000 at every level of husbands' earnings. The highest median earnings occur in the three important middle-income classes—those where the husband earns between $4,000 and $15,000.

On the other hand, the dispersion *within* such classes exceeds that elsewhere: the distribution of wives' earnings around the median varies between upper- and lower-income families. Hence, the median earnings figure of $3,000 is not representative, or even equally unrepresentative, at all income levels. For families where husbands earn less than $15,000, the median appears to reflect the distribution, with the total number of cases clustered closely around this figure. But at the two top earnings levels of husbands, the median earnings ($3,000 to $4,999) class for wives contains few cases and is one of the smallest of the entire distribution. Thus, almost 10% of the women in these top classes, whose husbands earn over $15,000, themselves earn over $10,000 and about twice this number earn between $7,000 and $10,000. Such earnings cannot be considered insignificant even next to husbands' earnings of $15,000 to $25,000. Yet the existence of such families is in no way suggested by the median wives' earnings of $3,000.

THREE HYPOTHETICAL FAMILY TYPES

The tables discussed above reiterate the uselessness of any simple formula to describe the impact of working wives on total family income. Women's earnings influence consumption and saving choices as well as the impact of financial stringency. To illustrate the possibilities, three models may be outlined, corresponding roughly to families where husbands report low, median, and high earnings. These cases pose hypotheses which cannot be tested with existing data. They probably suggest, however, more useful questions about women's earnings and family incomes than the questions which are currently used to elicit such data.

Husbands with Low Earnings

As has been suggested, the 3.4 million families with no earnings by either husband or wife include both a young student population and the older retired population. Families with husbands reporting very low incomes also contain sizeable numbers of such people, but these families clearly depend upon the wives' earnings for their well-being. The source for the preceding tables (Current Population Reports, Series P-60, No. 85) provides five dollar earnings classes *below*

$2,500. In each of these, the *median earnings of working wives exceeded the highest earnings of their husbands.* Thus, of 350,000 families where the husband earned less than $500 or suffered financial loss, the median earnings of the wife amounted to $2,745. Of approximately 200,000 families where the husband earned between $1,500 and $2,000, the working wives earned, at the median, $2,589. And so on.

Some of these families probably consist of a young married couple reporting low earnings because they have worked only part-time upon graduation from school or college. Others may include a disabled husband or one who is unemployed; in such cases, the wife's earnings would represent a smaller part of total family *income* than of husband-wife earnings because of benefit payments to the husband for his financial loss. Many families will leave this group in the following year, to be replaced by others entering the job market or temporarily unemployed. But a significant number of these families represent low-wage poverty. Thus, the contribution of working wives will be highly significant, if not crucial, to the family's survival either in poverty or over a short period of financial stress.

Husbands with Earnings Around the Median

The second case, more typical, describes the middle-income family where both partners work. The wife's earnings may very well have propelled the family into middle-income status, but families are less likely to be temporary inhabitants of their income class. These are rarely the newly married: most of these husbands and wives are over 25, although the wives may or may not have emerged from the so-called child-bearing years. Judging from the increase among married women and mothers in the labor force over the past two decades, these families will become more common in the future. But although their number and importance will not decline, the diversity of occupation, age, and year-round or part-year employment prevents any generalization about the type of work these women will do. Currently, most are crowded into recognizable women's occupations. Their earnings, generally low, reflect the effective ceiling on wages imposed by such concentration in these fields.

A variety of case histories can be imagined, from the large family where the mother's earnings help provide "basic necessities" to the small family where the working wife provides college tuition or a trip to Europe. How rising income relates to the birthrate needs particular exploration if income rises result from the earnings of married women. The recent decline in the U.S. birthrate has been partly attributed to the increase of the number of women in the labor force, but the distinction between cause and effect is not clear. Since the fastest growing group of working women consists of mothers of young children, it could be argued that child-bearing is no longer much of a deterrent to employment. Since employment increases income, there may be a simple correlation between a rise in income and a decrease in the birthrate. Feminists will argue that working women have found other functions for themselves than that of child-bearer and child-rearer. But this type of husband-wife dual-earner family will continue. It now represents and will more clearly become the typical American pattern into the foreseeable future.

Husbands with High Earnings

The last group of families, those in which husbands earn over $15,000 and where a significant fraction of the wives are also high-income earners, pose both economic and noneconomic questions. These groups contain professional women and business or government executives. For such women, employment probably represents a deliberate choice of a career, as opposed to a job; their commitment to professional progress can be combined with marriage in a variety of ways. Some signs exist among young couples that joint maximization of incomes (or of preferences) can lead to increased mobility of wives; sharing of home responsibilities between both partners evidently occurs more frequently at all ages.

As for children, some evidence exists to show that highly educated women, with high levels of participation in the labor force and earnings from employment, tend to care for their own children by withdrawing from employment more than do women with lower educational levels. But "temporary" withdrawal can also be a matter of weeks or months.

In many cases, child-care can be combined with part-time employment, for, among the group of professional and managerial women earning sizeable incomes, opportunities differ significantly from those in other occupations. Earning considerably higher sums than their less-trained sisters, they can obtain a higher total income from working fewer hours. Part-time work may therefore provide continuous employment during the years children are at home. Thus, the accountant retires from the large firm of auditors during her pregnancies; but she continues to practice her profession, working out of her own home for as many or as few clients as she wishes. The security analyst, operations researcher, or market specialist works for her former firm as a two- or three-day a week consultant, with more time at home for her children. These schedules in no way represent "dropping out" of the labor force, a characteristic that has been attributed to women of child-bearing years.

Only professional women have the ability and saleable skills to achieve this kind of labor force attachment. It is a professional attachment. For them, the status of part-time carries none of the stigma—low skills, undependability, or lack of motivation—attributed to part-time workers at low-income levels.

If more occupations become open to women, the number and percentage of dual-earner families in upper-income classes will increase. Most women work for the same motives as men, i.e., to earn an income. But this is not the only motivation for either sex. It is a rare man who, offered a promotion from assistant manager to branch manager, takes it because he and his family "needed the money." The Carnegie Commission on Higher Education (1973: 25) observes:

> Highly educated women are frequently motivated to work, not just for the income they will receive, but because they find their work intrinsically interesting and rewarding. Along with educated men, they want to develop and utilize their mental capacities to the greatest possible extent, to avoid wasting their previous investment in education and training, and, if holders of advanced degrees, to share with men the rewards that come from research accomplishment. These include the satisfaction of achievement, as well as the more obvious rewards associated with acquiring a distinguished reputation.

Consequently, women should be able, like men, to refuse jobs which underutilize their education and training and thus to demand more pay for what they can contribute.

CONCLUSIONS

The conclusions of this somewhat impressionistic discussion can be briefly summarized. The significance of women's contributions to total family income has usually been dismissed by quoting an average amount or share earned. For many years, the earnings for working wives have amounted to about 25-27% of total family income. From this figure and from other assumptions, it has been generally argued that married men constitute the "breadwinners," the "primary earners," and that "most families" depend upon working husbands for most of their income. Such statements are, at best, oversimplifications and, at worst, highly misleading. Data on the distribution of families with working wives by occupation, by year-round and part-year employment, by age, by earnings of husbands, and by earnings of wives illustrate a diversity which reveals the conventional explanations as being simplistic or sexist.

Although more research and much more data are needed to draw a complete picture of the distribution of income by individuals and by families, much available information lies unanalyzed. Nevertheless, enough evidence exists to put full stop to the common practice of relying on averages and aggregates to diminish the significance of women's contributions to family income.

NOTES

1. Partly this is a data problem; the decennial *Census of Population* figures on family income become rapidly obsolete as descriptive of working women and the yearly surveys provided by the *Current Population Reports* lack the total coverage of census data. A useful discussion of the first, with some analysis of the second, is contained in Symrot and Mallan (1974).

2. Stories in *Advertising Age* indicate that some firms have finally realized that if women, in fact, are working in greater numbers, they cannot at the same time be at home watching television. Therefore, some products formerly advertised during the daytime have shifted at least part of their appeal to prime evening time or even later night spots.

3. The calculated mean or median could be modified by quoting other measures of dispersion, including the standard deviation. Because such statistical refinements cannot yet be understood by the general public, simple averages—like the 27% discussed—have been publicized often and extensively. I question whether analysts who rely on this particular figure are being completely responsible in their presentations, especially when they omit any discussion of its deficiencies.

4. The Bureau of the Census defines "head of family" as "usually the person regarded as the head by members of the family. Women are not classified as heads if their husbands are resident members of the family at the time of the survey."

REFERENCES

Carnegie Commission on Higher Education (1973) Opportunities for Women in Higher Education. New York: McGraw-Hill.

KATONA, G., J. N. MORGAN, J. SCHMIEDSKAMP, and J. A. SONDQUIST (1968) 1967
    Survey of Consumer Finances. Ann Arbor: University of Michigan, Institute for Social
    Research, Survey Research Center.
SYMROT, D. and L. B. MALLAN (1974) "Wife's earnings as a source of family income."
    Washington, D.C.: Social Security Administration, DHEW Publication No. SA 74-11701,
    April 30.
U.S. Bureau of the Census (1972) "Money income in 1971 of families and persons in the
    United States." Current Population Reports, Series P-60, No. 85. Washington, D.C.:
    Government Printing Office.
U.S. Department of Labor (1972) Manpower Report of the President. Washington, D.C.:
    Government Printing Office.
––– Bureau of Labor Statistics (1972) Monthly Labor Review (April).
––– (1970) "Marital and family characteristics of workers, March 1970." Special Labor
    Force Report 130.

10

SEX DISCRIMINATION IN CREDIT
The Backlash of Economic Dependency

JANE ROBERTS CHAPMAN

A credit manager of a metropolitan department store was asked a few years back why he refused to open an account for a woman with a high-paying professional job, excellent references, a savings account, and all the other attributes of credit-worthiness. "She could get pregnant tomorrow," was his answer. And in that response lies several tales. The Center for Women Policy Studies undertook to unravel those tales in a project which investigated the availability of credit to women.[1] The project focused on the development of information on the legal and economic barriers which hamper women borrowers.

INTRODUCTION

The notion that it is natural for women to be economically dependent on men is formalized in domestic law, social structures, attitudes, and economic institutions which have been centuries in development. But the rationale for these elaborate processes, in its simplest terms, is the assertion that "she could get pregnant tomorrow." Only about three million women give birth to children each year. But 42% of all women work, and 13 million women work even though they are mothers of children under 18 years of age. Yet

AUTHOR'S NOTE: Portions of this chapter appeared in the January 1975 issue of *Challenge: The Magazine of Economic Affairs* under the title, "Women's Access to Credit."

the notion persists that women cannot be considered reliable economic entities because they have the capacity to become pregnant: lives are ordered on the basis of it; and thus are policies made and implemented.

The denial of consumer credit and mortgages is a good example of an economic problem which besets women (and their families) because of both real and perceived economic dependency. Real dependency exists because women in some cases do not or cannot earn in the market the money which supports them. As economist Carolyn Shaw Bell (1974: 12) puts it:

> The income women spend . . . accrues chiefly because of their dependence, partial or total, on income earned in the first instance by men, who share it with women in their families, or pay taxes to provide transfer income to women receiving benefits under Social Security, Veterans payments or public assistance programs.

Perhaps because of the genuine dependency of some women, institutions tend to make policies as though all women were dependent. In the past the law similarly classified all married women and significantly hampered their rights. Most of this legal dependence on the husband has been eliminated through married women's property acts and other state legislation. But it is indicative of lenders' acceptance of the idea that women are dependent on men that all the credit problems faced by women relate either to their marital status or to the possibility of a change in marital status. By making it difficult for women as a class to acquire credit, lenders are perceiving a level of economic dependency which no longer exists.

Easily available credit is one of the lures used by business to encourage greater consumption—in some cases, consumption of unneeded products. When credit is viewed as merely the means to indulge a bottomless appetite for material goods, then the whole issue of whether or not women have equal access to it seems of marginal importance. But, in fact, credit is one of the factors contributing to an individual's economic status. Lack of credit or of a credit record can present severe handicaps to women in home buying, in financing an education, purchasing durable goods, or setting up their own businesses. For example, home buyers who cannot get their full income counted are obliged to choose less desirable housing, possibly in neighborhoods far from their places of work or otherwise inconvenient. Women who cannot get educational loans must change their plans for higher education in ways ranging from working at low-paying jobs during the school year to completely dropping out of school.

In a broader context, the inability to get credit is a contributing factor in the disadvantaged status of women. As with other handicaps in the areas of taxation, insurance, and employment, it must be viewed as a part of a pervasive problem. The interrelationships emanate from the underlying concept of women as economic dependents. Thus, credit problems are significant in a sense above and beyond their immediate importance. They are an example of the fashion in which legal, economic, and social aspects of the status and role of women interrelate with disabling effects.

The barriers which confront women seeking credit can be classified into five general types:

(1) Single women have more trouble obtaining credit than single men (particularly in regard to mortgage credit). Some of their problems are based on the presumption that they will marry and not pay debts incurred before marriage.

(2) Creditors generally require a woman upon marriage to reapply for credit, usually in the husband's name. Similar reapplication is not asked of men when they marry.

(3) Creditors are often unwilling to extend credit to married women in their own names.

(4) Creditors are often unwilling to count the wife's income when a married couple applies for credit. This is particularly serious when mortgages are being sought.

(5) Women who are divorced or widowed have trouble establishing or reestablishing credit. Women who are separated have a particularly difficult time.

As a result of considerable publicity given to the issue over the past two years and the steady pressure of women's groups,[2] most of the blatantly discriminatory practices have ceased or become more covert. The Equal Credit Opportunity Act (ECOA) took effect in late 1975. It has not been operative long enough to monitor its impact.

But, by and large, resistance by lenders to making credit available on an equal basis has diminished somewhat or been driven further underground. In many ways, the latter practices are more difficult to eliminate and call for a several-pronged attack based on a thorough understanding of the reasons used to rationalize differential treatment for women.

The two potential bases usually cited as justification of sex-discriminatory policies are legal disabilities and economic unreliability. Some lenders still believe that they cannot extend credit to married women because domestic laws at the state level, such as those requiring husbands to support wives, make married women unable to contract in their own right. However, every state has a law, usually entitled "Married Women's Property Act," that was enacted to nullify the common law disabilities of married women (Kanowitz, 1969: 40). These acts establish the right of women to be considered legally capable of entering into financial agreements. However, some other state laws have been cited as obstructing that capability. They are domestic relations laws requiring husbands to support their wives, community property laws, and multiple agreement laws. Legal research has established, however, that these laws, in fact, present only very limited disabilities and only in a limited number of situations (Gates, 1974; Polikoff, 1974).

Federal legislation outlawing discrimination in the granting of credit on the basis of sex or marital status became effective in October 1975—the Equal Credit Opportunity Act. It will undoubtedly have an impact on credit discrimination; however, if lenders remain unconvinced that women do pay their bills as reliably as men, it will not prove to be a sufficient remedy. Another means of opening up credit to women has been to learn more about the economic reliability of women—that is, their performance as borrowers and consumers, and whether or not there is any justification for treating men and women differently.

With respect to the economic handicaps of women which might render them less credit-worthy, lenders point to the low earning power of women generally, their greater tendency to enter and leave the labor force, and to the notion that divorced persons are less credit-worthy. In addition, there is at work here an old myth, seldom acknowledged publicly, that women are not financially reliable—that they are by nature poor credit risks. If the stories about women being poor credit risks can be exposed as myths and dispelled, then legislative enforcement and the pressures of women's rights groups can carry an added force. A review of the available empirical information on these economic issues follows. It is intended to provide the basis for development of the range of remedies needed to combat the problem.

CREDIT-WORTHINESS AND HOW IT IS DETERMINED

Making determinations about who gets credit and who does not is inherently a selective process. But it is in the public interest that the criteria on which the decisions are based be reasonable and that they be applied impartially and through techniques that are free from bias. While there is some variation from institution to institution, most creditors rely on four basic credit criteria, often referred to as the "four Cs"—capacity (to repay), collateral, character, and credit record. An extensive literature has developed around the translation of these criteria into guidelines for individual credit decisions (see, for example, American Institute of Banking, 1974).

In days gone by, when credit consisted primarily of a loan from a local bank or an account with a local merchant, decisions were easier. The applicant was more often known to the creditor and the use of credit was limited primarily to essentials such as housing, medical expenses, or automobiles. Now the story is quite different; consumer credit outstanding in 1974 totaled $190.1 billion (Booth, 1975: 46). Slightly less than half of all American families had outstanding installment debt in the first part of 1970, and 50% of all families used at least one credit card during that year (Katona et al., 1971: 19-20).

These millions of transactions range from loans for setting up a business or buying a home to the use of a credit card to charge toothpaste in a drug store. This means that credit decisions are not only complicated by the immense volume of applications which must be processed, but also by differences in an individual's credit-worthiness which depend upon the nature of credit being extended. Someone who is credit-worthy (i.e., willing and able to repay) where a BankAmericard is involved might be justifiably turned down for a mortgage or for an automobile loan.

The volume of applications for credit makes it impractical, in most situations, to evaluate applicants through personal interviews. It also makes it less valid for credit managers to base decisions on their own attitudes about who is likely to repay. In order to deal with a large-volume credit economy, lenders and retailers have adopted what are referred to as "credit scoring systems" for evaluating credit-worthiness. Some of the systems are based on statistical analysis of the institutions' past loans or accounts.

Credit scoring systems consist of a group of characteristics on which the prospective borrower is "graded." The list of potential variables is quite large and, in theory, if analysis indicated that people with red hair or six toes were less credit-worthy, then these traits could be included on the application as part of the scoring system.' Typically, however, the scoring systems include about 7-10 items such as length of time on present job or whether the applicant's home is owned or rented. Some characteristics are considered more valuable or more damaging than others. For example, before passage of the Equal Credit Opportunity Act, it was lawful to award points on the basis of marital status. A divorced person might score 0 or −5 while a married person would score 10 for marital status. On a scale of 100 points, the screening process might decree 70 points as the cutoff below which credit is not granted, or at which more in-depth scrutiny of the applicant's credit record is warranted.

Scoring systems are often considered to be objective methods of dispensing credit. But the fact is, whether the creditor makes decisions based on "hunches" or on the most sophisticated, computer-based numerical system, sex bias can influence the outcome. If a system ranks women applicants on the basis of variables which are not good predictors of their propensity to repay, it eliminates women from consideration on the basis of their sex, not on the basis of their credit-worthiness. And, without doubt, some credit scoring systems have done just that.

The most obvious example of indirect bias in credit scoring has been to ask if the applicant has a telephone in his/her own name. Commonly the telephone listing of a married woman is in the husband's name. But this is a matter of security and social custom, and it is difficult to see how the fact that the listing is in this fashion could possibly give the lender an accurate clue as to the married female applicant's credit-worthiness. Fortunately, the regulations which implement the Equal Credit Opportunity Act specifically outlaw the use of this question in credit scoring, allowing the creditor to ask only if there is a telephone in the applicant's home.

Some scoring systems include length of time on job as a positive indicator of credit-worthiness. Yet it is not unusual for women, even those practicing professions, to have an interrupted career pattern. But this pattern does not necessarily mean that women as a class are unlikely to pay their debts or even that women with interrupted careers are unlikely to pay their debts. More probably it means that such women will curtail indebtedness to conform to income.

Without a credit history it is difficult for women to demonstrate their reliability when submitting an application. This makes the credit bureau a crucial factor for the woman who seeks to maintain a financial identity. Relatively few women have credit records because, when they marry, their records are merged with their husbands, and creditors have, until recently, almost uniformly insisted that accounts be converted at that time to the husband's name and that all future accounts be taken in the husband's name. Good credit ratings then become the property of the husband, regardless of how faithfully the wife contributes to the making of that record. Practices like this are direct descendants of the attitudes summed up in the oft-quoted *Commentaries* (p. 413) by Blackstone: "The husband and wife are one person in law. . . . The very being or legal existence of the woman is suspended during the marriage, or at least is incorporated and consolidated." The one person, in other words, is the husband. If the couple separates, the newly single woman has no credit identity. Bad credit ratings, interestingly enough, follow both husband and wife, even when they separate or divorce, and even if the wife has had no part in creating the bad record.

Credit bureaus frequently claim that their practices are set in response to the needs and requests of the member firms. Creditors, on the other hand, often maintain that it is the credit bureau which is the source of the problem because, when they request information on a married woman, the credit bureau says it has no record of her. As a result, regardless of who is initiating the practice, a woman wishing to establish her own economic identity may have great difficulty doing so. After November 1976, a creditor will be required by law to give new applicants the option to have accounts held in both spouses' names with both names recorded at the credit bureau. Thus, even married women with no earnings may begin to establish a credit history.

CREDIT RELIABILITY ACCORDING TO
SEX AND MARITAL STATUS

Since bias can be introduced into any decision-making process —whether "objective" or subjective—it is difficult to determine what groups are most credit-worthy. Nevertheless, it is necessary to review and evaluate the information that is available in order to develop policies and remedies which are in the public interest. If one is concerned with tracking down the economic justification for differentiating between men and women in granting credit, there is some information on which to base a judgment that women are equal or better credit risks than men. There is no information which indicates that they are worse.

The whole question of credit reliability is one which has received surprisingly little attention, in view of the prevalence of credit transactions in this country. There are a number of books dealing with credit management—"how-to" books for the credit manager as well as institutes and seminars for managers and new employees. But by and large, these are "theoretical" in the sense that they are not based on analyses of the actual performance of borrowers.

The few studies which are available deal fleetingly, if at all, with the significance of sex and marital status as indicators of reliability. Perhaps the most comprehensive review of the literature and issues in credit reliability is the National Bureau of Economic Research study, *Measures of Credit Risk and Experience* (Fiedler and Pech, 1971). It is a 357-page volume which devotes virtually no attention to the relevance of sex and marital status in the extension of credit.

Retail Accounts, Banks Loans, and Installment Credit

The findings of studies and industry surveys point to the conclusion that women who borrow or open retail accounts perform in as credit-worthy a fashion as do men. Department store accounts of single women have been found to incur serious delinquency with significantly less frequency than those of single men. A retail trade association analyzed the accounts of six large department stores and found that 6.6% of the single female accounts became delinquent, while 8.4% of the single male accounts were delinquent (Kerr, 1974: 440).

A study in the mid-1960s which measured risk on installment credit found that, for both married and single women, the bad account probability was substantially lower than for men with the same marital status (Smith, 1964).

The earliest study to consider the determinants of credit risk —conducted in 1941 by David Durand—found that women are better credit risks than men, a fact which the author said "seemed puzzling to a number of credit executives." In the area of personal borrower characteristics, Durand (1941: 74) concluded that

> The classification of borrowers by sex and marital status indicates that women are better credit risks than men; and the superiority appears to be statistically significant. No significant difference, however, is evident between the risk characteristics of married and single persons.

Durand also found that there are some variations according to a consumer's occupation. Professional persons and clerical employees appear to be good risks. And most clerical employees were then, as now, female.

Some banks have undertaken systematic analysis of their past accounts. Still others have identified high risk groups on the basis of a more superficial monitoring of delinquency patterns. Because the surveyed institutions have been guaranteed privacy, they cannot be identified, but it is possible to report that not one lending institution interviewed during the Center for Women Policy Studies' credit project had found a higher rate of default on the credit extended to women than that to men. One large West Coast bank found that divorced men were poorer credit risks than divorced women or people in other marital statuses. Another found that divorce was not an indicator of credit reliability for either sex.

Lenders maintain that statistically based discrimination is accepted by legal precedent and by years of business practice. Critics of statistical discrimination oppose it for two reasons. First, the statistical analysis can be based on prejudiced premises. If the choice of variables and the methodology reflect bias against a class of people, then it is of no use for the results to be applied impartially. Variables which are common to one sex or marital status could be weighted in such a fashion as to eliminate women from "eligible" status even if sex or marital status were not directly identified. Some variables might, in fact, be poor indicators of the financial reliability of the groups in question and therefore should be validated before utilization. Second, if a group of people is considered high risk and their credit is limited accordingly, those individuals who are in the group but are not high risk are penalized.

Mortgages

A study of mortgage lending practices in Hartford, Connecticut, conducted by the U.S. Commission on Civil Rights (1974: 33), found with regard to discrimination on the basis of sex, "the major problem is not that mortgage procedures or criteria *permit* opportunities for decisions on the basis of discrimination. Rather traditional mortgage lending criteria followed by Hartford mortgage lenders virtually *require* sex discrimination." The Housing and Community Development Act of 1974 prohibits sex discrimination in housing, and the law extends to the practice of "discounting," or ignoring part or all of a working wife's salary when determining the size of mortgage for which a couple can qualify. The Equal Credit Opportunity Act forbids discounting, as well, and is potentially a much stronger tool for fighting credit discrimination. It is as yet unclear what impact these laws can be expected to have. But it is safe to suggest that it will be difficult to eradicate such a deeply entrenched economic practice. The inflated cost of real estate is eliminating more and more families from home ownership. So the discounting practice becomes increasingly crucial as the housing crunch continues.

None of the literature on mortgage risk suggests that in two-earner families, where a wife's income was counted, the result has been higher delinquency rates. A study by John P. Herzog and James S. Earley (1971) found that marital status is unrelated to delinquency and foreclosure risk. Several loan-related characteristics were found to be relevant—the loan-to-value ratio, the presence of junior financing, and loan purpose. The only significant borrower characteristic was occupation. A second study published the same year (von Furstenburg, 1971) also found loan characteristics more important than lender characteristics. It was determined that as the loan-to-value ratio rises, it becomes increasingly important as a predictor of default risk. This may indicate that the payment-to-income ratio is not as important as had been thought, thus making it less valid to discount the working wife's income on the basis of its uncertainty. Home loan economist Josephine McElhone (1973) asserts that the task of accurately projecting a family's income is quite complex and beyond the capacity of a lender, and therefore renders the arbitrary discounting of women in certain age groups an unproductive policy.

Mortgage lenders voice considerable concern over whether married women can be counted on to remain employed over the course of a mortgage. Doubts about the reliability of women's income as a factor in their economic independence and, thus, in their access to credit and business opportunities can be considered in two ways. First, how unreliable *is* women's income compared with men's? And second, how relevant is the fact that some women have interrupted work lives so far as credit-worthiness is concerned?

There are some changes in the employment profile of women which deserve the attention of lenders. There has been a significant change in the employment status of women as a class over the past 15 years. An influx of millions of women into the labor force occurred during the 1960s—with the most rapid increase coming from women who are married and have children. Their labor force participation rate is now 41% compared with 29% in 1960 (U.S. Department of Labor, Manpower Administration, 1974). This movement has not been tied to a major national emergency, but to economic and social changes and, thus, should not be characterized as temporary. It is not yet clear how many more women will join the work force during the coming decade, but labor force projections indicate that the proportion of women who work will certainly be greater in 1980 than it is now.

Credit extenders often voice doubt over the permanence of women's employment. But the fact that most women work from economic necessity makes voluntary job-leaving an unlikely luxury (U.S. Department of Labor, Women's Bureau, 1971: 1). In fact, a study published in 1972 found that, in the manufacturing sector, the propensity of women to voluntarily leave their jobs has decreased considerably over the past decade. Historically, the fact that a high proportion of women were employed in an industry has meant that that industry would have a high quit rate. But by 1965, this was no longer true: "as the relative proportion of women workers increased [in an industry] the quit rate decreased" (Armknecht and Early, 1972: 35).[3] Available statistics on labor turnover also indicate that the net difference in turnover of men and women in the labor force is much smaller than the conventional wisdom would suggest (U.S. Department of Labor, Women's Bureau, 1969: 2-3, 5).

The available information on work-life expectancy of women is based on 1960 data (Garfinkle, 1967), and therefore does not reflect the great changes of the past 15 years. However, even these data show that a married woman 35 years old, in the labor force after the birth of her last child, averages 24 more years of labor activity. For divorced, widowed, or single women the figures are higher, and knowledgeable economists have agreed that the working life for women in various age and marital groups has lengthened since the original research was done. A great deal is known about female labor force activity, and the available profile of the female labor force is certainly sufficient for purposes of forming credit policy.

The degree of discounting in home mortgage transactions often varies according to the age of the woman, because of the view that women under 35 years are in the child-bearing period and likely to quit their jobs abruptly. Just because a woman is in the "child-bearing" years does not mean that she will (a) have children; (b) leave her job; or (c) quit work if it means a drop in family income which would result in delinquency or foreclosure on the home. McElhone (1973) suggests

> that even if a lender can estimate the probability of a wife's continued labor force participation, his selection of a weight for her income may be quite inappropriate unless he can also estimate the probability of unemployment for her, her husband, and for the average male who is sole support of his family, and unless he knows how her husband's unemployment will affect the wife's labor force behavior.

WOMEN ENTREPRENEURS

Most concern regarding the impact of credit discrimination focuses on women as consumers, homeowners or students—that is, in the conduct of their private lives. An overlooked area of credit discrimination is that in commercial loans for female entrepreneurs. The very combination of the words female and entrepreneur seems unnatural because American enterprise is nothing if not masculine. But women will achieve neither independence nor equality until they influence a significant share of American business. One of the factors that keeps them out of business is lack of financing. This sort of discrimination is particularly difficult to quantify, because of the highly individual set of circumstances surrounding each application.

Businesswomen themselves report a variety of manifestations of bias. For example, a male co-signer is frequently required before banks are willing to loan a woman money for her business. One woman surveyed during the Center for Women Policy Studies' project reported being denied a loan after refusing to provide the co-signatures of both her former husband and her teenage son. Women who have operated a business jointly with their husbands may find their lines of credit greatly curtailed after the death of their husbands.

Problems in borrowing venture capital may not always keep a woman from launching a business, but they almost invariably mean she must think small at the outset. A large proportion of businesswomen surveyed had started their businesses with personal savings or loans from family or friends, rather than venture capital from banks. Many women also report that their growth opportunities could not be maximized because loans for expansion were unavailable. Women who control relatively large businesses are likely to have acquired them by inheritance or marriage, and there are relatively few of these individuals (Robertson, 1973).

Because the vast majority of female-owned businesses are small, it would seem to follow that the Small Business Administration could meet the needs of those firms failing to secure loans from conventional lenders. The Small Business Administration is an independent federal agency, and its major loan program requires that the applicant have been unable to obtain adequate funding from private sources. However, in 1974, women received only 1,946 out of 27,485 loans distributed by the SBA (7%). This compares favorably with the preceding year, when women received 125 out of 33,948 loans (less than .4 of 1%).[4] In mid-1974, an amendment to the Small Business Act took effect, prohibiting sex discrimination in SBA lending.[5] Unfortunately, no specific enforcement provisions were adopted with this measure.[6]

Some SBA programs are limited to use by individuals who are socially or economically disadvantaged.[7] A strong case could be made for the contention that women are socially and economically disadvantaged as a class. Women workers, after all, earn only 59 cents for every dollar earned by men doing comparable work. Women are disproportionately represented among the poor and underrepresented in management, political life, the professions, and all other indices to economic influence and well-being. It would be possible to designate women a disadvantaged group, by Executive Order, and this would contribute to reducing the formidable financial barriers which now exist for women business owners.

A second federal agency with the potential to support the growth of female enterprise is the Office of Minority Business Enterprises (OMBE), which is part of the Department of Commerce. There is no special program for women at OMBE, or any other part of the Department of Commerce, despite the fact that female enterprise is, if anything, even more feeble than black enterprise.

There is an indirect but very real barrier which stands in the way of women being more affirmatively brought into federal lending programs, as well as receiving their due in private lending. This barrier is the almost total lack of information about women entrepreneurs. In order to design remedial programs or to attack credit discrimination at its roots, it is necessary to know something about the group in question. How many female entrepreneurs are there? In what types of businesses are they concentrated? How did they get their venture capital? What size are the businesses? These questions can be answered only in exceedingly general terms because data on businesses collected by the government and privately is not generally available by sex and marital status. Analysis of limited data from the Bureau of Census' 1970 "Report on Occupational Characteristics" yields some information. The report found that about 1.2 million women were self-employed or an employee of their own corporations, as compared with 5.8 million men in the same categories. There are some uncertainties in the data which make it difficult to use. A much more reliable analysis could be done by using information from income tax returns which is currently retrievable, but which has never been analyzed.

CONCLUSIONS AND RECOMMENDATIONS

There is no significant legal reason why women—married or single—cannot obtain credit. There is no documented economic justification for denying credit to women. There are assuredly economic differences between men and women, but it has not been demonstrated that these differences make women more risky as borrowers. Indeed, to discriminate against women is presumably not even in the best interests of the lenders.

The interests of creditors and women are more complementary than conflicting. Since 42% of all women have their own wages to dispose of and borrow against, it would seem that creditors, by clinging to outdated concepts of the role of women, are bypassing a substantial market. In addition, the very fact that married women are in the labor force means they are out of the home. This results in the need for new services and products (Bergmann, 1971: 8). Creditors able to meet these needs will doubtless secure more of the business of working women. Families with two earners also tend to use credit more frequently than either female-headed or male-headed, single-earner families (Goulet, 1973: 39). Elimination of the practice of discounting without doubt would have an impact on the real estate and home mortgage lending business, because if a lender disregards a wife's earnings, a family supported entirely by the husband's income can obtain a mortgage of two and a half times that available to a family with equal income but where 60% is contributed by the wife (McElhone, 1973: 11).

The years 1974 and 1975 saw the beginnings of the development of new policies regarding women and credit. There were stirrings at several levels—institutional, state and local, and national. If these beginnings are to grow into a meaningful change—a change which moves toward the recognition of women as individuals in their own right, with their own right to an economic record and economic opportunities—then action is needed on four fronts: consumer action, lender education, research, and legal action.

Virtually every major women's organization has taken some action regarding credit—ranging from resolutions endorsing nondiscriminatory legislation to citywide surveys of lender practices and consumer boycotts. In many locales, the time for surveys and publicizing the problem has passed. Understandably, effort in these cities and states will be increasingly focused on education or monitoring enforcement of existing legislation. But important work still remains to be done in consumer action at both the local and national levels. For example, intensive negotiations, coupled with an organized boycott of specific institutions, might have an impact in the retail area. Support should be marshalled from consumer and civic groups as well as women's organizations.

At the policy level, presidents and vice presidents of banks often issue directives regarding nondiscriminatory behavior. But, privately, they concede that the directives are often not implemented at lower levels. If credit managers in banks and other establishments are not convinced that delinquency rates will not rise if women are granted credit, it is likely that federal legislation will succeed in reducing blatant discrimination, but that the female population will one way or another still not have equal access to credit.

The possibility of educating credit managers and bank personnel on the relationship of economic and equity issues has not been fully exploited. The banking and credit industry regularly undertakes to instruct its personnel in the concepts of credit management. They should also be trained on the rights and potential of specific market groups such as women, youth, and divorced persons. Some material could be directed to new personnel, other kinds of information could be introduced in professional meetings and regional banking conferences. A course might be developed for the American Institute on Banking which would cover various aspects of sex discrimination.[8] Such a course could familiarize credit personnel with the somewhat unfamiliar notion of women as economic persons. For example, it might contain information on the employment patterns of women. What amounts to almost a revolution in the work force behavior of women has taken place during the careers of many credit managers. Further, personnel could be informed of indirect sex bias which can occur in scoring systems and other elements of credit policy.

As an example of action at the state level, the Washington State Human Rights Commission and the Association of Washington Business have developed credit seminars which instruct creditors about their obligations under the state anti-discrimination statute. The program recommends that high-level personnel institute in-house policies to educate those persons who initially review credit applications as to what practices are prohibited.

In the area of research, mortgage lenders have expressed interest in having detailed tables of work-life expectancy for women in various age groups. But it is, in fact, not useful to credit policy-makers to continue to undertake studies which would demonstrate with high probability the propensity of women with "X" number of children and "X" years of work experience to remain in the labor force. Further research on the working patterns of women is not going to demonstrate credit-worthiness generally and could be badly misused in the mortgage market. Discounting has been widely practiced. But the ECOA regulations attempt to deal with the issue by prohibiting lenders from basing their decision on an applicant's child-bearing or child-rearing plans or on statistical information on the labor force activity of the applicant's population group.

Further research effort should be concentrated directly in the area of risk and reliability. It might be that the credit-granting industry is in the best position to undertake such research using the information peculiarly within its grasp—the data on performance on past accounts. Two caveats are important here. First, sex bias must be eliminated from the methodology in this sort of research; and, second, the research should cover a large enough sample to provide significant findings. It would not do for a small retailer to look at a few bad accounts and draw conclusions from them.

Ultimately, significant change is likely to be spurred by strong federal legislation prohibiting sex discrimination in credit. Although 29 states and the District of Columbia have enacted some law in this area, most are inadequate in their coverage and poorly enforced (Polikoff, 1974). The federal legislation which took effect in October 1975 provides women with a strong weapon against lenders who do not voluntarily alter discriminatory practices.

Sex discrimination in home financing is illegal under the Fair Housing Act, which was amended to include sex in August 1974 (Housing and Community Development Act). The remedy under this law is not as strong as the remedy under the new comprehensive statute, but women's advocates should be able to use both laws to bolster the elimination of offensive practices. The comprehensive law, which applies to all forms of credit—consumer, business, educational, as well as home financing—also permits class actions and punitive damages. But it is thought that the maximum allowable damages are too low and fail to provide incentive to creditors to avoid litigation.

When a combination of forces comes to bear on American business, then and only then will financial barriers break down for women. Among these forces will be legislation, lender education, and citizen action. Another will be competition. The First Women's Bank, chartered in New York State, has opened for business in New York City. Feminist credit unions are operating in several states. Added to those women-controlled lending institutions are the increasing number of women who own and operate their own businesses.

A few relatively small credit unions, banks, and businesses cannot be expected to have a direct impact on the majority of lenders and creditors. But they represent a trend to be watched. If a significant group of lenders and merchants should actively seek women as credit customers, the prospect of consumer defections from male-owned enterprises could ultimately influence the relaxation of credit discrimination.

Finally, there is no way to devise a genuine solution to sex discrimination in credit without dealing with both the real and presumed economic dependency of women. It is real dependency which keeps women too poor to qualify for credit. It is the presumption of dependency which exists because of the lenders' ignorance of how many women work or what they earn which keeps banks frozen into outmoded policies.

NOTES

1. The project is in its second year and has been sponsored through grants from the Ford Foundation.

2. Among the organizations which have undertaken credit discrimination projects are the Women's Equity Action League and the National Organization for Women, both of which have prepared credit action kits. It is common for local NOW chapters to monitor retail creditors in their area. Numerous State Commissions on the Status of Women have held hearings and prepared reports on credit discrimination.

3. One of the reasons put forth for this change is the lamentable fact that women's voluntary job mobility is limited by sex discrimination in hiring.

4. These figures do not include loans to (a) corporations owned by women; (b) partnerships which include a man even if a woman is the most active partner; and (c) loans for which collateral is signed by both husband and wife (even if the wife receives the loan).

5. The amendment provides that in carrying out the programs administered by the Small Business Administration, including its lending and guaranteeing functions, the Administration shall not discriminate against any person or small business concern applying for or receiving assistance from the SBA.

6. Injunctive relief would likely be available to stop discriminatory practices or policies, but a private action for damages could be sustained only if it would be considered to be implied.

7. These are the Minority Enterprise Program, the 8(a) Contracting Program (which facilitates competition for federal contracts by disadvantaged businesses), and the Economic Opportunity Loan Program.

8. The American Institute of Banking conducts three programs in which sex discrimination materials could be introduced: (1) courses for which AIB develops textbooks and materials; (2) bankers' schools, of which there are about 81; and (3) in-house curriculum development. AIB develops materials for many banks' own training divisions.

REFERENCES

American Institute of Banking (1964) Installment Credit. Washington, D.C.: American Bankers Association. (reprinted in 1971)

ARMKNECHT, P. A. and J. F. EARLY (1972) "Quits in manufacturing: a study of their causes." Monthly Labor Review 95, 11 (November).

BELL, C. S. (1974) "Economics, sex and gender, an attempt to explain to social scientists and others how economics deals with women." Working Paper No. 7. Wellesley, Mass.: Department of Economics, Wellesley College.

BERGMANN, B. (1971) "The economics of women's liberation." Proceedings of the American Psychological Association (September).

BOOTH, S. L. (1975) 1975 Finance Facts Yearbook. Washington, D.C.: National Consumer Finance Association.

DURAND, D. (1941) Risk Elements in Consumer Installment Financing. New York: National Bureau of Economic Research. (technical edition)

Equal Credit Opportunity Act (1975) Title VII of Public Law 495, Depository Institutions Act.

FIEDLER, E. R. and M. R. PECH (1971) Measures of Credit Risks and Experience. General Series 95. New York: National Bureau of Economic Research.

GARFINKLE, S. (1967) "Work life expectancy and training needs of women." Manpower Report No. 12 (May). Washington, D.C.: Government Printing Office.

GATES, M. J. (1974) "Credit discrimination against women: causes and solutions." Vanderbilt Law Review 27 (April): 409-441.

GOULET, J. (1973) "A preliminary investigation of credit availability to women." Unpublished report submitted to Center for Women Policy Studies, November 1973. (based on analysis of University of Michigan Institute for Social Research four-year panel study consisting of a constant sample of 1,436 family units)

HERZOG, J. P. and J. S. EARLEY (1971) Home Mortgage and Foreclosure. New York: National Bureau of Economic Research.

Housing and Community Development Act (1974) Public Law #93-383 (August 27, 1974), Sec. 808(a) and (b).

KATONA, G., L. MANDELL, and J. SCHMIEDESKAMP (1971) 1970 Survey of Consumer Finances. Ann Arbor: Survey Research Center, University of Michigan.

KANOWITZ, L. (1969) Women and the Law, The Unfinished Revolution. Albuquerque, N.M.: University of New Mexico Press.

KERR, R. F. (1974) "Statement," in Hearings Before the Subcommittee on Consumer Affairs, Committee on Banking and Currency, on H.R. 14856 and H.R. 14908, June 21. Washington, D.C.: Government Printing Office.

McELHONE, J. (1973) "Mortgage lender discounting of secondary incomes: its rationale and impact." Delivered at Federal Home Loan Bank Economist Conference, Atlanta, Georgia, May.

POLIKOFF, N. D. (1974) "Legislative solutions to sex discrimination in credit: an appraisal." Women's Rights Law Reporter (Summer).

ROBERTSON, W. (1973) "The ten highest ranking women in big business." Fortune (April): 80-89.

SMITH, P. F. (1964) "Measuring risk on installment credit." Management Science 2 (November): 327-340.

U.S. Bureau of the Census (1970) "Report on occupational characteristics." Washington, D.C.: Government Printing Office.

U.S. Commission on Civil Rights (1974) "Mortgage money: who gets it?" Clearinghouse Publication 48 (June).

U.S. Department of Labor, Manpower Administration (1974) 1974 Manpower Report of the President. Statistical Appendix. Washington, D.C.: Government Printing Office.

U.S. Department of Labor, Women's Bureau (1971) Underutilization of Women Workers. Washington, D.C.: Government Printing Office.

――― (1969) Facts About Women's Absenteeism and Labor Turnover. Washington, D.C.: Government Printing Office.

von FURSTENBURG, G. (1971) "Technical studies of mortgage default risk: an analysis of the experience with FHA and VA home loans during the decade 1957-66." Ithaca, N.Y.: Center for Urban Development Research.

THE CONTRIBUTORS

NANCY SMITH BARRETT is Professor of Economics and Chair of the Department of Economics at American University, Washington, D.C. She is the author of several books on economic theory and policy and has published widely on the labor market status of women.

CAROLYN SHAW BELL is Katharine Coman Professor of Economics at Wellesley College. She is currently Chair of the Federal Advisory Council on Unemployment Insurance and is a member of the Joint Council on Economic Education. In addition to her many scholarly journal articles in the areas of human resource economics and microeconomic analysis, Professor Bell is the author of *The Economics of the Ghetto* (1971), *Consumer Choice in the American Economy* (1967), and co-author with S. Schensul and W. Fisher of *Coping in a Troubled Society: An Environmental Approach to Mental Health* (1974).

JANE ROBERTS CHAPMAN is a founder and Co-Director of the Center for Women Policy Studies, Washington, D.C., and an editor of the Sage Yearbooks in Women's Policy Studies. Her recent publications include "Women's Access to Credit," *Challenge* (January 1975) and "Essays in the Social Sciences: Economics," *Signs* (Autumn 1975).

MARGARET GATES, a founder and Co-Director of the Center for Women Policy Studies, is an attorney and Adjunct Professor of Law at the Georgetown University Law Center. Her recent publications include "Credit Discrimination Against Women: Causes and Solutions" (*Vanderbilt Law Review*, April 1974) and "Women and

Policing: A Legal Analysis," which appeared in *Development of Female Police Officers in the United States* (1974).

MARTHA W. GRIFFITHS is a former member of the U.S. House of Representatives. In 1973 Mrs. Griffiths chaired the Joint Economic Committee hearings on the economic status of women and now chairs the Homemaker Committee of the National Commission on the Observance of International Women's Year.

HILDA KAHNE is Assistant Dean of the Radcliffe Institute, where her current research is focused on career patterning of women in selected professions—psychology, physics, and public administration, in particular. Her most recent major publication was a chapter entitled, "Employment Prospects and Academic Policies," in Ruth Kindsin (editor), *Women and Success: The Anatomy of Achievement* (1974).

PAMELA ROBY is Associate Professor of Sociology, Chairperson of the Community Studies Department, and Director of the Extended University Bachelor's Degree Program—all at the University of California, Santa Cruz. She is co-author of *The Future of Inequality* (1970), editor of *Child Care—Who Cares? Foreign and Domestic Infant and Early Childhood Development Policies* (1973), and editor of *The Poverty Establishment* (1974).

HEATHER L. ROSS is Assistant Director in the Office of Policy Analysis, U.S. Department of the Interior. Ms. Ross was previously Senior Research Associate at the Urban Institute and an economist at Mathematica Inc., where she was an originator of the New Jersey Income Maintenance Experiment. She is co-author (with Isabel Sawhill) of a forthcoming Urban Institute book entitled, *Time of Transition: The Growth of Families Headed by Women.*

IRENE TINKER is Director of the Office of International Science, American Association for the Advancement of Science. She was the first President of the Federation of Organizations for Professional Women (1972-1974), and was a member of the U.S. delegation to the UN Commission on the Status of Women (January 1974). Dr. Tinker has written extensively on comparative problems of political and cultural development, with emphasis on Southern Asia, Africa, and the United States.

ETHEL L. VATTER is Professor Emeritus at the New York State College of Human Ecology, Cornell University. Her most recent writings in such publications as the *Journal of Home Economics, Gerontologist, Family Coordinator,* and *Human Ecology Forum* have dealt with family income (supplemental effects of federal food programs and income maintenance), working wives, affiliated families, and quality-of-life indicators.

BARBARA M. WERTHEIMER is Senior Extension Associate and Director of Trade Union Women's Studies at the New York State School of Industrial and Labor Relations, Cornell University. She was formerly the head of the national educational program of the Amalgamated Clothing Workers of America and co-authored the 1975 volume, *Trade Union Women: A Study of Their Participation in New York City Locals.* She is currently at work on a book tentatively entitled, *We Were There: The Story of Working Women in America.*